86 on his new harmonic language

THE FORGING OF THE 'RING'

BY THE SAME AUTHOR

Richard Wagner. Sein Werk. Sein Wesen. Seine Welt (Zürich/Freiburg i. Br., 1956)
Gespräch um Wagner (Bayreuth, 1961)
Vom Holländer zum Parsifal (Zürich/Freiburg i. Br., 1962)
Wagners Dresdener Bibliothek (Wiesbaden, 1966)
Wagner (Zürich/Freiburg i. Br., 1968)
  Italian edn (Milan, 1973)
  Japanese edn (Tokyo, 1973)
  English edn (in preparation)

CURT VON WESTERNHAGEN

The forging of the 'Ring'

RICHARD WAGNER'S COMPOSITION SKETCHES FOR
DER RING DES NIBELUNGEN

Translated by Arnold and Mary Whittall

Wagner:
The moment of joy is when the nebulous idea transmitted
to my pencil suddenly stands before me, clear and plain.
Orchestration, by comparison, is already a public process.
(*From Cosima's diary*)

CAMBRIDGE UNIVERSITY PRESS
CAMBRIDGE
LONDON · NEW YORK · MELBOURNE

Published by the Syndics of the Cambridge University Press
The Pitt Building, Trumpington Street, Cambridge CB2 IRP
Bentley House, 200 Euston Road, London NWI 2DB
32 East 57th Street, New York, NY10022, USA
296 Beaconsfield Parade, Middle Park, Melbourne 3206, Australia

Original German language publication *Die Entstehung des 'Ring'*
© 1973 Atlantis Musikbuch-Verlag Zürich
English translation © Cambridge University Press 1976

First published 1976

Printed in Great Britain at the
University Printing House, Cambridge
(Euan Phillips, University Printer)

Library of Congress Cataloguing in Publication Data
Westernhagen, Curt von
The forging of the 'Ring'
Translation of *Die Entstehung des 'Ring'*
Bibliography: p. 244
Includes index
1. Wagner, Richard, 1813–83. *Der Ring des Nibelungen*. I. Title
ML410.W15W1853   782.1'092'4   76–7140
ISBN 0 521 21293 6

Contents

FÜR ELISABETH

Preface

When all's said and done, the head is only able to grasp a
work of art in the company of the heart.
(Goethe to Schiller)

This book approaches Wagner's greatest work by a different route from those pursued by any other interpretations and commentaries. It is the first to make use of the unpublished sketches in exploring the process of the composition of the *Ring*, in the belief that the exposition of that process is the only commentary that can truly aid understanding of the completed work. It was not undertaken with a view to proving or disproving any particular preconceived theory, but confines itself to recording and collating the observations that result from a comparison of the sketches and the score. No analytical sophistries have been attempted, bearing in mind Wagner's mockery of those for whom music is 'a curiously abstract thing, floating somewhere between grammar, arithmetic and gymnastics'. On the other hand, I need hardly say that I owe a debt to some musical theorists, above all to Ernst Kurth, whose theory of the energetics of music probably comes closest to the reality of Wagner's work.

The book is intended to appeal to the music lover who is familiar with the elements of musical theory and able to read a vocal score. Nowadays, too, gramophone recordings of the *Ring*, of which four complete performances are available at present, provide a unique aid to the study and understanding of the score, and one that was formerly inconceivable.

Performers should also find much of interest here, in that the differences between the sketches and the score – the expansion of certain passages, the introduction of syncopation, changes of interval in the vocal writing – give an indication of what was uppermost in the composer's mind: this applies above all to the part of Brünnhilde in *Götterdämmerung*. Similarly, the conductor will draw guidance from the notes on instrumentation and performance written down on the sketches, the revision of the orchestral writing, highlighting individual parts or embedding them in denser textures, and the alterations to melodic lines.

I do not believe that any work of art, least of all this one, ever came into existence in a vacuum; on the contrary, it bears the perceptible impression of the creator's personality and experiences, even though not in the sense of direct biographical revelation. The biographical data in the text are intended to convey something of the personal background.

My books have been accused of betraying my 'love' of Wagner, and the same charge will probably be made against this one. I shall have to console myself with Goethe's comment on Herder's review of contemporary poetry, that an undertaking of that nature, consisting of 'a meagre distribution of praise and blame', is completely worthless if it lacks 'loving sympathy'.

Finally I should like to express here my gratitude to all those who have assisted me in different ways in this task, which has taken more than a decade with continual interruptions. Above all, to Frau Winifred Wagner, who generously allowed me to use and photocopy the original manuscripts; to Frau Gertrud Strobel, who prepared the sketches for photocopying, and to Herr Wolfgang Wagner, who gave permission for this to be done in the studio of the Bayreuth Festival; to Professor Walter Salmen of Kiel and Professor Carl Dahlhaus of Berlin for their valuable practical advice; to Dr Daniel Bodmer of Atlantis Verlag, Zürich, for his decision to publish the book, whose many musical examples made it an expensive and elaborate undertaking; and last but not least to Mrs Mary Whittall, for the sympathy with which she has translated the book in the spirit of the English language, and to Dr Arnold Whittall of London University for his valuable specialist advice in the translation.

Preetz (Holstein) January 1976   Curt von Westernhagen

Key to the musical examples

Sketch
Composition sketch

Score
Full score
*(Generally, in the case of the sketches, and always, in the case of the score,
the examples do not quote all the parts in full, but only the relevant ones)*

Notes in parentheses ( )
Deleted in the original manuscript

Words of the text in parentheses
The vocal part is omitted, and the words are given only for orientation

Words in square brackets [ ]
Author's annotations

[?]
Indicates a doubtful reading of the manuscript

·/.
Wagner's own mark to indicate a repeat

Unimportant alterations and additions made to the sketches by the composer
are incorporated in the examples without comment; more significant ones
are indicated by square brackets.

Marginal references

The numbers in the margins refer to the pages of the scores of the *Ring*
published by Schott. Those in upright type refer to the eleven-volume edition of the study score, those in italic to the 1908 edition of Klindworth's vocal
score. The study score includes Jameson's English version of the text.

Translators' note

The text of the *Ring* is not translated, except where the meaning of isolated
words is the point at issue. Quotations from all other German sources are
presented here in new translations, without reference to the English translations that already exist in some cases, such as *Mein Leben*. The page
references in all cases are to the German editions listed in the bibliography.
The translation of the passage from Cosima's diary quoted on p. 87 is
reproduced here by kind permission of Thames and Hudson Ltd.

The significance
of composition sketches

> You can't get to know works of art or of nature when they
> have been finished; you must get a grasp of them while they
> are coming into being in order to gain any degree of under-
> standing of them.
> (*Goethe to Zelter*)

> It is to be hoped that an expert may some day be given access
> to these priceless documents, with authority to reproduce at
> least a few important passages and make a general report in
> terms intelligible to the ordinary musical amateur.
> (*William Ashton Ellis*, 1904)

When Otto Strobel died in 1953, after many years as curator of the
Wagnerarchiv, Wagner's English biographer, Ernest Newman, mourned it
as an exceptional loss that his death put paid to his project of tracing the
genesis of Wagner's works in the light of the sketches: Newman considered
that the work would have been more important than Beethoven's sketches
for the *Eroica*, as a revelation of the conscious and unconscious creative
processes of a musical genius of the first rank.[1]

Strobel had given me some idea of his *modus operandi* shortly before his
death, with an example from *Die Meistersinger*: in his manuscript the stages
in the writing of Pogner's address 'Das schöne Fest, Johannistag' were
illustrated by a series of facsimiles, from the first idea, by way of the
composition and orchestral sketches to the score itself. It was the method
that I subsequently applied, in *Die Musik in Geschichte und Gegenwart*,[2] to
the opening of 'O sink hernieder, Nacht der Liebe' in *Tristan und Isolde*,
but which, let it be said at once, I have not used in the present analysis of
the sketches of the *Ring* for reasons that I shall give.

Newman was right: Gustav Nottebohm's publication of Beethoven's
sketches a hundred years ago, especially those of the *Eroica*,[3] opened a new
epoch, not only in Beethoven studies, but in the investigation of the
processes of musical creation as a whole. A large number of other publications have followed since then – some as large in scope as Joachim von
Hecker's *Untersuchungen an den Skizzen zum Streichquartett cis-moll op.
131*[4] – until a start was made in 1952, with the sketches for the *Missa
Solemnis*,[5] on the publication of the first complete critical edition of what is
estimated to be more than five thousand sheets of sketches.

---

[1] Cf. *The Sunday Times*, 22 March 1953.
[2] Vol. XIV, coll. 88ff. (Kassel, 1968).
[3] 1865 and 1880. New edition: *Zwei Skizzenbücher von Beethoven aus den Jahren
1801 bis 1803*, ed. by Paul Mies (Leipzig, 1924).
[4] Universitätsbibliothek Freiburg/Breisgau (1956).
[5] Ed. by Joseph Schmidt-Görg (Beethovenhaus, Bonn, 1952).

There is an obvious, twofold gain from these studies. They yield an insight into the psychology of musical creation, especially with regard to the relative contributions of the conscious and the unconscious mind, and the comparison of the separate stages of the work sheds light on the composer's stylistic intentions.

Such considerations encourage the idea of making similar studies of the work of other composers – provided that a comparable quantity of sketch material survives. Even then the process can only really be worthwhile if, as in the case of Beethoven, the material serves to illustrate the conceptual and the technical development of a particular work.

With Wagner the first condition – quantity of material – is fulfilled with astonishing abundance in the case of the *Ring*: apart from a number of preliminary sketches of individual motives, the Wagnerarchiv holds 470 (half-size) sheets of composition sketches (for *Das Rheingold, Die Walküre, Siegfried* and *Götterdämmerung*) and 263 (three-quarter-size) sheets of orchestral sketches (for *Siegfried* and *Götterdämmerung*). Further, some material survives for *Siegfrieds Tod*, the original version of *Götterdämmerung*: a folio-sized sheet of separate sketches, now in the Library of Congress in Washington, and the beginning of a composition sketch, dated 12 August 1850, which, until 1936, was in the Collection Louis Barthou in the Bibliothèque Nationale in Paris, but is now available only in a facsimile.

Whether Wagner's sketches also meet the second condition, that of providing as much information as Beethoven's do, necessarily depends on the degree of similarity between their respective methods of creation. When somebody once said that he carried on the tradition of Beethovenian melody, Wagner firmly denied it: Beethovenian melody was *sui generis*; but then he went on: 'I would not have been able to compose in the way I have, if Beethoven had not existed.' (Cosima's diary, 10 December 1880, BBL 1937, p. 161.) In making that reservation and that admission he summed up his relationship with Beethoven as concisely as anyone could. He was not, however, alluding to the claim he made early in his career, which has been repeated *ad nauseam* – generally for polemical purposes – that the choral finale of Beethoven's Ninth Symphony marked the end of purely instrumental music; it ought to be well enough known by now that he later withdrew the claim by both word and deed, not only hailing Bruckner as Beethoven's successor, but also expressing the wish, after he had finished *Parsifal*, to write one-movement symphonies himself, which would have 'no element of drama' in them (GLRW, VI, p. 752). What he meant was something 'technical', in a very far-reaching and lofty sense of the word, given that he regarded the 'technicalities' as being the only aspects of music that could be talked about or taught. And the one outstanding technicality in the case of Beethoven was the art of motivic development, which 'from a single starting point', as Wagner once said of the *Egmont* over-

ture (GLRW, VI, p. 388), shapes the whole work organically. Or, as Hans
Pfitzner described his own experience:

> The exhilarating, interesting, valuable, delightful thing about all
> musical form, in the last analysis, is that one idea gives birth to the
> next; one principal idea, as it were, produces all the others from itself,
> thus ensuring their organic relationship and cohesion: and not just
> the 'themes' in the textbook sense, but absolutely everything that
> 'happens' in the movement, grows out of this seed or stem and
> flowers from it.[6]

The course of Wagner's development placed him unerringly on the right
path to make this discovery, in that he had the opportunity to make the
acquaintance of *late* Beethoven at a very early stage of his own career: in
1829, at the age of sixteen, he procured a much treasured copy of the E♭
major quartet, op. 127, which had had its first performance only four years
earlier. In the same year he copied out the score of the Ninth Symphony – the most reliable means of gaining understanding of the technique of a composition, according to Newman – and made a piano reduction
of it,[7] by no means a poor one, to judge by the specimens, which he vainly
offered Schott for publication in 1830. In the accompanying letter – the
earliest by him that survives – he wrote: 'The closer my acquaintance with
the high worth of the work, the more saddened I have been by the thought
that it is still so much misunderstood, so much disregarded by the majority
of the musical public.' (6 October 1830.)

A poor performance in Leipzig planted seeds of doubt in his mind, but
these were eradicated when he heard the first three movements in 1839,
played by the orchestra of the Paris Conservatoire under Habeneck. This
performance revealed Beethoven's secret to him: his music is all melody,
down to the runs and passage work. Thirty years later he confessed that he
had never again heard the regular, pianissimo, semiquaver figures of the
violins in bars 116–123 of the first movement played with so much understanding as by those Parisian players trained in the lyrical Italian school.

His instinctive comprehension of Beethoven's music was matched by the
ambition to gain a complete understanding of his musical technique; this is
attested by what he says of Beethoven's processes of melodic construction
and development in *Oper und Drama* (1850–51): that he did not present a
completed melody but the 'act of its birth' (RWGS, III, p. 312). He also
exchanged views on the subject around the same time with his friend
Theodor Uhlig, the writer and violinist in the Dresden court orchestra, who
recorded them in a work on 'the choice of motives and the manner of their

---

[6] *Die Ästhetik der musikalischen Impotenz* (Verlag der *Süddeutschen Monats-
hefte*, Munich, 1920).

[7] Otto Daube, '*Ich schreibe keine Symphonien mehr*' (Cologne, 1960), pp. 94ff.

deployment in large-scale instrumental compositions', which unfortunately has not survived.[8]

Wagner was preoccupied with these questions at the date of *Oper und Drama* because he was then thinking about the *Ring*, the text of which he finished on 15 December 1852. He had discovered the principle of motivic development by accident in *Der Fliegende Holländer*, and he wanted to apply it in the *Ring* in full consciousness of what he was about. The composition had 'turned out to be a firmly entwined unity', he wrote ecstatically to the conductor August Röckel after finishing the composition sketch of *Das Rheingold*; 'there is scarcely a bar in the orchestral writing that does not develop out of preceding motives' (25 January 1854).

Between the musical vision of the opening of *Das Rheingold* that Wagner experienced in La Spezia on 5 September 1853, and the start on the composition sketch on 1 November, he heard a performance of the E♭ major and C♯ minor quartets by the Maurin-Chevillard quartet, which must have seemed a favourable augury: 'if that were the only thing I could remember of that visit to Paris, it would still qualify as unforgettable' (ML, p. 585).

Once again he heard recapitulated all the 'technicalities' that he had 'inherited' from Beethoven and was now on the point of using – motivic development, the differentiated texture, the melodic flow – all the distinctive characteristics of his own second creative period, particularly the last of them: while he was working on *Tristan* in 1859 he took drastic measures to illustrate the 'inexhaustible, onward-flowing melodic stream' of the *Eroica* to the young composer Felix Draeseke, by singing him the first part of the first movement in a single outpouring until he ran out of breath.[9] 'I declare, Beethoven and I, we are the only two melodists, our line is the great one.' (Cosima's diary, 2 February 1880, BBL 1937, p. 155.)

He transmitted the findings of his passionate, lifelong study of Beethoven by word of mouth and in his writings. His 'programmatic elucidations' are worlds away from the usual poeticizing 'interpretations'. True, there could be nothing more audacious than Wagner's exposition of the C♯ minor quartet, according to Albert Schweitzer, but it is not a matter of 'comments' that might raise a smile: 'here "the poet speaks"'.[10] Wagner himself said later of the famous programme note made up of quotations from Goethe's *Faust* that he compiled for his epoch-making performance of the Ninth in Dresden in 1846, that what was expressed in the first movement could not be put into words, though he had tried in his time. His intention, by this reference to one of the greatest works of poetry, had been to induce in the audience that 'elevation of sensibility' without which Beethoven can

---

[8] Theodor Uhlig, *Musikalische Schriften*, ed. by Ludwig Frankenstein (Regensburg, n.d. [1913]).

[9] Erich Roeder, *Felix Draeseke*, vol. I (Dresden, n.d. [1931]), pp. 102ff.

[10] Albert Schweitzer, *Bach* (Leipzig, various edns), p. 417.

neither be performed nor appreciated. Although he could not help associating the A major symphony with a Dionysian rite – 'I swear I could paint pictures of it' – he added: 'But if anyone were to do so he would see at once that he was worlds away from the music.' (Cosima's diary, 1 December 1878, BBL 1937, pp. 59f.)

Nothing, therefore, could be more superficial than to pair Wagner with Berlioz, for example; the *idée fixe* as a poeticizing motive of reminiscence has very little in common with the Leitmotiv (the term was not coined by Wagner), which is simultaneously the germ-cell of the musical organism. Wagner regretted Berlioz's loss of the 'musical thread' in the love scene in *Roméo et Juliette*, because he kept to the narrative structure of Shakespeare's balcony scene, instead of 'sublimating' it according to its emotional content, which could only be reproduced in the music.[11]

But while opinions can always be disputed, one outcome of Wagner's attitude to Beethoven is beyond dispute and is all the justification it needs: the success of his perfomances of Beethoven's works. As Wilhelm Furtwängler declared in 1918:

> There is one thing to Wagner's credit that he will never forfeit: he was the first to show, by his words and even more by the performances he gave, imbued with the whole force of his passionate personality, just what Beethoven really was.[12]

In spite of this evidence of Wagner's affinity to Beethoven and his work, it is still surprising to discover that he thought similar methods of musical analysis would also be appropriate to them both. He read with interest Theodor Helm's technical analysis of Beethoven's string quartets, which first appeared in instalments in the Leipzig weekly *Musikalisches Wochenblatt* in 1881; he found some of it very good and to the point, and expressed the wish that something similar could be done for his own works. When Cosima objected that popularity would have to precede analysis, he replied that things like the late quartets could never be popular unless they were 'studied', by which, in the context, he obviously meant technical analysis. Without it, he said, one would not even know the right tempi, since Beethoven's markings are often misleading; the quartet he had heard in Paris, well though they had played as far as melody was concerned, had made some bad mistakes.[13]

On the other hand he remained unacquainted with Nottebohm's study of

[11] *Über Franz Liszts Symphonische Dichtungen* (RWGS, V, p. 182); cf. also Schweitzer, *Bach*, the chapter 'Dichterische und malerische Musik'.

[12] 'Anmerkungen zu Beethovens Musik', *Ton und Wort* (Wiesbaden, 1954), pp. 11ff.

[13] Theodor Helm, *Beethovens Streichquartette*, 3rd edn (Leipzig, 1921). Mentioned GLRW, VI, p. 435; Cosima's diary 29 November 1881; BBL 1938, p. 6. The continuing validity of Helm's analyses is proved by the references to them by Hecker and by Walter Riezler (*Beethoven*, Zürich, 1951, p. 280).

the C♯ minor quartet,[14] and with his edition of two of Beethoven's sketch-books (originally published in 1865 and 1880). The analysis of the *Eroica* sketches would have reminded him of some of the characteristics of his own creative methods, as we encounter them in the *Ring* sketches: the weighing and testing of the developmental possibilities inherent in motives and figures; the tireless unravelling of figurations in order to release all their latent energy; the widening of intervals as a means of lending greater energy to the later versions of motives; even the occasional notes on instrumentation, which testify to the association of a timbre with an idea from its inception.

According to Nottebohm the sketches also indicate what was the 'active force' directing the inner logic of the composition: namely, 'that Beethoven constantly related a subsequent [idea or motive] to a precedent'. That is virtually identical to the claim, already quoted, that Wagner made after completing *Das Rheingold*, that 'there is scarcely a bar in the orchestral writing that does not develop out of preceding motives'.

Above all, Beethoven's sketches, like Wagner's, show that the concept of motivic development and motivic relationship ought not to be too narrow in its application. The decisive factor is not what appears to *us* to be the initial shape of a melody, but what it meant to the composer. 'The two versions, the sketch and the final form, seem to have nothing in common', is Kurt Westphal's opinion of the sketch of the second theme of the first movement of the Eighth Symphony.[15] That is even more typical of Beethoven than of Wagner, though it is sometimes the case with the latter as well.

It is possible to fail to recognize the genetic connection altogether: Ludwig Finscher sees nothing more than a 'conventional contrapuntal bass line'[16] in the earliest form of the 'Wahn' motive, as it survives in the first outline sketch for the prelude of Act III of *Die Meistersinger*, dated '22 May 62 / a.m.'. The line fulfils the formal function of the later 'Wahn' motive, but for Wagner it already fulfilled the expressive function, too; for it was on that same morning of 22 May that he wrote to Mathilde Wesendonk the letter in which he describes how he suddenly got the idea for the orchestral introduction to the third act: he was going to have the bass instruments play 'a soft, yielding, profoundly melancholy passage expressing the greatest resignation'.

There cannot, therefore, really be any doubt that, as Otto Strobel had already established, this was the original form of the 'Wahn' motive, even

[14] In *Beethoveniana* (Leipzig, 1872).

[15] *Vom Einfall zur Symphonie: Einblick in Beethovens Schaffensweise* (Berlin, 1965), pp. 12f.

[16] Ludwig Finscher, 'Über den Kontrapunkt der *Meistersinger*', in Carl Dahlhaus, ed., *Das Drama Richard Wagners als musikalisches Kunstwerk* (*Studien zur Musikgeschichte des 19. Jahrhunderts*, vol. XXIII) Regensburg, 1970), p. 308. The first sketch of the prelude to Act III of *Die Meistersinger* was published in facsimile in the *Bayreuther Festspielbuch 1951*, p. 90.

though no more like it than the 'caterpillar' is to the 'butterfly', to borrow the simile Westphal used in the Beethovenian instance referred to above.

Finally there is that union of intuition and reflection, characteristic of Wagner too, that 'imagination that has passed through reflection' in Nottebohm's perceptive phrase, which is typical of Beethoven's work on his sketches. It was nevertheless far from being the case, as some excessively rationalistic analysis might lead the reader to suppose, that he cobbled away at a banal first idea until he had made something striking out of it.

Nottebohm is nearer the mark when he conceives of Beethoven starting out from an 'original total idea'. But perhaps Ernst Kurth's psychology of music offers the most appropriate means of uncovering the essence of this idea. According to his theory it takes the form of psychic impulses in the depths of the unconscious, beneath the level of perceptible sound, which, after rising into the conscious mind, insist on breaking out in sound. 'The essential function of all musical theory is to observe the transformation of specific impulses into sounds.'[17] This would account for how the 'original total idea' can already be very fully formed and very striking, while the first attempts to transform it into sounds still lag a long way behind.

'You are going to ask me, where I get my ideas from. I can't answer that with any certainty', Beethoven confessed to a young musician,

> they come unasked, indirectly, directly, I could take hold of them in my hands, out in the country, in the woods, on walks – aroused by moods that transform themselves into words for the poet, and for me into notes that ring, bluster, rage, until finally they are arrayed before me as music.[18]

Wagner admitted to the same reaction to the initial musical idea. 'Is there anything else like a melody, a direct gift from Heaven?' he exclaimed, referring to Beethoven (GLRW, VI, p. 395). And while working on *Parsifal* he said of himself, 'what distinguishes me from composers nowadays, and gives them an advantage over me, is that I cannot compose without having an "idea"; but they can' (GLRW, V, p. 71). A large number of such moments of creative inspiration are on record: on walks in bad weather and good, in the Sihltal near Zürich, on the shores of the Vierwaldstättersee, on steep mountain paths, in the avenues of the Hofgarten in Bayreuth. The inspiration is almost always 'open-air music'.

'Oh, the way it just comes to you! If I sit down at the piano it's only in order to remember, I don't get any new ideas there.' (DMCW, I, pp. 704ff.) The simile of a flash of lightning that Wagner used of the musical inspiration of the Wanderer–Erda scene in the third act of *Siegfried* gives some notion

[17] Ernst Kurth, *Romantische Harmonik und ihre Krise in Wagners Tristan* (1st edn, Bern and Leipzig, 1920), pp. 1ff.
[18] Quoted in Riezler, *Beethoven*, p. 102.

of what the experience of an initial idea was like, lighting up for an instant and then receding again into darkness, to be resurrected with the aid of his 'productive memory' (KLRW, II, p. 258).

'But then the working out begins in my head', Beethoven continued, on the occasion referred to above. 'Once I know what I want, the fundamental idea never deserts me, it rises, it grows upwards, I hear and see the image in its full extent, standing before my spirit as if from a single casting.'

Wagner's description of this second phase is found in a letter to King Ludwig:

> Why there is so little in the world that has been wholly completed, can probably be explained in part by the fact that true genius manifests itself not just in the all-embracing speed of the conception of a great plan, but also, specifically, in the – certainly! – passionate, even painful perseverance that the full realization of the plan demands.
> Nothing will come of scribbled jottings in a case like this; from an artistic point of view, what transfixes us like a flash of lightning is a miraculously linked, delicately articulated piece of jewellery, in which every stone, every pearl, every link in the chain has to be fixed in its proper place, like a work of art in its own right, with painstaking diligence. (KLRW, II, pp. 256f.)

In the phase of 'working out' (Beethoven), of 'realizing' (Wagner) the musical idea, during which a decisive role is played by conscious judgment, rejection and selection, intuition still has its contribution to make; as Wagner said of his work on the *Ring* itself: there is nothing in the text that was inserted later, nothing that was made specially to fit a preconceived scheme, nothing that was carried out for the sake of a stylistic mannerism. 'This imposes a continual obligation to be inventive in composing the music, because the only means of advancing from one bar to the next really is with the aid of true inspiration.' (KLRW, II, p. 295.)

'From one bar to the next' – but at the same time, like Beethoven, never losing sight of the whole, of what had gone before and of what was to follow, which, in view of the immense scale of his work, is if anything harder to comprehend in Wagner's case.

> He had before him a task such as had faced no other composer in the whole history of music...At every point in the score he would have to look both before and after, seeing the whole in each part, and each part as contributing to the whole. (NLRW, II, p. 389.)

Thus far, analytical comparison of Beethoven's and Wagner's creative methods would illuminate both and confirm conclusions drawn about each separately.[19] But there is one factor that sets them fundamentally apart: the

---

[19] Klaus Kropfinger's attempt to establish a parallel between the 'incorporation of the slow introduction in the body of the first movement of Beethoven's B♭

combination, in Wagner's case, of music and verse text. Combination, or even collaboration, because the two make their effect simultaneously, as they were conceived simultaneously; it is only due to the techniques peculiar to writing verse and composing music that the work was realized in two stages at different times.

> Before I begin to write a single line of verse, or even to outline a
> scene, I am already intoxicated by the musical aroma of my creation,
> I have all the notes, all the characteristic motives in my head, so that
> when the lines have been written and the scenes satisfactorily con-
> structed, then so far as I am concerned the opera itself is already
> finished

Wagner confessed in a letter to Karl Gaillard on 30 January 1844, while he was composing *Tannhäuser*. And the following year, after he had finished the score, he wrote that the whole of his productive power, and especially his musical productive power, was founded on the fact that he shaped and developed his material in such a way that even he himself could not distinguish between 'what is done by the poet and what by the musician' (letter to Gustav Klemm, 20 June 1845).

The principle of 'simultaneity' is somewhat qualified in the case of the *Ring* by Wagner's emphasis on the priority of the 'form' over the 'motives'; he assured Liszt in a letter of 11 February 1853:

> So far as the form is concerned, [the music] is completely finished
> within me, and I have never been so much in one mind over the
> musical realization of anything as I am now, in respect of this text. All
> I lack are the little pleasures of life that are necessary to induce the
> cheerful temper essential if the motives are to pour out readily and
> joyfully.

That the *Ring* is thus a special case in Wagner's *œuvre* as a whole is in accordance with the whole history of its inception and composition: while the text was written backwards, from *Siegfrieds Tod* (*Götterdämmerung*) to *Das Rheingold*, the creation and development of the motives proceeded in the other direction, more systematically, moreover, than in any other work. There are two further elements to complicate the contrary directions of these two strands of development: motives and themes are introduced in the third act of *Siegfried* that are known to have been conceived in a different context altogether; and, as the two sheets of sketches show, Wagner made a start on the composition of *Siegfrieds Tod* as early as 1850 and, knowing how he worked, it is reasonable to assume that other motives and melodies had occurred to him at that time. (The assumption is borne out in one

> major quartet, op. 130' and the allusions to the prelude in the course of Act I
> of *Tristan* is very stimulating but not altogether convincing. (Dahlhaus, ed.,
> *Das Drama Richard Wagners*, pp. 259ff.)

instance: what eventually became the Valkyries' motive had its inception in the Valkyries' chorus sketched in 1850.) Taken in conjunction these different factors compel us to understand the 'simultaneity' of the poetic and musical conceptions in a rather broader sense. Studying the composition sketches will illustrate this by individual examples.

But even here it is possible to demonstrate how great was the *fundamental* authority wielded by the poet of the *Ring* over its composer. 'To my delight, I discovered that the music for these lines took shape with the utmost ease and naturalness, completely as if of its own accord', Wagner affirmed after he had finished the text of *Der junge Siegfried* (letter to Liszt, 20 November 1851). It is indeed the case that the melodic line, its tensions and its articulation, is discernible in the declamation of his 'free, rhythmic verse', though admittedly with a certain range of possibilities of variation, as emerges from occasional alterations and modifications in the setting.

Although the declamation is the most obvious indication of how the music is already implicit in the text, however, it is far from being the only one. There are the archaisms in verbal forms and inflexions, used, not for archaism's own sake, but to amplify or compress the verbal expression; there are the instances of onomatopoeia anticipating or emphasizing characteristic instrumental effects, a kind of *instrumentation verbale* in themselves;[20] the famous interjections, which are essentially musical, like Aeschylus's, and, like his, provoked the derision of contemporaries; the idiosyncrasies of the syntax, which are dictated by the melodic contour, for instance the placing of a relative clause before the noun it qualifies, as the analogue of a rising melodic phrase; the preliminary outline design of musical schemes, which provide the foundation of the structure of periods, acts, the separate music dramas and their sequence.

The progress of the action is essentially musical too, in that it advances, not by means of dramatic dialectic, but by intensifying an underlying atmosphere, allowing the pressure to mount until the event bursts out like lightning from cloud. The same is true of the narrations and of the retelling in narrative of events that the audience has already seen enacted; these repetitions, by the variations in their setting, recall musical variation form. Even Wagner's decision, after completing the texts of *Siegfrieds Tod* and *Der junge Siegfried*, to compose a tetralogy taking the tale back to its primeval beginnings, was musically rather than dramaturgically motivated; it enabled him, like a symphonist, to begin with simple 'Nature motives' and gradually to extend and deepen them to become the 'vehicles for the promptings of the passions'; by tracing the transformations undergone by one such motive one can see, as Wagner said, 'the kind of variation that is capable of shaping the drama'.[21]

[20] Léon Guichard, *La musique et les lettres en France au temps du wagnérisme* (Paris, 1963), p. 104. The *wagnéristes* experimented with an *instrumentation verbale* as an independent means of literary expression.

[21] *Über die Anwendung der Musik auf das Drama*, RWGS, X, pp. 176ff.

The opportunity to observe the effects of the interpenetration of the textual and the musical factors is the extra element in the analysis of the *Ring* sketches that distinguishes it from the analysis of Beethoven's sketches. Apart from those characteristics of the text mentioned above, there is the important contribution of what is unsaid, even unconscious, in the text: the latent music of silent looks, the physical actions expressed only in the music, the reminiscences and anticipations, the mysterious relationships. The knowledge that one of the most pregnant relationships, the motivic connection between the prelude of *Das Rheingold* and the Erda scene, was established retrospectively, is due solely to the discovery of the differences in the composition sketch of the prelude; it is an increase in the poetic density of the myth born of the spirit of music.

'It's strange!' Wagner wrote to Liszt while composing *Siegfried*. 'It's only now that I am composing that the true essence of my text is being revealed to me: everywhere I am discovering secrets which until now have remained hidden even from me.' (6 December 1856.)

In view of the quantity of the material and the abundance it yields, it is astonishing that, apart from investigations of the *Siegfrieds Tod* sketches by Newman, Robert Bailey and myself (cf. the following chapter), and isolated publications about the *Ring* sketches by Strobel and myself, virtually no work has been done in the field at all.[22] What has been done shows that isolated test-borings, however interesting in themselves, are not enough.

For that reason I set myself the task of deciphering the composition sketches bar by bar, a matter of no small difficulty in those passages of *Götterdämmerung* where the pencil notation was not inked over afterwards. I then selected examples which were particularly informative, either for their deviation from the eventual version, or for their similarity to it, and which thus helped to reveal the mystery of the creative process and the stylistic intention and motivation of the work.

Two possible methods of presenting my findings were open to me:

1. Synoptic presentation, whereby individual findings would be grouped together under subject headings. This seems an instructive method at first glance, but for the reader it would have the disadvantage of forcing him to skip about constantly from page to page in the eleven volumes of the Schott study score (or the four volumes of the vocal score).

2. Presentation that would follow the order of the scenes, with the inclusion of synoptic comments within the scenes where necessary. Apart from its greater convenience for the reader, what really decided me to choose this method was the advantage it had of allowing every passage analysed to be seen in its context, and not in isolation. Moreover they are also seen in the right context in the history of the composition of the work,

[22] Werner Breig contributes a study of the motive of the Annunciation of Death ('Das Schicksalskunde-Motiv im *Ring des Nibelungen*') to Dahlhaus, ed., *Das Drama Richard Wagners*, which takes the composition sketch into account. See below, the chapter on *Die Walküre*, Act II.

which I have done my best to enliven and illuminate by the composer's own remarks.

Of course the selection of the examples is necessarily subjective and is bound to suffer from omissions, and equally there will be some dispute over the interpretation and even the readings: two good reasons why the sketches should continue to be the subject of discussion. But let us hope that the discussion, if it is to remain fruitful, will not make the mistake of treating composition as a 'curiously abstract thing, floating somewhere between grammar, arithmetic and gymnastics', as Wagner remarked ironically of his – contemporary – 'teacher in a conservatory'.[23]

Just as the publication and evaluation of Beethoven's sketches opened a new epoch, not only in the study, but also, more pertinently, in the experience and understanding of his work, so too the study of Wagner's composition sketches, in which this book is a first step, will contribute to a richer and deeper understanding of the content and the form of his works, especially of the greatest of them.

The importance that Wagner himself attached to these sketches is revealed by a letter to Otto Wesendonk, asking him to surrender the score of *Das Rheingold* to King Ludwig:

> Many heartfelt greetings to your dear wife! She shall keep for ever something that is of more value than the fair copy of the score that you have been asked to return. (31 July 1865.)

---

[23] *Über das Dirigieren*, RWGS, VIII, p. 274.

Siegfrieds Tod: the 1850 sketches

Liszt also tells me that he is setting in motion . . . a commis-
sion from Weimar for me to compose *Siegfried* [*Siegfrieds
Tod*].

(*Wagner to Theodor Uhlig*)

One of the items shown at the Wagner Memorial Exhibition in Leipzig in
1913 was a folio sheet with musical sketches for *Siegfrieds Tod* on both
sides, from the manuscript collection of Gustav Herrmann of Leipzig. It is
now in the Gertrude Clarke Whittall Foundation, in the Library of Congress
in Washington. From the fact that the stave lines were drawn with a rastrum
(a pen specially devised to draw the five lines at once), Robert Bailey[1] has
deduced that the sheet must be dated after 27 July 1850, the day on which
Wagner wrote to Theodor Uhlig, 'I've already provided myself with manuscript paper and a rastrum from Dresden: whether I am actually capable of
composing anything, God alone knows! But perhaps I shall get into the way
of it again.'

On the recto there are a song of the Norns ('In osten wob ich') and
Siegfried and Brünnhilde's duet ('Zu neuen thaten' and 'Mehr gabst du,
wunderfrau'). The verso has: four bars, plus an upbeat, of a melody
without a text; the continuation of the Norns' song ('Einen wurm zeugten
die riesen'); two versions of the Valkyries' song ('Nach süden wir ziehen')
(Act I, Scene 3); the continuation of Siegfried and Brünnhilde's duet ('Ein
wissen doch wahr' ich wohl'), as far as 'Brünnhilde zu gewinnen' with the
text, and as far as 'Brünnhilde zu erwecken!' without text.

In another Wagner anniversary year, 1933, the February number of the
French periodical *L'Illustration* published a facsimile of the composition
sketch, dated 12 August 1850, of the whole of the Norns' scene and the
opening of the Leavetaking scene from *Siegfrieds Tod*, to which the
sketches on the Herrmann manuscript (or the Washington Sketch, as Bailey
calls it) constitute the preliminary studies. The composition sketch belonged
at that date to the Collection Louis Barthou, which was on deposit in the
Bibliothèque Nationale in Paris. The facsimile was accompanied by an
article by Gustave Samazeuilh, paying tribute to the 'précieuse trouvaille'.

Wagner himself writes in his autobiography:

> Still weary from my exertions on *Oper und Drama*, . . . I sat down at
> my . . . Härtel grand, for the first time for a very long time, to see what

---

[1] 'Wagner's musical sketches for *Siegfrieds Tod*', *Studies in Music History*
(Princeton N.J., 1968), pp. 459ff.

sort of a start I could make on the composition of my massive heroic drama. I quickly sketched the music for the Norns' song, which I had outlined only approximately in that first version; but when I set Brünnhilde's first address to Siegfried, my courage deserted me completely, since I couldn't help but ask myself what singer, within the next twelve months, was going to breathe life into the heroic figure of this woman. (ML, p. 541.)

The date of the earlier sheet of sketches, as deduced by Bailey, and the date given on the second sheet, lead to the conclusion that Wagner's memory was at fault here, since he wrote *Oper und Drama* later, not finishing it until 10 January 1851. The point is significant for revealing that he had already occupied himself with the musical realization of the material before writing the book in which he expounded the theoretical basis of his concept.

The first brief assessment of the composition sketch came from Ernest Newman in 1937, in the second volume of his *Life of Richard Wagner*,[2] where he drew attention to certain features which were retained in the composition of *Götterdämmerung* twenty years later. He also expressed the view that we could be thankful that Wagner had not persisted at that time with this composition 'in the style of *Lohengrin*'.

I was spurred on by this to attempt to obtain a photocopy of the original from the Bibliothèque Nationale, but I was informed on 18 December 1961 that, as the manuscript did not belong to a 'collection publique', the library was not in a position to provide a photocopy of it. After further enquiries I finally discovered on 7 February 1963 that: 'Le manuscrit de Wagner, de la Collection Barthou, a été adjugé 11.500 francs à un Monsieur Lévy dont malheureusement l'adresse ne figure pas au procès-verbal. [Signed] Etienne Ader, Commissionaire Priseur.' And from the evidence of Georges Blaizot, expert près la Cour d'Appel, this transaction took place on 17 June *1936*! If I recount the tale in such detail here, it is in the – admittedly faint – hope that the manuscript's trail may yet be picked up again. Meanwhile we must be grateful to *L'Illustration* for having saved a facsimile, at least, of a manuscript that is literally priceless.

I made one attempt to assess it in 1962, in my 'new Wagner studies', *Vom Holländer zum Parsifal*.[3] Then in 1963, in a Wagner number of the *Neue Zeitschrift für Musik* (vol. 124, no. 5), I published it in facsimile and in transcription and discussed, in particular, the stylistic differences between the corresponding scenes in *Siegfrieds Tod* and in *Götterdämmerung*.

Bailey discussed the sketch in greater detail in his 1968 paper, with the benefit of being able to refer to the unpublished Herrmann manuscript. He appended a 'composite transcription' of the two sketches to his analysis,

---

[2] Second edn (New York, 1946), pp. 159ff.
[3] (Freiburg im Breisgau and Zürich, 1962), pp. 38ff.

reaching, with the insertion of the text, to Siegfried's 'Brünnhilde zu erwecken!'

I cannot concur in Bailey's opinion that the interest of the 1850 sketches does not lie 'in the more or less coincidental resemblance of an early turn of phrase to one in the later *Ring*'; the sketches would have little intrinsic value, were it not for the occasional glimpses of traits of the later version. I shall mention such traits individually in their contexts, namely:

1. in the introduction to *Das Rheingold*;
2. in the second and third acts of *Die Walküre*;
3. in the prologue to *Götterdämmerung*.

Whether one calls the second manuscript a 'composition sketch', as Newman and I do, or an 'orchestral sketch', as Strobel and Bailey do, is not of any great importance, incidentally, since neither term is precisely applicable where Wagner's compositional methods are concerned. The composition sketches for *Das Rheingold* and *Die Walküre* have much more detail in the way of indications of instrumentation and stage directions than do those for *Siegfried* and *Götterdämmerung*, for when Wagner started the latter he had already decided to make orchestral sketches as well. In no circumstances, however, can the Herrmann manuscript be regarded as a composition sketch, since it fails to satisfy the essential criterion of being a continuous piece of composition.

Das Rheingold

There is scarcely a bar in the orchestral writing that does not
develop out of preceding motives.
(*Wagner to August Röckel, 26 January 1854*)

The only surviving sketches of individual motives for *Das Rheingold* are the
earliest versions of the Weia–Waga melody and the Nature motive, both on
the same sheet of paper, now in the Wagnerarchiv.

Ex. 1*a*

Ex. 1*b*

Hörner in Es

The Rhinemaidens' melody is as yet incomplete here, and moreover the
minor alteration made while the composer was actually writing it out, which
gives the melody a new 'turn', betrays that it was still at a developmental
stage. The divergence of the text from the eventual version puts the sketch
at a date before the writing of the verse text, that is, at least eighteen
months before Wagner began composition of the music. A note in the
margin of the prose sketch (March 1852),

> Weia! Waga!
> Woge du Welle!
> Walle zur Woge...

with words crossed out and altered, shows how Wagner was trying to bring
about a conciliation between the sound of the words, evoking the
'Eiapopeia' of German children's rhymes as well as Jacob Grimm's
'heilawâc' ('heilige Woge': 'sacred wave'), and the melody which had
already taken basic shape in his mind.[1]

---

[1] There is evidence that Wagner had read the Middle English *Sir Tristrem* with
its fascinatingly strange and archaic strophic form. In this work it says of

It cannot be said with certainty whether the Nature motive sketched on the same sheet dates from the same time, since Wagner not uncommonly used old sheets of paper for his sketches. If it is so early, then it predates the 'vision' of La Spezia (5 September 1853), which is perfectly possible, as Wagner says in his autobiography that the prelude 'came upon' him when he was half asleep, in exactly the form that had been gestating within him but he had been unable to perceive before (ML, p. 580).

The note in the Annals, on which the description in *Mein Leben* is based, is as follows: 'Afternoon rest on the sofa: waking with conception of the orchestral introduction to *Das Rheingold* (chord of E♭ major): sinking into the rushing of the water. Decided at once to return and begin work.'

The sketch of the Nature motive is also in a provisional form, of which there will be more to say in connection with Erda's scene, but it is already in E♭ major and marked 'Horns': that is, the key and the instrumental timbre were already part of Wagner's original conception. The further development, with the transition to a higher octave, is an attempt to prefigure the rise in the dynamic tension. What 'came upon' Wagner in La Spezia was the outcome of that rising tension, not a careful motivic development, but an irresistible natural event.

Prelude and Scene 1

The composition sketch of *Das Rheingold* in the Wagnerarchiv consists of thirty-eight sheets of manuscript paper, used on both sides, and one further sheet used on one side only; each sheet has fourteen staves on a side; the notation is in pencil, inked over later. The beginning is dated '1 Nov: 53', the finish '14 January 1854. R.W.'. The sketch is mostly written on two staves, occasionally on three, and like all the other *Ring* sketches it survives complete. Since no orchestral sketch was envisaged in the case of *Das Rheingold*, the characteristic instrumentation is already noted in at this stage. It is interesting to see that where the overall key of longer periods is not always evident from the key signature at a given juncture, Wagner writes the appropriate letter of the alphabet against the passage. This confirms Alfred Lorenz's theory of Wagner's 'construction of form by means of harmony'.[2]

The start of the composition sketch implicitly refers to the prior existence of the Nature motive in the sketch described above; the first two bars (marked 'Animated, wind, *p*') are preceded by the note 'first, slowly, preparation for the Rhinegold motive'. The Nature motive, which is what Wagner means here by the Rhinegold motive, established the theme of the

Ysoude (Isolde): 'Sche seyd: "wayleway!"' The dictionary notes that this is an exclamation often to be found in Chaucer, also written 'walawa', and it appears to be the refrain of an old song. This rhyme must have haunted Wagner so much that he gave it to his Rhinemaidens in 1852: 'weialaweia!'

[2] *Der musikalische Aufbau des Bühnenfestspiels Der Ring des Nibelungen*, 2nd edn (Tutzing, 1966), pp. 15ff.

Das Rheingold, prelude and start of Scene I (composition sketch)

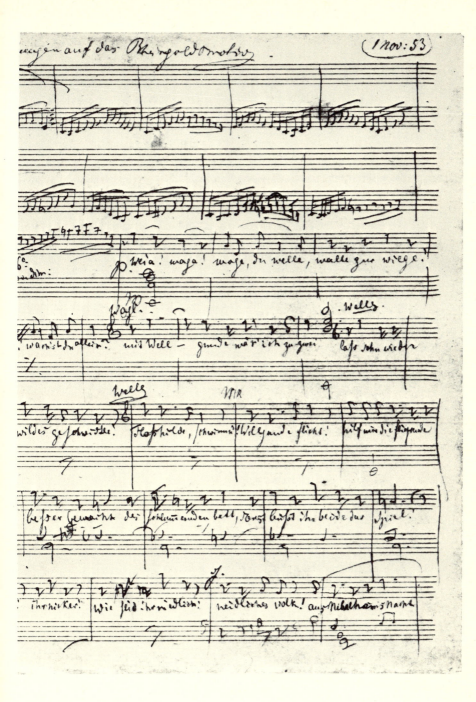

orchestral introduction. Its further development is indicated in words: 'etc. (climbing)'.

The third bar of the sketch introduces the new element that Wagner owed to the 'vision' of La Spezia: the dream of a torrent of water, which presented itself to him musically as an irresistible swell of melodic figurations over the constant, unchanging chord of E♭ major: 'With the sensation that the waves were now rushing high above my head, I woke with a sudden start from my half sleep.' One might expect that this musical vision would have resulted in a free fantasy. Instead, after establishing the wind theme, the composition sketch develops it in four strictly compartmented sixteen-bar variations, each raising the dynamic tension further. The first of these is written out in full, while the first bar only of each of the other three is sketched with the annotation '16' and, in the case of the last, '15 / the 16th poco dim:'.

While the instrumentation for the first variation is given simply as 'strings', for the others it is more specific: 'viola and cello' for the second and 'violin II and viola' for the third; while the specification of all these individually, as well as 'violin I' for the first time, against the last variation demonstrates that all were conceived as playing together from their first entry here. Only the double basses are absent, and they are reserved for the pedal E♭.[3] One must also bear in mind that although the 'climbing' wind theme is not expressly written out in full in the sketch, it provides the ever-present melos, heard simultaneously with the string figurations.

As described thus far the composition sketch of the prelude corresponds in formal layout to the full score. The distinguishing features are these:

1. The extent of the separate periods: even the initial establishment of the theme is more expansive in the score and prolonged as far as the canon for eight horns (thirty-two bars), and an eight-bar coda, with the theme fragmented, is added at the end.

2. More important, however, is the difference in the motivic material: the 'melodic figurations' of the sketches

Ex. 2*a* Sketch

Ex. 2*b* 1850 composition sketch

---

[3] It is not a pedal point, strictly speaking, but the bass note of a chord sustained for a very long time.

bear no similarity to the corresponding motives in the score:

Ex. 3*a* Score

Ex. 3*b* Score

The latter appear to be variants of the Nature motive, ex. 1*b*, although, as we shall see when we reach the Erda scene, their origin was probably rather different.

Ex. 2*a*, on the other hand, recalls the figure accompanying the Norns' song in both the 1850 sketches (ex. 2*b*). This shows that, first, reminiscences of the *Siegfrieds Tod* sketches were present in Wagner's mind when he came to compose the *Ring*, and, second, those associations were musical rather than conceptual (the figure in the Norns' scene relates to the movement of the rope, that in the *Rheingold* prelude to the flow of the Rhine).

In the composition sketch the last bar of the prelude prepares for the '*p*' of Woglinde's 'Weia! Waga!' with a 'poco dim: ', while in the score the last bar of the prelude has a crescendo marking, so that now the subsequent *p* is a Beethovenian piano subito – an effect which was further intensified in the 1876 performances by Wagner's asking the violins accompanying Woglinde to produce an extreme *pp*. This unexpected reversal of the crescendo, according to Heinrich Porges in his record of the rehearsals at Bayreuth, created the impression of the elemental billows of the prelude suddenly compressed into a human figure, 'slender and free, as though sprung from the void' (Schiller).[4]

The E♭ is retained as the bass note for the 'Weia! Waga!' passage, in the sketches as in the score, so that the accompanying A♭ major triad is sensed as a sustained second inversion anticipating the return of the E♭ major harmony. The harmonic refinement is already there in the first committing to paper.

One notices immediately that the composition sketch is already marked

30 5

32 5

[4] All the references to Porges are to his *Die Bühnenproben zu den Bayreuther Festspielen des Jahres 1876* (Leipzig, 1896). 'My dear friend!. . . Even before you wrote to me, I had thought of you for an office of the very greatest future importance to my undertaking. I had decided to ask you to follow all my rehearsals very closely, just as you did with the 9th Symphony, and to note and write down all my remarks, even the most intimate, about the interpretation and performance of our work, so that a tradition is established in writing.' (Wagner to Porges, Bayreuth, 6 November 1872.)

with abbreviated stage directions, which can only have been intended for the composer's own convenience here. For instance, when Alberich is trying to climb the rocks (sketch: 'Meno mosso'; score, in German, not Italian: 'holding back somewhat in tempo') there is the note: 'climbs up / laughter / Woglinde downwards / Alberich down / Woglinde up / laughter / he tries to follow her'. Wagner always had the stage movement, the 'choreography', in his mind's eye while he was composing (GLRW, VI, p. 77).

49 *12*

As the Rhinemaidens glide up and down, the accompaniment naturally lacks the motives of exx. 3*a* and 3*b*; instead, figures developed from ex. 2*a* are indicated, which only occasionally suggest the wave motive of ex. 3*a*, for instance where Alberich sings admiringly 'Wie scheint im Schimmer ihr hell und schön!'

46 *10*

Ex. 4 Sketch

In the score a solo clarinet enters here in place of the strings. Although that instrument is not specified in the sketch, the sound of the clarinet will have suggested this particular figure to Wagner's imagination.

Indications of instrumentation are very sparse in this scene in the sketch, unlike the prelude – they appear as *aides-mémoire*, for instance at the darkening to C minor at Flosshilde's admonition 'Des Goldes Schlaf hütet ihr schlecht!' Here, where the lighter colour of flutes and clarinets is replaced by oboes and cor anglais in the score, the sketch already notes 'oboes'.

35 *6*

Occasionally a subordinate instrumental part will take off from the vocal line or the accompanimental figurations and assume an independent melodic significance. This polyphonic flowering, quite spontaneous in effect, is so typical of the mature style inaugurated with *Das Rheingold* that it can be illustrated by a handful of examples.

At Wellgunde's 'Heia, du Holder!' the first flute part detaches itself from the rest of the accompaniment, which is following the vocal line, and floats independently above the dialogue in long, sustained notes. The effect is already touched in lightly in the sketch:

56 *15*

Ex. 5 Sketch

70 *19*   Similarly, at Flosshilde's 'süßen Trost schüfe die Traute dir', an upper part develops out of the vocal line in the sketch and continues above Alberich's gruff 'Holder Sang singt zu mir her', and is assigned to a solo violin in the score:

Ex. 6 Sketch

(Ex. 6 also illustrates Wagner's practice of making verbal annotations on the sketch: 'quaver movement' against the chords written in the bass line and 'B♭ tonalities' over Alberich's entry.)

74 *21*   Another way of introducing a degree of polyphony consists of the repetition of a four-bar vocal phrase in sequence by an instrument, while the voice accompanies it in counterpoint:

Ex. 7*a* Sketch

Ex. 7*b* Sketch

The interesting thing is that these are not cases of ornamentation added to the score at a late stage, but instances of an innate tendency of Wagnerian melody to break out in polyphony from the moment of inception.

Alberich's complaint, with the orchestra's motivically significant echoing

83 *24*
87 *25*   of his cry of 'Wehe!' already present in the sketch, is followed by the Rhinemaidens' first trio in E♭ major (introduced by the Weia–Waga melody

and again based on the second inversion of the chord of the subdominant), which was written out directly in three parts without any alteration.

97 *28*   Even the orchestral passage during which Alberich chases the three maidens, with its wealth of motivic references and modulations – August Halm describes it as a review of all the themes heard so far, with the attributes of a Beethovenian development section[5] – even that passage is written out in the sketch with only one unimportant emendation like a choreographic scene; the handwriting betrays the speed at which it went

103 *29*   down on the paper. Even the change from 6/8 to 9/8 time (written as 3/4 in the sketch) is already taken into account.

105 *30*   In the introduction to the moment at which the rays of the sun strike the gold (in the dominant of C major), the composition sketch shows the later insertion of a bar between each of the vocal phrases, so that the voice part does not overlap with the fanfare stating the motive of the gold, and this is how it eventually appears in the score.

111 *32*   The melody of the Rhinemaidens' second trio (in C major) is also outlined in the sketch as it is to appear in the score, the initial cries of 'Rheingold!' written in three parts, everything else in two, or only one. The sustained chord of the seventh in the cry of 'Rheingold!' is particularly incisive in this condensed notation:

Ex. 8 Sketch

The Ring motive makes its first appearance in the dialogue that follows,

136 *40*   developing out of the Rhinemaidens' singing, at the words 'Der Welt Erbe gewänne zu eigen, wer aus dem Rheingold schüfe den Ring'; it does not flow up and down so smoothly in the tenths of the form it takes in the sketch as it does in the thirds of the final version. Above all the relationship of the second half of the phrase to the first is more strictly symmetrical in the score than in the sketch, increasing the effect of an incantation:

Ex. 9*a* Sketch

---

[5] *Von Grenzen und Ländern der Musik* (Munich, 1916).

Ex. 9*b* Score

138 *41* At Flosshilde's 'klug zu hüten den klaren Hort', the rising thirds given to the woodwind in the score creep gently in, to die away piano in a reminiscence of Alberich's threatening:

Ex. 10 Sketch

Over and over again we can see how motivic reminiscences of this kind arise as involuntary musical associations.

140 *42* The passage that follows, beginning 'Nur wer der Minne Macht versagt',[6] shows the conscious effort Wagner sometimes applied to the shaping of apparently simple melodies:

Ex. 11 Sketch

[6] The 'entsagt' in the score is due to a copying error. Writing to Princess Marie Sayn-Wittgenstein on 28 May 1854, with the news that he had finished *Das Rheingold*, Wagner still quoted the word as 'versagt'.

In the score at this point quaver rests are added after 'Macht' and 'Lust', to give a musical emphasis to 'versagt' and 'verjagt', which are already thrown into prominence by the rare end-rhyme. The movement in thirds in the accompaniment is abandoned in the fourth bar, and in the fifth, evidently for the same effect, the G minor chord is replaced by a diminished seventh chord. The monotone pizzicato of the double basses is relieved in the second and fourth bars by pianissimo chords on the five tubas and the contrabass trombone. In brief, everything has been made more three-dimensional, more monumental. On the other hand, the triplets rising chromatically towards 'Zauber' – 'a melodic phrase that almost slithers along the ground', as Halm describes it – are already present in the sketch.

146 *44*　　The Rhinemaidens' third trio, 'Lieblichster Albe' (E major), presents a reprise of the first, 'Schäme dich Albe' (E♭ major), shortened and a semitone higher, and like the first it is introduced by the Weia–Waga melody on the second inversion of the subdominant chord. Wagner avoids the risk of mere repetition, even in the sketch, by lengthening the note values in the vocal line, while the accompaniment remains the same:

Ex. 12*a* Sketch

[contrapuntal study]

But the note '9/8', added later, shows that he was still not satisfied and wanted to broaden the vocal line even more by changing the time signature. He did so in the score, so that the three girls' voices now appear to float freely above the brisker accompaniment:

Ex. 12*b* Score

151 *45*　　As the trio ends the sudden entry of the Rhinegold fanfare ('horns', in three parts, in the sketch; solo trumpet in the score) is accompanied by an

immediate modulation from A major to C major in the sketch, while in the score one bar in A minor is inserted to raise the tension gradually.

After the Rhinemaidens' lighthearted frolicking, the theft of the gold seems all the more horrifying. This passage, filling a whole page of the sketch and written in a bold, dynamic hand, undergoes some telling changes in the score. The orchestral interlude following the trio is lengthened by four bars in which the Ring motive is stated twice (the stage direction is 'Alberich, his eyes fixed unblinking on the gold'). The melody of 'doch listig erzwäng' ich mir Lust?' is given a demonic colouring and incidentally it is not a threat openly addressed to the Rhinemaidens: the sketch, though not the score, has the express direction 'heimlich' ('to himself'):

Ex. 13*a* Sketch

Ex. 13*b* Score

The original line 'Das Gold entreiß ich dem Riff' was changed to 'entreiße dem Riffe das Gold' when Wagner came to set it. It is one of a number of textual changes made primarily for vocal reasons but not affecting the meaning. In this instance the change places 'Gold' at the climax of the crescendo instead of the short 'i' of 'Riff'. The tempo of the Renunciation of Love is even more explicitly defined by the 'Adagio' of the sketch than by the 'langsam' ('slow') of the score.[7] While the distorted statement of the Rhinegold fanfare now heard ends in the sketch with a chord of the seventh that persists in the ensuing violin arpeggios, in the score it resolves on to the

[7] In his later works Wagner gives his tempo directions in German, instead of the usual Italian: not out of chauvinism, but because he regarded tempo as something that should be capable of modification, and the Italian terms seemed to him to be too rigid in their definitions. Performers will find comparison of the terms he used in the sketches with those in the score illuminating.

155 *46*

166 *49*

second inversion of the C minor chord – the key of the great heroic lament. The Rhinemaidens' cries for help are expanded and distributed among the voices separately. Most important of all, the string passages of the transformation music are changed from shortwinded quaver runs in 6/4 into broad semiquaver passages in 9/8

Ex. 14*a* Sketch

Ex. 14*b* Score

and swell to the *ff* of the chord of the ninth in order to die away, as in the sketch, in the *p* of the Renunciation motive.

It is immediately noticeable that the changes Wagner made while he was sketching or later, when he came to the score, never relate to the form. Even before Alfred Lorenz's study of the musical structure of the *Ring* (first edition, 1924), Halm, in 1916, singled out the Rhinemaidens' scene as a 'magnificent conception of musical form':

> Does anyone seriously believe that these well-organized relationships, these measured proportions of length and weight in the music, just appear by a happy accident from a poem in which the creative musical spirit took no part, in which, indeed, it did not play the dominant part?

It was this that enabled the form outlined in the dramatic text to take shape with complete assurance even in the composition sketch, needing no alterations later. As to whether it was the outcome of conscious or unconscious design, the outline of the orchestral introduction in the composition sketch gives every reason to assert that here, too, there was an initial creative vision, the formal shaping of which was undertaken in full consciousness. We can conclude from this, too, that even where there is no explicit evidence of it, consciousness and unconsciousness worked together in the creation of the form.

Two of Wagner's letters contain illuminating allusions to his work on the composition sketch of the first scene. 'Friend, I stand amazed!' he told Liszt in a letter which is undated but was at all events written before 16 November 1853:

> A new world is revealed to me. The great scene in *Das Rheingold* is
> finished: the abundance I see before me is greater than I ever dared to
> hope. Now I believe my capabilities are limitless: the making of music
> floods through every fibre of my being.

This proves that the first scene was composed – or rather, written down
on paper – in just a fortnight. The shortness of the time demonstrates the
force with which the music poured out of him, and puts to rout all the
various allegations about the artifice of his creative methods and the
theories about his composing at the piano. And we learn, too, of his own
astonishment at the abundance and potential of the motives he set out in the
first scene.

Liszt's setting of lines from Schiller's *Die Künstler* prompted Wagner to
write about his own, different processes in the first scene of *Das Rheingold*,
in a letter dated 4 March 1854. An immense change had taken place in his
attitude to poetry, musically speaking: he could not produce a melody to
Schiller's lines for a king's ransom. The only way to deal with them would
be by an effort of the musical will, deliberately inducing 'harmonic outpour-
ings', in order to get the melody flowing.

> I know all this from my own experience, and now I am in a process of
> development where I have turned to a totally different method of
> creating: this – imagine it – is how the *whole* of the orchestral intro-
> duction to *Das Rheingold* is based on the one chord of *E flat*!

In view of the novelty of the compositional method he had developed, the
assurance with which he employs it from the very first in the sketch is all the
more amazing.

Scene 2

Wagner noted down the following scheme towards the end of the transition:

(Valh: D♭ major)
renunciation – then: world inheritance – last
Valhalla.

The first line denotes the goal of the tonal progression: following the E♭
major (the dominant of the dominant) of the introductory scene, the gods
enter the action of the tetralogy as they will leave it, in its principal key, D♭
major. The rest of the note identifies the motivic material of the transition;
'world inheritance' means the Ring motive.

Just as the first part of the interlude was enlivened by the transformation
of the quavers in the sketch into semiquavers in the score, so the final part is
178 52 accelerated by halving the note values of the Renunciation motive:

Ex. 15*a* Sketch Ex. 15*b* Score

This is mitigated in part by different tempo markings: in the sketch the Renunciation motive is still governed by the 'Allegro' of the transition, and the 'Lento' only starts with the statement of the Ring motive; while in the score the 'very fast' is already slowed down to 'somewhat slower' at the statement of the Renunciation motive.

181 *53*   There is a note against the piano crotchets that follow, floating serenely upwards 'to disperse the mist', whereby Wagner reminded himself to score them for wind instruments: flutes in the event. Then in the last eight bars we hear the Ring motive developing into the Valhalla motive.

184 *54*   The Valhalla motive is written straight out, fully harmonized, on two staves without a single emendation: a complete piece of music in miniature. Wagner may have been unsatisfied initially with the structure of the theme, according to Mathilde Wesendonk's reminiscences,[8] but there is not the slightest trace in the composition sketch, at least, of any attempt to alter it. The only difference at this stage is that the instrumentation is still noted as 'trombones dolce' and, for the metallic demisemiquaver triplets, 'trumpets'. But in the fair copy of the score started on 15 February 1854, the basic theme is given to the quintet of tubas that Wagner devised specially, while the varying admixture of trumpets and trombones enhances the clarity and assurance of its contours. What was in his mind then was the impression that had overcome him on the Julier pass, on the road to St Moritz from Chur, on 16 July 1853: it was in that tranquillity that he imagined Wotan and Fricka in their majesty (BBL 1937, p. 54). The silhouette of the fortress steadily emerges in the morning light, in the varying shading of the three groups of brass.

    To object to the 'brevity' of the two-bar motive is to overlook, first, that it is a condition laid down by the way it develops out of the Ring motive and, second, that it nevertheless possesses great thematic potential.

    Wagner wrote to King Ludwig on 16 September 1865 about his decision to use the new kind of tuba:

> In the orchestration of the 'Nibelungen' I have used some instruments [the tubas], which I first came across some time ago, in Paris, at Sax the instrument maker's, who invented them. When I have tried to find the same instruments, or at least adequate substitutes, in military bands here [in Munich], and when I was in Vienna, too, there has been nothing that would do, indeed people doubt whether the Sax

[8] *Richard Wagners Briefe*, vol. v (Leipzig, 1912), p. ix.

instruments are really practicable or suitable for my purposes. But as I go on with the orchestration, my need for something of the kind is becoming really pressing, and it is essential that I should pay an immediate visit to the Sax workshop, to have a good look at the instruments, so that I can then make up my mind.

The proposed journey did not take place.

The only occasion on which Wagner could have visited Sax's workshop was during his brief stay in Paris, 9–28 October 1853, immediately after the La Spezia vision, and before he started the composition sketch of *Das Rheingold*. *Mein Leben* (p. 732) has an account of the negotiations with Sax in 1860, over the possibility of using saxophones instead of hunting horns in the finale of the first act of *Tannhäuser*, but by then the scores of *Das Rheingold* and *Die Walküre* had already been finished.

The difficulties in finding the tubas he wanted crop up again in Wagner's correspondence with Hans Richter about the concerts in Vienna and Budapest in 1875, which were to include excerpts from the *Ring*. 'The tubas etc. have been ordered in Munich,' he wrote on 25 November 1874, 'we shall have to play the new instruments in first.' 'Wicked man, I suppose it's gone clean out of your head that I need the new instruments for the excerpts from *Götterdämmerung*', he complained on 29 December. And as late as 23 February 1875 he wrote from Vienna: 'The tuba business was a close shave!'

While the structure of the first scene of *Das Rheingold* consists of a series of songlike sections, built round the variation form of the three trios, the outstanding element of the second scene is the 'dramatic dialogue [which furnishes] the principal material of the musical realization, too'. It was the successful exploration of the potential of dramatic dialogue in this role which Wagner later claimed as his contribution to opera, though he did not claim to have invented the form as such (RWGS, IX, p. 308). The apparent simplicity of this scene is precisely what helps to demonstrate the characteristics of his new style by a series of examples, both where sketch and score agree and, especially, in the rare instances of divergence between them.

The Valhalla motive has been ushered in by the transformed Ring motive, and then twice stated as a theme in its own right. Similarly, other new motives are introduced in turn in a kind of embryonic form which anticipates their first full statements. The significant thing is that this is already the case in the composition sketch, which shows that it was spontaneous rather than the product of deliberation. At the end of the second statement of the Valhalla theme, 'hehrer, herrlicher Bau!', we can see in the sketch how one of the most fruitful motivic germs came into being as if incidentally: the last bar of the cadence is bracketed and replaced by two new bars.

Ex. 16*a* Sketch

Ex. 16*b* Score

195 *57*

206 *61*

210 *63*

The motive heard here, assigned to a solo trumpet in the score, recurs later, transposed to C major and sung by Wotan as an expression of hubris: 'das Spiel drum kann ich nicht sparen!' Shortly afterwards it accompanies Freia's flight from the giants, as a downward plunging sequence in E minor ('All[egr]o non troppo') – an example of Wagner's quite frequent use of variations of one and the same motive to express contraries. The many forms that this motive subsequently undergoes have been pursued by Richard Sternfeld right through to its final metamorphosis at Brünnhilde's valediction, 'Ruhe, ruhe, du Gott!'[9]

226 *70*

230 *71*

The Spear motive, which is so prominent later, is also tried out first in embryonic form in the sketch, piano, three times one after another, until it is played in full at Fasolt's 'die dein Speer birgt' with the note 'Tr[umpets]' (horns and bassoons, *ff*, in the score). The Treaty motive that derives from it, 'Weißt du nicht offen, ehrlich und frei', appears at once in stretto between the voice and the orchestra.

218 *67*

The first time the giants, 'die dort die Burg mir gebaut', are mentioned the ponderous rhythm of their motive is anticipated in the accompaniment, piano; then again at Freia's frightened cry, 'mich Holde käm' er zu holen', forte; then at last, as Fasolt and Fafner enter, it is presented in full as a theme, fortissimo.

[9] 'Wotans Lebenstrieb', *Richard-Wagner-Jahrbuch*, vol. v, pp. 233ff.

The nucleus of Freia's motive, as goddess of love, is stated twice as the
224ff. *69ff.* violent run-up to her Flight motive, then taken up in an expressive cello and
oboe melody accompanying Fasolt, and finally given a full, expansive
272 *87* rendering ('Adagio' in the sketch) at Loge's praise of 'Weibes Wonne und
Wert'. Apart from the far richer polyphonic writing in the score, the
sketch's semiquaver passages are expanded and smoothed down in the form
of triplets, the 'slowest' musical figures which Wagner always imbued with
special expressive power.

Ex. 17*a* Sketch   Ex. 17*b* Score

The same happens again every time Freia's motive recurs. There are two
particularly effective changes in the score, as against the sketch:

Ex. 18*a* Sketch

Ex. 18*b* Score

278 *88* The bite of 'verlacht' ('laughed to scorn') is underlined by its repetition by
the oboes and clarinets, and the final cadence is elaborated in the first violin
279 *88* part.[10]

Ex. 19*a* Sketch

---

[10] The final cadence of the song *Der Engel* (1857) is very reminiscent of this, but
transposed from the key of D to G.

Ex. 19*b* Score

Even Loge's highly characteristic flickering motive has been anticipated long before his appearance on the stage, in Wotan's part:

214 65

Ex. 20*a* Sketch   Ex. 20*b* Sketch

If it were not already there in the sketch at that point, it might reasonably be supposed that Wagner inserted it there while working on the score, with the benefit of hindsight. As it is, there can be no doubt that the anticipation at that point predates the composition of the full motive. Furthermore, the chromatic elaboration of the motive in the orchestral part is already very detailed in the composition sketch: in two and three parts, one and sometimes two parts written in semiquavers and the rest in quavers, and always in such a form that the harmonies are unmistakable.

296 95

Loge's praise of the Nibelungen treasure, 'den schimmernd Zwerge schmieden, rührig im Zwange des Reifs', is already accompanied by the motive of their hammering in the sketch, long before the scene changes to Nibelheim. The rhythm is slightly different, but the bass line is already making its characteristic descent.

Ex. 21*a* Sketch   Ex. 21*b* Score

Besides this technique of the 'organic' growth of new motives, the other important new attributes of 'dramatic dialogue' are the melodic character of the vocal line and its interweaving with the orchestral melody. Wagner always expressly rejected the idea that his vocal writing was a kind of glorified recitative. The alterations he made in the process of composition show that he attached great importance to the smallest note values, and he expected singers and conductors to observe them just as strictly. 'No recitative, there's no such thing in my music!' he proclaimed during the rehearsals of the 1876 *Ring*: 'It's all "arias"!' And during the rehearsals for *Parsifal* in 1882 he justified his claim: 'The exact observance of the rhythm gives the musical speech the character of simplicity and naturalness.

Operatic recitative has inured us too much to histrionics.' (*Wagner-Gesamtausgabe*, xxx, p. 166.)

'Recit.' appears as a note only once in the sketch, at Loge's 'Doch ihr setztet alles auf das jüngende Obst', and that is replaced in the score by 'free, but lively and harsh' (for four bars).

Nor, as Lorenz stresses, does the origin of Wagner's vocal writing lie in recitativo accompagnato. Although the convention, from the Venetians and Neapolitans to the scenas of the Romantics, offers many instances of profound emotional expression, they are formally fragmented: the more striking they are in individual characteristics, the more diffuse their structure – 'precisely the contrary to Wagner's *unifying* genius!' (p. 63).

This unifying force is based on the principle of motivic development and motivic relationship, which links the instrumental motives genetically not only to each other but, as we have seen, to the vocal melody as well.

Further evidence that the vocal writing does not proceed from ordinary declaimed speech, as recitative does, appears when one realizes that, from *Das Rheingold* onwards, it makes fewer and fewer concessions to the accentuation of natural speech. The process is neither random nor arbitrary but rather the result of listening to the secret melody of speech, as 'words, transfigured by the spirit shining through them, already stand ever on the threshold of musical conformation' (Porges, with reference to *Siegfried*, Act III).

The avoidance of declamation and the 'spiritual transfiguration' of the words take the musical form of broadening the narrow compass typical of recitative by enlarging the intervals in the melody, sometimes introducing leaps that had previously been thought unsingable:

Ex. 22*a* Sketch

Ex. 22*b* Score

Ex. 23*a* Sketch

Ex. 23*b* Score

Ex. 24*a* Sketch

Ex. 24*b* Score

Ex. 25*a* Sketch [crossed out]

Ex. 25*b* Sketch [emended]

The melody is expanded, which simultaneously makes the rhythm more elastic and more vigorous.

245 77   The sole purpose of the change in the following example, which even entailed a rare cut in the text, was to strengthen the rhythmic vigour of the voice part at a dramatic highpoint:

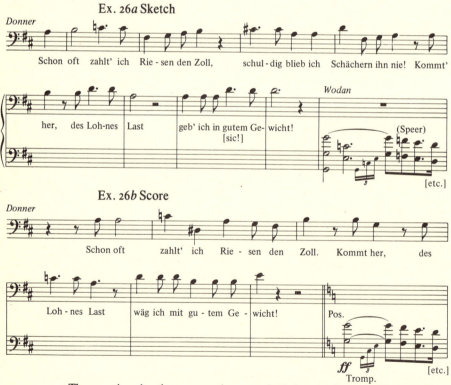

The version in the score gives a vivid impression of Wotan's Spear motive – *ff* in the trombones, striding down through more than two

octaves – being launched now by the energy of the phrase sung by Donner.

Alterations which add to the lyric quality of the vocal writing are equally illuminating, especially in Fricka's part, where Wagner took pains to avoid the intonations of a nagging wife. Already in the sketch he changed her 'So ohne Scham verschenktet ihr Frechen', so that it started a fourth lower, with the effect of making the female voice sound, in this dark register, sorrowful rather than accusing:

199 *59*

Ex. 27*a* Sketch [with the second version on the lower stave]

Ex. 27*b* Score

217 *67*   'Die im bösen Bund dich verrieten' is rather colourless in the sketch; in the score, where it foreshadows the thirds of Alberich's curse, it has acquired grandeur:

Ex. 28*a* Sketch

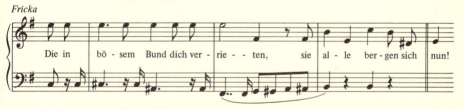

Ex. 28*b* Score

344 *112*   Finally, the arresting 'Wodan, Gemahl!',[11] another case where Wagner changed the phrase to its final eloquent form in the sketch, and where it is

---

[11] The spelling 'Wodan' is used throughout the composition sketch.

already, in addition, a rare example of a soprano solo accompanied by a *pp* tremolo on the drums:

Ex. 29 Sketch [with the revised version on the middle stave]

At her wheedling 'Um des Gatten Treue besorgt', it is the alteration by a mere semitone that relieves the melody of the suspicion of sentimentality:

Ex. 30*a* Sketch

Ex. 30*b* Score

Halm comments that Wagner's sense of the syntactical congruence of speech and music, which made him one of the great masters of declamation, is perfectly exemplified here in the way the – shortened – antecedent is not so much closed as left open by the second inversion triad on 'besorgt'.[12] He could not have known when he wrote that that the chord already took that form in the hastily written sketch, in other words that Wagner really did 'sense' rather than calculate it.

As Fricka goes on with 'zieht's in die Ferne ihn fort', Halm suggests that the change of harmony on 'fort' ('away'), an A major chord in an F major

---

[12] Halm regards it as a mistake on Schubert's part, in setting the line 'Das Meer erglänzte weit hinaus', to have written a perfect cadence on 'hinaus'.

context, is a simile for a look, or a longing to go, into the distance; the return to the main key, to its initial dominant-seventh chord, indeed, has a 'positively three-dimensional' effect. This harmonization, too, as well as the accompanying cello figure, which rises chromatically in a *Tristan*-like manner, is already formed in the sketch:

Ex. 31 Sketch

One concomitant of 'infinite melody' is that Wagner avoids perfect cadences and links separate periods together to form a chain. Then, when there is a significant pause in the dialogue once in a while – for example, following Fafner's 'Ew'ge Jugend erjagt, wer durch Goldes Zauber sie zwingt' – and we actually hear a tonic chord prolonged for five and a half bars, enriched and given plagal shading by three motives in conjunction, it is, in Lorenz's words, 'one of the most heavenly closes in all music' (p. 67); a pause at this point is the only fitting thing, because the gold casts its spell over everyone present in that great D major period.[13] One might suppose that the combination of motives at this juncture was the outcome of deliberation, perhaps not worked out until the composition of the full score. Far from it: they are already combined in their final form in the composition sketch, complete even with the sharply dissonant chord D–G–B♭–F♯–A:

Ex. 32 Sketch

The astonishing thing is the assurance, even elegance, with which Wagner handles the technique of motivic combination, as if he had merely taken it over from generations of precursors. As Loge comes to the end of his narration, and speaks of the Rhinemaidens lamenting the theft of the

[13] On the subject of 'infinite melody', cf. also Ernst Kurth, *Romantische Harmonik*, part VII.

gold – 'Um den gleißenden Tand, der Tiefe entwandt, erklang mir der Töchter Klage' – the cry of 'Rheingold', the song of the Rhinemaidens, and the fanfare motive of the gold itself – the last brilliantly breaking through from A major to C major – are so woven together with the independent lyric melody of the voice part that the listener is not even conscious of the art that has gone to create the moment. This combination, too, is already there in the sketch, lacking only the slur in the woodwind and horn parts in the final cadence.

The key structure is another interesting feature of this whole period. As we shall see, there is always a strong impulse to repeat a motive in its original key if it is to be emphasized – an appeal to perfect pitch, in fact. For instance, at 'Nacht-Alberich buhlte vergebens um der Badenden Gunst', which is accompanied by the Weia–Waga melody, Wagner originally modulated from D major, via B minor to A♭ major in the composition sketch, i.e. to the motive's original key, but then he wrote 'A major' over it and erased the still just legible B♭ key signature: evidently he decided not to interrupt the flow of sharp keys for the sake of a fleeting quotation, remembering his own condemnation of anyone who modulated obviously without good reason as a bungler.

By contrast, a little earlier, when fragments of the Valhalla theme are quoted playfully in duple time at Loge's 'In Höhen und Tiefen', and then the whole theme is quoted in conclusion in triple time, Wagner did not hesitate to modulate from A major to the original D♭ major, and expressly marked the resulting harmonic transition 'F major' in the sketch, so that it is clear that the colourful mediant progression, A major, F major, D♭ major, was a perfectly deliberate conception.

Orchestral timbre is another feature anticipated in the sketch: the 'pizz.' of the cellos and double basses that so poignantly underlines the quaver rest in the vocal part after Fricka's reproachful 'allein' ('alone'); the timbre of clarinets bubbling upwards as she expresses her disapproval of the Rhinemaidens' seductive wiles; the mournful thirds of the oboes accompanying Loge's 'Fröhlich nicht hängt Freia den Rauhen über dem Rücken', as the giants carry Freia away;

281 *89*

252 *80*

255 *80*

199 *59*

310 *100*

325 *105*

Ex. 33*a* Sketch

Ex. 33*b* Score

(ausdrucksvoll)
[Vc., Db., as in the sketch]

336 *109*   the octave Ds sustained by the strings for eight bars after Loge's 'Von Freias Frucht genosset ihr heute noch nicht', which embraces the Golden Apples theme like the shimmer of a paradise lost;

Ex. 34 Sketch

297 *95*   even such specks of colour as the *pp* strokes on the triangle and cymbal after Fricka's 'Gewänne mein Gatte sich wohl das Gold?' are already presaged in the sketch:

Ex. 35 Sketch

'I would have finished the first half [i.e. the first two scenes] of *Rheingold* by the end of this month,' Wagner wrote to Hans von Bülow on 25 November 1853, 'but unfortunately I was prevented by a very severe feverish cold and its aftermath, from which I am only just recovering now.' And in a letter of 17 December to Liszt he wrote:

I am spinning a cocoon round myself like a silkworm, but at the same time I am spinning the thread out of myself. I have written no music for five years. Now I am in 'Nibelheim': today Mime was bewailing his lot. Unfortunately a bad feverish cold laid me low last month and I wasn't fit enough to work for ten days; but for that I would certainly have finished the sketch this year. Often, too, my rather draughty situation robs me of the inclination: at the moment the air is ominously still. But I'm sure to have finished by the end of January.

Interlude and Scene 3

The transition to the third scene, the descent to Nibelheim, already bears an amazingly close resemblance to the score in the sketch. The only change involves four bars quite near the beginning, which were crossed out and 352 *115* replaced by chromatic sequences offering a variation on Loge's motive. This very complicated fashioning of the motive – chromatically descending semiquaver figures with climbing quaver runs in contrary motion – is more faithful to the score in the way it is written out here in the sketch than was possible for it to be later in the vocal score, which had of course to be playable. The handwriting betrays that this orchestral passage was not constructed, piece by piece, but written down in one burst.

The irresistible force with which Wagner's conception flooded from him must be relayed in performance. From Porges's accounts of the rehearsals we know that he wanted the predominating mood in this passage to be a 'demonic delight in annihilation'. At the same time, however, the strictest attention must be paid to the abundant variations in the composer's phrasing and dynamic markings: 'for only so would these structures, executed in the style of monumental art, acquire that distinctive individuality of physiognomy wherewith they confront us face to face'.

358 *116* Lorenz remarks of the onset of the second part of the interlude (marked 'acceler.' in the sketch and 'getting faster' followed by 'very fast' in the score): 'Observe that the key of B♭ is the relative minor of D♭ major, the key in which the might of Wotan, Alberich's antagonist and counterpart, is presented' (p. 25, note 1). The composition sketch now confirms that Wagner employed this key symbolism quite consciously: just as he noted 'D♭ major' before the second scene so here he expressly wrote 'B♭ minor'.

The only indication of instrumentation is 'trumpets' against the second 363 *117* statement of the Rhinegold fanfare (trumpets and bass trumpets in the score), leading into the variant of the Flight motive which plays so important a motivic role later.

Ex. 36 Sketch

366 *118*   The score gives a detailed specification regarding the size and disposition of the eighteen anvils and exactly how they are to be employed, and the way the Hammering motive is sketched confirms that Wagner in no way intended the effect of a blank wall of noise but an orchestra of percussion instruments.

Ex. 37 Sketch

372 *119*   The last feature of the transformation music to mention is that, having written out the Ring motive, plunging downwards *ff* in the strings, in the last two bars, Wagner thought of an alternative harmonization, which he wrote out on the stave below:

Ex. 38 Sketch

II, I *120*   Not only is the location of the third scene a most unusual one for the operatic stage, but it inhabits a sound world that is even more unusual. Each of the four male voices – two tenors and two basses – is treated in a quite distinct manner, one might even say orchestrated: Wotan's bel canto; Alberich's declamatory delivery, often rhythmically unbridled and verging at one point on free recitative; Mime's wails, coloured by short sobbing acciaccaturas; Loge's ironic hauteur, given a cold glitter by playfully interwoven coloratura – the whole spectrum of the possibilities of vocal expression was already fully envisaged by Wagner when he was writing the sketch.

    Coming after the scrawl of the interlude, the calligraphy of the chords of
5 *122* the Tarnhelm motive is almost ceremonious by contrast (marked 'wind' in the sketch, eight muted horns in E in the score). Wagner's notation was often more strictly correct in the sketches than in the score, where ease of reading has priority, and so it is informative to see he regarded the enharmonic change of E minor to F♭ minor as not taking place until the sixth bar:

Ex. 39 Sketch

The letter to Liszt quoted above – 'today Mime was bewailing his lot' – gives 17 December 1853 as the date when the dwarf's elegiac lament was sketched: 'Sorglose Schmiede, schufen wir sonst wohl Schmuck unsern Weibern, wonnig Geschmeid...' It must have given Wagner a great deal of satisfaction: 'rather good and fine', he noted in the margin of the sketch, and later he advised Bülow: 'You must see that it is sung well and clearly, then "Weiber" and "Geschmeid" ["wives" and "trinkets"] will be really mouthwatering.' (16 January 1854.)

At Mime's 'Nehmt euch in acht; Alberich naht', the key of G minor used hitherto is abandoned and the change to Alberich's key is again expressly marked: 'B♭ minor'.[14] The climax of his bullying of the other dwarves, 'Zittre und zage, gezähmtes Heer!', backed by the ring's magic power, was already revised in the sketch, with the insertion of two bars where Alberich kisses the ring, but it was not until the score that Wagner arrived at its eventual lapidary form:

Ex. 40*a* Sketch

[14] The demonic scene between Hagen and Alberich in Act II of *Götterdämmerung* (written eighteen years after *Das Rheingold*) is also in B♭ minor.

[inserted in the sketch]

Ex. 40*b* Score

The Rhinegold fanfare, which would only have checked the melodic flow, is left out; most prominent of all, Alberich's imperious cry acquires an emphatic reverberation in the major third at the top of the accompanying brass chord (cf. Kurth, p. 158).

66 *140*   The surprising leap from B♭ minor to A minor, as Alberich rounds on the two gods – 'Was wollt ihr hier?' – is also there in the sketch. A 'harmonic *salto mortale*', its abruptness concealed by the use of a single line, suddenly puts us in the 'wrong key', as Lorenz observes (pp. 26f.). The composition sketch shows that this abrupt change was carefully chosen: Wagner actually wrote down the key signature of A major to start with, then crossed it out and wrote 'A minor' above it. His purpose in making this downward transposition of one semitone is explained in Julius Hey's account of the 1876 rehearsals in Bayreuth: 'The sound of Alberich's voice ought to create as much surprise as the sudden low E in the orchestral bass and the A minor based on it.'[15]

The ensuing dialogue between the gods and Alberich, with its mounting

[15] *Richard Wagner als Vortragsmeister* (Leipzig, 1911), p. 165.

dramatic tension, is written down very fluently on two or three staves. Only

80 *146*   at the Nibelung's 'Wie ich der Liebe abgesagt' does the score differ from the sketch. While the latter quotes the Renunciation motive in C♯ minor, the score puts it in its original C minor, trusting to the power of the

83 *147*   listener's perfect pitch. The change to the Valhalla key of D♭ major at 'Auf wonnigen Höh'n' is common to both versions.

78–88   The sketch provides various markings to slow the tempo for Alberich's

145–9   great outpouring, 'Die in linder Lüfte Weh'n' to 'aus stummer Tiefe zu Tag!', but some of them are dropped from the score, evidently with the aim of allowing the period as a whole to make a more uniform, elemental effect.

    The various forms of Loge's flickering motive, brightening the subterranean gloom of the scene, are sketched with complete certitude, notably the delightful woodwind scherzo (staccato quavers) accompanying Loge's

90 *150*   'Wen doch faßte nicht Wunder...' In the sketch the voice part is in unison with the cellos, in counterpoint to the orchestral motive, but the line in the score is more in keeping with Loge's character:

Ex. 41*a* Sketch

Ex. 41*b*

110 *157*   The ponderous motive of the giant serpent, identified in the sketch by the word 'snake' above it, is another to be altered: the quavers in the sketch, to which it uncoils in the last three bars, become crotchets in the score.

    The notes on instrumentation are generally confined to the alternation of

74 *143*   strings and wind, for instance in the motive illustrating the rising heap of gold (marked 'wind'): 'Das ist für heut', ein kärglich Häufchen!':

Ex. 42*a* Sketch

Ex. 42*b* Score

Fag., Bs. Cl.

p ——— *p* ———   [etc.]

Vc., CB.   *p*

This is a particularly good example of how the instrumentation – a striking conjunction of wind and string timbres in this case – already adheres to the motivic idea as such, is indeed identified with it.

That is even more true of the toad's unimportant motivic figure, 'Krumm und grau, krieche, Kröte!', which owes its individual character entirely to the timbre of the cor anglais in a low register, an effect already prescribed in the sketch.

118 *160*

Interlude and Scene 4

121 *161* The short first part of the transition music is conceived as an epilogue to the third scene, as the continuous flow of the handwriting makes abundantly clear in the sketch. The plummeting *ff* sequences in the strings, constructed

123 *162* from the Ring motive, which conclude this section, are marked 'with violas' (first and second violins and divided violas in the score).

Just as the key suddenly jumped down a semitone as Alberich turned on the gods in Scene 3, so here, again disguised by the use of a single line, it

127 *163* rises a semitone at the entry of the anvils, as the sustained low F of the bass and contrabass tubas is interpreted by the low strings as the tonic of F minor, which then leads into the ensuing C major as minor subdominant.

This introduces the second section of the interlude, now the prelude of the fourth scene, in the form of variations on Loge's motive, combining fragments of various other motives. In spite of its apparent complexity the section was sketched in a single burst, apart from a minor alteration at the beginning of the first variation:

Ex. 43 Sketch

cresc.

(crossed out)

This figure which, in Kurth's words (p. 518), 'starting in the depths, seizes hold of the upward impulse and forces its way to the heights with stubborn strength', ushers in the orchestral interlude. Kurth cites this motive in this place as an example of those figures, some allied to Leitmotive, some independent of them, which have a great significance for the dynamism of Wagner's compositional technique. These 'development motives', as Kurth calls them, have been largely disregarded, but they are increasingly frequent in the *Ring* from *Die Walküre* onwards: the fact that they are already found in the composition sketch confirms that they are not decorative afterthoughts, as might be supposed, but had a structural function from the first.

The frequent changes of tempo in the interlude are not marked in the sketch: they result, as a matter of course, from the motivic variety of the passage, so the composer did not need to note them down to remind 139 *166* himself. The last of the variations (staccato *ff* quavers in place of the semiquavers played up till then) should be performed 'at considerable speed but not so fast as to detract from the clarity of the motive' (Porges, p. 35); the sketch includes a note of specific instruments, one after another: 'flute, violin, viola' (the eventual scoring is for woodwind, violas and cellos reinforced by bassoons).

At this point 'Loge's triumphant, mocking laughter' strikes on our ears 'with a harsh, shrill sound' (Porges, p. 35), which is transformed into harmless teasing by a playful variation of the motive, as soon as the gods emerge on to the mountain top with Alberich. The stage direction is 'Loge snaps his fingers, dancing' (the wording differs in the sketch and in the score, but the essence is the same). It is one of the psychological refinements of Wagnerian music drama that, unlike other characters, Loge reveals his true nature only in the two symphonic interludes. One might even suggest that perhaps Wagner himself found the character developing as it does only through the nature and the prompting of the music. 'It's strange!' he wrote later to Liszt, while composing *Siegfried* (6 December 1856), 'it's not until I'm composing that I become aware of the true nature of my text: everywhere I discover secrets that were hidden even from me until that moment.'

Like the others, the fourth scene was written out in one continuous outpouring, in spite of the huge span of its action and, even more, of its emotional compass. Sheet 29 of the sketch bears an interim date that has been overlooked hitherto:

1 Jan. 54
170 *176*   'nun löst, ihr Bösen, das Band!'[16]

This means that everything before that point was written, if we discount the ten days of illness, in fifty-one days or approximately seven weeks. Further-

[16] The score has the synonym 'jetzt' for 'nun'.

more, the remainder, the bulk of the fourth scene – Alberich's curse, Freia's return, the apparition of Erda, the invocation of the storm, the Rhinemaidens' lament, the gods' entry into Valhalla – was written in a fortnight, 1–14 January 1854.

The differences from, and anticipations of, the score continue to be

152 *171*

illuminating. Alberich's command to the enslaved Nibelungen ('he kisses the ring and murmurs a command beneath his breath'), as in the sketch of the third scene, again ends here with the colourless minor triad, with the fifth in the upper part (cf. exx. 40*a*, *b*). As the treasure hoard is brought up,

153 *171*

Alberich's key of B♭ minor is again expressly indicated. The score has some characteristic changes in the singer's part here: in one case two bars were contracted into one, intensifying the attack of the words, while in another

195 *184*

case four bars were expanded to five, in order to emphasize the antitheses of the text by means of the musical device of sequence. The idea of this expansion had already struck Wagner while he was still working on the sketch, and he wrote in '3 bars', twice, as a reminder.

Ex. 44*a* Sketch

Ex. 44*b* Score

196 *185*

On the other hand, the succeeding phrase, one that recurs at climactic points throughout the *Ring*, was written straight out in its definitive form, except for a quaver rest inserted in the score after 'verfallen', which had the effect of 'composing' the very syntax of the line:

Ex. 45*a* Sketch

Ex. 45*b* Score

Dem To - - de ver - fal - len   feß - le den Fei - gen die Furcht!

All the changes to Alberich's part illustrate a determination to combine the utmost verbal emphasis with the utmost melodic expression, an ambition achieved most convincingly, already in the sketch, in the Curse motive, hammering one third down on top of another.[17]

The notes of instrumentation are more numerous here than usual. A drumroll is specified for Alberich's summons of his slaves (a tremolo on the tamtam with drumsticks, *pp*, in the score). There is hesitation over the scoring as the treasure approaches: 'just pizz. in the basses here?? (or bassoon alone)' (three bassoons with pizzicato double basses in the score). When the Nibelungen actually enter with the gold the double basses are replaced by 'timp.' and the bassoons by 'tub. trombone' (kettle-drums, two tenor and two bass tubas in the score). At Alberich's 'Dorthin geführt, wie ich's befehl'!', the sketch adds 'trumpets: oboes: horns', transmuted in the score to cor anglais, clarinets, horns, trumpets, bass trumpet, trombones and tubas, gradually swelling from *p* to *ff*. One cannot help but recall Richard Strauss's dictum that a little brass may sound crude, but large amounts do not.[18]

The sombre colouring of the syncopated motive reflecting Alberich's hatred, after his release, is something else that is already foreseen in the sketch, with the note assigning it to the clarinets in their low register.

Ex. 46 Sketch

The dark colours associated with the Nibelungen are strongly contrasted with the bright colours of the gods. As Wotan gazes at the ring, 'Nun halt' ich, was mich erhebt', the sketch notes 'wind' and 'trumpets', which are translated in the score as the gradual unfurling of the full wind complement; the theme, 'swelling as if by magic from the initial piano to majestic grandeur', was, Porges tells us, to be played very calmly and broadly.

The sketch shows that Wagner's original idea was to modify the tempo during Alberich's Curse: he noted 'slow' before 'zertrümmert', 'livelier' after 'bind' ihn los' and 'slow' again at the end, at 'So segnet in höchster Not'. In the score, however, the initial 'slow' holds good for the whole

192 *183*

153 *171*

154 *171*

157 *173*

191 *183*

187 *182*

186–200
181–6

[17] On 'structuring with thirds' in Wagner, cf. Kurth, pp. 217f.
[18] In his edition of Berlioz's *Traité de l'instrumentation* (Leipzig, 1904).

period, another instance of preserving the overall line through greater uniformity of tempo.

The sketch notes 'clarinets, oboes' for the C major canon, formed from the Golden Apples motive, that accompanies Freia's return. The octave Gs of the entire string section, enveloping the melody like a nimbus for eight bars on end, are also indicated in the sketch:

Ex. 47 Sketch

The stage direction at this point differs from the score in the composition sketch: 'The gods become visible, as if waking from a state of unconsciousness: they step forward etc.' (Wagner had started by writing 'The gods who have been unconscious', but then crossed out the words 'welche betäubt'.) The unreal nature of the scene in Wagner's imagination is expressed even more precisely here than in the direction in the score: 'As the mist disperses, Donner, Froh and Fricka appear and hurry to the foreground.'

There are no important differences between the sketch and the score during the following episode, the ransoming of Freia up to the appearance of Erda. The occasional alterations are interesting for their demonstration of what prompted Wagner to make them. Fasolt's initial address is a case in point: the monotony of the dotted rhythm is alleviated in the score; above all the enlargement of the intervals makes the cadences in the fourth and eighth bars even more vigorous:

Ex. 48a Sketch

Ex. 48*b* Score

222 *192* The sorrowing variant of Freia's motive after 'So stellt das Maß' was also changed subsequently:

Ex. 49*a* Sketch

Ex. 49*b* Score

225 *192* On the other hand, the ensuing polyphonic canon on the Treaty motive, combined with the giants' rhythmic pattern and the smiths' motive, is sketched exactly as it remains in the score. Sketch and score also agree on
238 *198* the way Freia's motive shines through at 'Weh! noch blitzt ihr Blick zu mir her', with 'oboe' – the 'naive–tragic' instrument, as Wagner called it – already noted on the former.

After this brief lyric lull the action presses on towards its crisis, carried along on an F minor figure (marked 'lively') formed by fragmentation of the Ring motive, that climbs, sequence-like, to a height from which it abruptly plunges down *ff* and is transformed into Erda's motive in C♯ minor (marked 'slow'):

Ex. 50*a* Sketch   Ex. 50*b* Sketch

[development motive]   [Erda's motive]

This musical process of motivic development and transformation corresponds exactly to Wagner's explanation of the dramatic development. According to Porges: 'The lust for power exerts a demonic fascination over Wotan and as it gains the mastery within him it wakens a hidden subterranean force, which normally exercises its power under the mysterious cover of darkness.'

252–64
202–5

The Erda scene seems simple enough but the composition sketch brings to light some musical problems which had to be solved. One glance at it is enough to show that the amount and extent of deletions and alterations are far greater than in other passages of comparable length. There is little to be gained, it is true, from observing that the preceding bars in F minor, Wotan's 'Laßt mich in Ruh'', are crossed out and then rewritten, apparently without any significant changes. But the following passage in C♯ minor, especially its first half, has whole sections crossed out in light wavy lines and without alternative versions being proposed in the sketch; these are found only in the score, where there are also alterations to sections that were not crossed out in the sketch.

252 202

One important alteration, right at the beginning, needs a magnifying glass to discern. Lorenz has argued that the scene is not really in C♯ minor, but in D♭ minor: nobody will hear the *ff* octaves interjected by the trombones after the four bars of F minor as anything but D♭, and similarly the subsequent bass tremolo on A is bound to strike the ear as B♭♭; it is all written in C♯ minor merely to make it easier to read. It has already been mentioned, however, that Wagner preferred to notate the sketches in the 'correct' harmony: the presence of C♯ minor in the sketch would therefore seem to refute Lorenz's argument. It is only on looking very closely indeed that one sees the original B♭ key signature under the thick cluster of Xs written over it![19]

D♭ minor is certainly more appropriate to the key symbolism of the *Ring*: as Alberich's B♭ minor is the relative minor of Wotan's D♭ major, the principal key of the entire work, so Erda's D♭ minor is its mediant minor. It is typical of Wagner's creative methods to establish meaningful key relationships between the most important elements of the drama. It would be an

---

[19] Lorenz, pp. 25f., footnote. Lorenz did not know the composition sketch.

interesting experiment to write out a piano reduction of the Erda scene in Db minor: not only would it sound quite different to the inner ear, but one would also interpret its harmonies quite differently. But since the composition sketch and the score both have C# minor, let us be content with that in our analysis, to avoid confusion.

While Erda's motive was first written in the sketch in the subdominant, F# minor, in the score it goes straight into the tonic C# minor. The change, an unusual one in view of Wagner's normal confidence in his choice of keys, was motivated by his wish to establish the key of this crucial scene impressively and without any ambiguity. The progressions in the sketch as 'Erda appears': subdominant (2 bars), tonic (1 bar), subdominant (1 bar), tonic (3 bars) and so on, are certainly disjointed and unconvincing. The progressions in the score: tonic (5 bars), subdominant (5 bars), dominant seventh (4 bars), tonic, are by contrast both clear and compelling.

Ex. 51*a* Sketch

Ex. 51*b* Score

The alteration of the vocal line in the first two bars in the score, so as to make the most of the contralto's low notes, is equally effective. The repeated syncopation, at 'weiß ich' and 'seh' ich auch', missing from the sketch (cf. exx. 52a and b), is another improvement.

Ex. 52a Sketch

Ex. 52b Score

It emphasizes Wagner's wishes concerning the delivery of these lines:
'slowly and very expansively', so as to give the impression, Porges wrote,
'of Erda's spirit sinking back into itself like light fading'.

Finally there are bars of purely instrumental music that are cut in the
score or interwoven with the vocal line, adding to the combination of
individual characteristics and monumental grandeur that makes the Erda
scene so impressive.

Apart from the motive of the Gods' Downfall itself, a descending variant
of Erda's motive played over a chord of the Neapolitan sixth,

Ex. 53 Sketch

a rising variant in the tonic's relative major, E, is developed at 'Drei der
Töchter, urerschaffne', consisting of two related and contrapuntally interwoven motives:

256 *203*

Ex. 54 Sketch

It sounds like a quotation from the orchestral introduction to the first scene, but from the composition sketch we learn that this is by no means the case, genetically, but rather the reverse.

As it appears in the sketch, and as we analysed it at the beginning, the prelude is the 'vision' of La Spezia, but still imagined purely as a depiction of nature. Wagner had not yet seen how to instil into it a symbolic content worthy of the mythic drama it begins. It was one of the great moments in the writing of the *Ring* when he had the idea of projecting the two Norn motives of the Erda scene backwards, transposing them from E major to E♭ major and making them the principal motives of the orchestral introduction (cf. exx. 3*a* and *b*) instead of the figuration in ex. 2*a*. The remarkable thing is that they strike the hearer as variants of the simple triadic motive (ex. 1*b*), although, as the composition sketch shows, it had nothing to do with their origination.

It is true that when one hears the prelude for the first time one can have no means of knowing what the concept is to which the two motives relate, but one does have the sense that this orchestral introduction is more than a depiction of nature. For this reason the reminiscence of the prelude when the Norns are mentioned in the Erda scene is all the more striking, establishing an association which is strengthened, even surpassed, when the Rhinemaidens prophesy Siegfried's death in *Götterdämmerung*.

In Wagner the text and its concepts are always inseparable from the music and its form, and *Das Rheingold* is no exception: the refashioning of the prelude meant that the music accompanying Erda's appearance ceased to be an isolated episode: listeners involuntarily hear the latter as a varied reprise of the former, and their sense of musical form approves it.

It is not clear when Wagner had the idea of revising the original version of the prelude. The first draft of the score is the earliest manuscript to contain the new version, and that is dated 'Zürich, 1 Febr. 54' on its first page. In the case of *Das Rheingold* he omitted altogether what was usually the second stage of composition, the orchestral sketch: 'I am now writing *Das Rheingold* straight out in full score,' he wrote to Liszt on 7 February, 'I can't think of any way of writing out the prelude...comprehensibly as [an orchestral] sketch.'

This was still not the last stage in the prelude's complicated history. We have already noticed that the Nature motive ('Horns in E♭') is in a provisional form in Wagner's earliest sketch, but the same form persisted in the composition sketch and the first draft of the score, even in the canon for eight horns. The version of the motive eventually adopted first appears in the final draft of the score, the first page of which is dated 'Zürich, 15 Febr. 54'.

I, 11

Ex. 55*a* First draft score

Ex. 55*b* Score, final draft

It is an apparently insignificant alteration. But its effect is twofold: the larger interval, a fifth, coming right at the start, gives the motive a stronger lift, and the mediant (G) to which it now rises imbues the final note, too, with a latent tension. It is the simplicity of genius: at one stroke an ordinary sequence of notes has become a living tonal shape. The first draft of the score was written in ink and this alteration was made to it later in pencil, perhaps only after the pages had been sent back to Wahnfried. There are also small crescendo and decrescendo marks in ink that were subsequently crossed out in pencil. They are absent from the final draft altogether, which directs that the whole prelude is to be 'piano throughout'. The vocal score is misleading at this point: it implies a crescendo, but the increase in the volume of orchestral sound is solely the result of the gradual increase in the number of instruments playing; the first, small crescendo marks do not appear until the last eight bars.

The two principal motives, exx. 55*b* and 54 (and exx. 3*a* and *b*), are now filled with an *inner* dynamic, so that they no longer need an external one. Quite the contrary: in rehearsal Wagner required the horns to play the high notes, especially the ultimate G, 'with the greatest delicacy and piano throughout'. He also insisted, acording to Porges, on the great crescendo creating the impression simply of a natural phenomenon developing out of itself, that is, of an impersonal process. The listener was not to be conscious of listening to music any more but instead to be 'steeped in the primal feeling of all sentient life'.

Wagner gave the first draft of the full score to Karl Klindworth, who made the vocal score. The Munich antiquarian dealer, J. Halle, acquired it from his estate and sold it to Dr Kurt Lehmann of New York and Munich. Lehmann put it up for auction in New York in 1927 when it was bought by the Rosenbach Company of New York for $15,400. In 1928 it was acquired by Mr John H. Scheide of Titusville, Pennsylvania, and it is now in the Scheide Library of Princeton University. (I am indebted to Dr Daniel Bodmer of Zürich for this information.)

By a happy accident this copy was not quite complete: the first eight pages were missing when Klindworth received it. Via Liszt, these made their way into the possession of the pianist Louis Köhler of Königsberg, who returned them to Wahnfried in 1878. They are now in the Wagnerarchiv in Bayreuth.

The close of the fourth scene could almost be played from the composition sketch as from a vocal score. Some individual features should be mentioned.

If the Erda scene is understood as being in D♭ minor, the return to E♭ major, as Lorenz remarks, would be able to proceed without enharmonic confusion:

Ex. 56 [Written in D♭ minor (after Lorenz)]

Soll ich sor - gen und fürch-ten,   dich muß ich fas - sen,   al - les er - fah - ren!

[from *) written enharmonically in the score]

The stage action was constantly in the composer's mind while he was writing the sketch: he often wrote particular directions above the relevant bars, as in the following example, where 'Wodan ponders' for three and a half bars, then suddenly 'brandishes his spear' as he makes up his mind.

Ex. 57 Sketch

Some melodic and harmonic changes epitomize the stylistic intentions that motivated them. The octave leap at the end of the phrase which now, as it were, answers the octave leap at the beginning, expresses Fasolt's uncontrollable anger more vividly than the vocal line in the sketch:

Ex. 58a Sketch

Schänd-li - cher du!   Mir die - sen Schimpf?

Ex. 58b Score

Schänd-li - cher du!   Mir die - sen Schimpf?

Loge's 'Was gleicht, Wotan, wohl deinem Glücke?', which combines flattery with irony, must be completely innocent of any false sentimentality, according to Porges. That is deducible from the syncopation of the cadence, 'um das Gold, das du vergabst', which would seem highly insipid if the D♯ came, like a conventional *Lied* cadence, on a strong beat. Comparison with the sketch confirms that Wagner took trouble to effect this very nuance.

Ex. 59a Sketch

um das Gold,   das du ver - gabst.

Ex. 59*b* Score

um das Gold, das du ver - gabst.

While the highest note already falls, paradoxically, on the second quaver in the sketch, its removal to the sixth quaver in the score emphasizes the syncopation even more. Moreover the two syllables 'Gold' and '-gabst', containing the alliterative rhyme, now both come on the first beat of their respective bars, so that the latter has no need of other accentuation.

285 213   The following bars illustrate how the sketch clearly delineates quite complicated sound formations; the corresponding passage in the score occupies eighteen staves, combining woodwind with violin and viola tremolos (the revised key signature is written in words):

Ex. 60 Sketch

292 215   Donner's summoning of the storm is another example of how it was precisely the simple, easily assimilable melodies that often took the longest to arrive at their final form. At his very first words, 'Schwüles Gedünst schwebt in der Luft', the sketch shows the evidence of second thoughts about the relationship of the rhythm to the metre, so that whereas the voice originally entered on the first crotchet, its entry is now slightly postponed, to the third crotchet. Then the whole conjuration of the storm was crossed out with a vigorous wavy line and a new version written out immediately after it. This successfully sustained and even intensified the taut, springy rhythm. Compare, for instance, these bars:

Ex. 61*a* Sketch

Don - ner der Herr   ruft euch zu Heer!

Ex. 61*b* Score

Don - ner der Herr ruft euch zu   Heer!

Or the final cadence, where, in place of colourless repetition, a slight extension of the text now permits the insertion of the subdominant with the subsequent turn to the dominant and tonic.

302 *216*   The sudden darkening from B♮ major to B♮ minor, which, as Kurth says, 'almost visibly' darkens the whole atmosphere, is already there in the sketch. Against the four bars of triplets running up to the flash of lightning there is the query: 'or wind alone??' But eventually in the score the strings were left in with the woodwind.

320 *220*   The enlarging of the intervals in Froh's 'beschreitet kühn' is a stage in the development away from anything resembling recitative towards a 'German bel canto':

Ex. 62*a* Sketch

Froh

Fuß: be - schrei - tet   kühn   ih - ren

Ex. 62*b* Score

Fuß: be - schrei - tet   kühn   ih - ren

Only a few bars of the harp part in the finale are jotted down in the composition sketch, in a footnote. In 1875 Wagner entrusted the final arrangement of the six parts to the virtuoso harpist, Peter Dubez of Prague. 'Greatly obliged to you for the work as I am, I bitterly regret not having consulted an artist of your stature at an earlier stage. Now we shall have to see if the omission can be made good.' Dubez was also to arrange the harp parts in *Die Walküre* and in the third act of *Siegfried*. 'The writing for the harps is again very rich at the end of the last act of *Götterdämmerung*, which I will send you so that you can arrange that as well.' (8 December 1875.)

356 *228*   'One of the most marvellous refractions of colour', in Kurth's words (p. 148), only came about after a slight change in the sketch: it was not until the diminished chords were transformed into chords of the dominant seventh (of C minor) that the downward inflexion of the top part acquired its magical effect:

Ex. 63 Sketch

3 Rheintöchter

um   dich,   du   Kla - res,   wir   nun   kla - gen!

But while alterations of that and similar kinds were arrived at during the process of composition, the actual 'inspiration' or 'idea' is something completely independent of it. We know how the work was started, with the 'vision' of La Spezia, and by chance the origin of Loge's 'apostrophe' to the Rhinemaidens has also survived.

The Annals give this information:

> 1852:...October, November: writing the text of *Rheingold*. Nov.
> (weather mild) excursion up the Klönthal with Wille and Herwegh:
> felt worn out, exhausted; couldn't sleep: night in Näfels. Wallenstädt.
> (Loge's final apostrophe.) – Reworking of *Der junge Siegfried*.
> Completion of the text of *Der Ring des Nibelungen*. –

The same excursion is described in a letter Wagner wrote to Theodor Uhlig on 10 November 1852:

> You will have been waiting confidently for a fat letter for several
> days. I have been unable to write it. I finished my work a week ago,
> but I was quite exhausted, and since the weather turned out to be
> unexpectedly fine, I went with Herwegh and Wille...on a three-day
> trip in the Alps...Unfortunately, the trip didn't do me any good,
> since I was so restless that I didn't get to sleep at all in the place where
> we spent the first night and then the next day – in spite of being most
> dreadfully tired – I made myself go on a forced march to please my
> companions, which – as always when I have to force
> myself – completely finished me. And so it is only today that I have
> got round to starting your 'fat' letter.

These two accounts are supplemented by an oral reminiscence, recorded by Cosima in 1874. Talking about the condition of the artist in the world, 'his inattention where realities are concerned', Wagner told the story of how,

> once, when he was out with Dr Wille and Herwegh, he was so tired
> that he asked them to leave him at a particular spot and go on without
> him. Thereupon Dr Wille, with his usual lack of sensitivity, thinking
> he was just being lazy, gave him a push in the back to make him go on.
> Richard vented his fury in a foul oath, and in that instant Loge's
> apostrophe to the Rhinemaidens came to him, words and music. 'Oh,
> the way it just comes to you! If I sit down at the piano, it's only in
> order to remember, I don't get any new ideas there, I try to recover
> things that often occurred to me at the worst possible moments.'
> (DMCW, I, pp. 704f.)

360 *230*   The following is the only thing that can be meant by 'Loge's final apostrophe':

Ex. 64 Sketch

The rider 'words and music' might seem to indicate otherwise, since the original manuscript of the text of *Das Rheingold* bears the completion date 'Zürich 3 Nov. 52'. Otto Strobel inferred from this, so Frau Gertrud Strobel tells me, that 'apostrophe' alluded to Loge's soliloquy, 'Ihrem Ende eilen sie zu', which was a later addition to the text. Quite apart from the fact that Wagner would not have called a soliloquy an apostrophe, that conclusion also ignores the context of the 1874 anecdote: he was talking then about *musical* inspiration, and specifically of *new* ideas. Loge's soliloquy, which is relatively long and declamatory in treatment, could hardly be talked of in those terms. Ex. 64, by contrast, is a short, very pregnant musical idea, of the kind that might well occur to a composer in an instant. The likely solution to the mystery is that the parenthetical 'words and music' simply means that both occurred *together* to Wagner at that moment, the words as reminiscence, the music as something new.

376 233

Finally, the apotheosis of the D♭ major Rainbow Bridge motive, a free variant of the E♭ major Nature motive of the prelude, had four bars added to it in the sketch, obviously not merely as padding, but to allow the latent momentum in the melody to unfurl to its full extent.

Ex. 65 Sketch

14 Januar 1854. RW Und weiter nichts?? Weiter nichts??

The motive is here assigned to 'trombones', while in the score it is given to the softer timbre of a quintet of tubas, supplemented by bass clarinet, bassoons, bass trumpet and contrabass trombone.

At the foot of the sketch there is the note:

14 January 1854

RW

And nothing more?? / Nothing more??

'*Das Rheingold* is finished,' Wagner wrote to Liszt on 15 January 1854, 'but I am finished too!!!. . . Believe me, there has never been a composition like this before: it seems to me my music is dreadful; it is a morass of horrors and sublimities!'

And on 20 January he wrote to Frau Julie Ritter:

> After my return from Paris I buckled down to the composition of *Das Rheingold* – I threw myself into the work with such fervour that, in spite of a relatively long interruption when I was ill, I had already finished it by the middle of this month.

In the letter to Liszt he also disclosed why the work had so exhausted him: the thought that he had to accomplish, by the resources of his own mind and spirit, 'the agonizingly difficult task of forming a nonexistent world'. In fact everything about the sketch supports the view that working on it must have been like living through an improvised performance in his imagination: the shortness of the time it took, the uninterrupted flow of the conception, the continuous development and transformation of the musical motives, their omnipresence in his imagination and their association with the relevant elements in the text and the action, at the same time keeping the most remote tonal relationships in mind, the certitude of the instrumental colouring even when the sounds are exotic original inventions, the constant background awareness of the stage action, from the large-scale nature painting to the smallest movements of man and beast. Even the occasional alterations seem to be the outcome solely of a suddenly clearer view, a clearer hearing of that imagined performance. This applies above all to the one *great* emendation, the blending of the Norns' motive into the introduction of the Rhinemaidens' scene: this was not thought out or deliberated in advance, as the sketch shows – the idea was born from the spirit of music.

As always, Wagner felt compelled to account to himself for his creation. He confessed in a letter to August Röckel on 25 January 1854:

> The composition of *Das Rheingold*, so difficult and so important a work, is now completed and . . . it has restored a great confidence to me. It is now possible again for me to comprehend how much of the whole essence of my creative intention is disclosed only with the music: I cannot bear to look at the text without the music any more. In due course I expect to be able to let you see the music too.

Then he goes on, significantly:

> For the moment I will say just this much, that it has now turned out to
> be a firmly entwined unity: there is scarcely a bar in the orchestral
> writing that does not develop out of preceding motives.

But the creative process itself remains a mystery to him:

> Yet this is something which defies definition.

Die Walküre

'I'm working hard and expect to finish the text of my *Walküre* within a fortnight', Wagner wrote to Liszt on 16 June 1852. And he concluded the letter: 'My *Walküre* (the first drama) is turning out fearfully well! I hope to be able to present you with the whole text of the tetralogy before the summer is out. Writing the music will be a very easy and quick affair: it will only mean the *effectuation* of what is already *completed*.'

Such a statement, at a time when he had not written down a single note of the music of the *Ring*, demonstrates that the composition was ever-present in his mind while he was still writing the text: not the word-setting alone, but the musical impulses and the formal impulses which were identical with them. Quite how far he had gone at this stage in translating the impulses into sound and into fully formed motives is uncertain, except in the cases where he adopted motives or provisional forms from the 1850 sketch for *Siegfrieds Tod*, or where, as with the Spring Song, a music sketch has survived which was made at the time when he was working on the text. When we consider that we owe that particular sketch to pure chance, we are probably safe in assuming that he had already conceived other melodies in his head too.

In *Die Walküre* Wagner leaves the world of elemental beings and enters the world of humans, and the 'plastic Nature motives' of *Das Rheingold* here become the 'vehicles for the promptings of the passions'. Or, as he himself put it, in a letter to Brahms, when he was sending him the score of *Das Rheingold* in 1875, ironically alluding to Hanslick's strictures:

> I have sometimes been told that my kind of music is painted scenery.
> *Das Rheingold* will certainly be accused of it. However, you may
> perhaps be interested to see, in reading the scores of the rest of the
> *Ring des Nibelungen*, that I have been able to construct all kinds of
> musical thematic material from the scenery set up in the first part.

Five days after starting the composition sketch of *Die Walküre*, he exclaimed to Liszt, on 3 July 1854, 'You know, now it really *is* getting started! Extraordinary, these contrasts between the first love scene in *Die Walküre* and the scene in *Das Rheingold!*'

Act I

There are no separate sketches of motives for the first act in existence, apart from the sketch of the rhythm of 'Winterstürme' in the margin of the original manuscript of the text (Wagnerarchiv) and the sketch of a first version of the melody on a sheet torn from a notebook, which was published in facsimile in the *Neue Musikzeitung*, vol. xxx, no. 1.[1]

The composition sketch of the first act consists of nineteen sheets of manuscript paper, used on both sides, of fourteen staves each, notated in pencil and inked over afterwards. The beginning is dated '28 June 1854', the end '1 Sept. 54'. The music is sketched mostly on two or three staves, rising to as many as six in the introduction. Wagner did not envisage an orchestral sketch: the notes on the projected instrumentation are even more numerous than in the *Rheingold* sketch, and so are the indications of key, written in letters and words.

The handwriting is beautiful to begin with, but becomes increasingly hurried from the Spring Song onwards.

The first act of *Die Walküre* is a particularly good example of the circumstances of a period in Wagner's life impinging on what he was working on at the time: the sketch includes sixteen easily decipherable allusions to his relationship with Mathilde Wesendonk.

Prelude

Maintaining an overall view of the prelude in the sketch was less of a problem in *Die Walküre* than in *Das Rheingold*.

3 2   The dissonant Es layered above each other in three octaves, played by the woodwind and horns (the instrumentation is not noted here), are lightly intimated above the two staves of the low strings:

Ex. 1 Sketch

5 3   Detailed notes of the instrumentation begin with the stretto-like treatment of the Storm motive, where the notation spreads on to four and six staves:

---

[1] O. Strobel, *Skizzen und Entwürfe zur Ring-Dichtung* (Munich, 1930), p. 256.

Ex. 2 Sketch

13 4   The sketch notes 'clarinet, bassoon, bass clarinet' for the run of triplets leading to the dynamic climax, to which flutes and cor anglais were added in the scoring.

Scene 1

22 6   The Storm motive was emended in the sketch at the point where it dies away in the cellos and basses, so that it now forms a minor variant of the cello figure, later transposed to the major, which introduces the Spring Song:

Ex. 3 Sketch

25 9   The melody for solo cello as Sieglinde offers Siegmund the drinking horn is a bar longer in the score (a note on the sketch shows Wagner considered expanding it by two bars) and a slight alteration of the phrase structure makes its articulation more flexible, enhancing the significance of the ultimate goal of the rising sequences, the Love motive formed from the second motive of Freia's theme, the Flight motive.

Ex. 4a Sketch

Ex. 4*b* Score

26 *9*   The accompaniment does not enter in the score until one bar after the
melody has reached its dynamic climax.

33 *12*   The following passage, as they share the cup of mead, illustrates how the
instrumental colouring was an integral factor in the initial idea: 'she' is
written against the phrase marked 'clarinet', 'he' against the cello phrase.

Ex. 5 Sketch

It is interesting to compare this with the passages of dumbshow during the
pauses in the chorale in the first scene of *Die Meistersinger*: viola and cello
for Walther, oboe and clarinet for Eva.

39 *14*   The last two bars of Sieglinde's exclamation, 'Nicht bringst du Unheil
dahin, wo Unheil im Hause wohnt!', are marked with a portamento,
something Wagner rarely uses, in both the sketch and the score.

Ex. 6 Sketch

40 *15*   The polyphonic orchestral passage after 'Hunding will ich erwarten' is
sketched in very exact detail, with ample notes of the orchestration for the
two contrapuntally linked melodies, which Wagner meant to be played as if
they were dialogue. 'L. d. m. M.?' ('Liebst du mich Mathilde?' – 'Do you
love me, Mathilde?') is written above the solo oboe part in the last eight
bars. The accompanimental horn chords were initially written in regular
quavers, but were already changed in the sketch to the crotchet syncopation

that now obtains, strengthening the 'rather marked rhythm' that Wagner wanted for the passage.

Scene 2

42 *16*

After the rhythm of Hunding's motive (like the giants' motive in *Das Rheingold*) has been anticipated twice, the motive itself is played in full, marked 'horns' in the sketch instead of the score's tubas. Hunding's question, 'Du labtest ihn?', is marked with a portamento arc at 'lab-test' in the sketch, but it is omitted in the score. The words, that is, should be 'blurted out quickly', not smoothly.

52 *21*

Following Sieglinde's 'Gast, wer du bist, wüßt' ich gern', there is a note in the margin: 'Answer, when I get back from Sitten. 13–14 July.' Wagner had agreed to conduct Beethoven's A major symphony and the *Tannhäuser* overture at the Swiss Confederation Music Festival in Sitten, but only on condition that he should see for himself that the arrangements were satisfactory: in fact he found the preparations so inadequate that he turned tail and fled. 'If everything goes well, I shall get on with the composition of *Die Walküre* again, from 1 August', he wrote to Liszt on 31 July, from on board the steamer *Stadt Zürich*. 'Work – *this* work – is the *only thing* that enables me to endure life.' Sheer vexation, however, prevented him from getting on with the composition at once, and he finally dated the resumption of work on the sketch: '*3 August!!*' The note beside the date, 'W. d. n. w., G.!!!' ('Wenn du nicht wärst, Geliebte' – 'Were it not for you, beloved') relates to the adjacent stage direction and Siegmund's words: 'Siegmund looks up, gazes into her eyes and begins: "Friedmund darf ich nicht heißen"'':

Ex. 7*a* Sketch

The tempo direction, 'a little slower', is not given in the score.

66 *27*

Originally Hunding's 'Die so leidig Los dir beschied' was meant to come immediately after Siegmund's 'drum mußt' ich mich Wehwalt nennen, des Wehes waltet' ich nur'. Wagner had already started to write the words, when he crossed them out again and inserted a six-bar oboe melody expressing Sieglinde's 'profound sympathy', with the marginal note 'D. b. m. a.!!' ('Du bist mir alles' – 'You are everything to me').

Ex. 8 Sketch

D. b. m. a.!! *Sieglinde* (drückt *tiefes Mitleiden* aus)

(Die so leidig Los dir) [crossed out]

The tempo direction, 'a little livelier', was left out of the score.

69 *28*   Sieglinde's impetuous reproof of Hunding is made even more impulsive in the score by a slight rhythmic adjustment:

Ex. 9*a* Sketch

Fei - ge nur fürch - ten den,   der waf - fen - los   ein - sam   fährt!

Ex. 9*b* Score

Sieglinde (etwas lebhaft)

Fei - ge nur fürch - ten den, der waf - fen - los   ein - sam   fährt!

The additional direction, 'rather lively', accords with the change.

72 *29*   The expressive and skilfully written five-part string accompaniment to Siegmund's 'Mit wilder Tränen Flut' was written straight out without change in the sketch, whereas the vocal part shows numerous crossings-out and alterations. In rich part-writing of this kind, Wagner frequently added the vocal line last, in order to assimilate it contrapuntally and harmonically to the orchestra, which is here the dominant partner, but at the same time he tried to give it as self-sufficient a melody as possible.

80 *32*   As Siegmund gravely ends his narration, 'Nun weißt du, fragende Frau', the introductory motive of the cellos and double basses was lengthened in the sketch by two bars, so that, as it now is, it offers a formal counterweight to the two following four-bar periods:

Ex. 10 Sketch

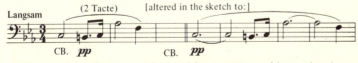

Langsam   (2 Tacte)   [altered in the sketch to:]

CB. *pp*   CB. *pp*

81 *32*   The two bars for low strings with pesante markings, that immediately follow, already have the explanatory stage direction, 'Hunding stands up', in the sketch.

Ex. 11 Sketch

(Hunding erhebt sich)

When the singers are provided with neither chairs nor table, however, choreographic figures of that kind are left up in the air.

87 *34*   In the episode of mime following Hunding's 'Harre mein zur Ruh'', one passage of eight bars and another of six bars are crossed out: evidently in order to simplify the sequential continuation of the melody. It is particularly noticeable here, and in the following scene, that the projected instrumentation is carefully chosen to contribute to the atmosphere of dim half-light, especially the piano pulsation of the horns above the long, sustained chords of the low wind.

At the first statement of the Sword motive the note is 'oboe' and at the second 'cor anglais' with 'oboe' tailpiece; the score differs only in replacing the final bar, with a descending minor second on the flute, by a bar's rest instead.

Ex. 12 Sketch

Scene 3

92 *37*   The scene begins ten bars later in the sketch, that is, not until the pulsating A on the horns. Above it stands the note 'G. w. h. d. m. verl.??' ('Geliebte, warum hast du mich verlassen??' – 'Beloved, why did you leave me??').

94 *37*   Siegmund's monologue, 'Ein Schwert verhieß mir der Vater', was written down in great haste, but not one of the subordinate parts was forgotten: neither the melody for solo cello (with the note 'Vc.') accompanying 'Ein Weib sah ich...', nor its continuation by the first violins. 'Oboe espr.' is noted against the Sword motive's statement in E minor (first oboe, 'expressively', in the score). When it is repeated once more, now in C major ('trumpet'), a harp is heard for the first time, a sound that Wagner had held in reserve until that moment. The woodwind triplets arching delicately above the motive and the urgent syncopations of the strings are also noted in. At the end of the monologue, the sketch has two versions of

112 *42*   the vocal line at 'tief in des Busens Berge glimmt nur noch lichtlose Glut', the first a third higher than the second, which is as in the score and which, with the *pp* chords of the trombones, further deepens the gloom of the 'nächtiges Dunkel'.

113 *43* Sieglinde's reappearance is preceded by a four-bar cello figure (marked 'lively'), from which triplet figurations subsequently develop in the violins and violas:

Ex. 13*a* Sketch

Ex. 13*b* Sketch

These 'development motives' are already there in the sketch, which confirms Ernst Kurth's opinion that they are not merely ornaments. The important thing, he says, is to grasp their psychological origin, the conditions that govern their dynamic character.

> They are separate lines of force of the great sustaining current of the infinite melody, and for that reason 'accompanimental motives' falls far short as a descriptive term for them; rather, they are components of the formal development... Their essential significance for the High Romantic style lies in their capacity for continual rebirth as separate linear elements at every point within the great harmonic compositional flow, separating the threads of the harmonic weave and thus displaying, in the small and separate parts, the creative will that seeks to break out in the infinite melody. (Pp. 517ff.)

118 *44* The perspectives opened up by considerations such as these should not lead us to overlook apparently minor details, however. The line in Sieglinde's narration, 'ein Fremder trat da herein: ein Greis in grauem Gewand', closes on an E in the sketch; it was not until the score that Wagner substituted the G♯, the leading-note effect of the mediant instantly raising the tension:

Ex. 14 Sketch

The development motives, which figure merely as tentative suggestions in the earlier passage, grow far more vigorous and turbulent towards the end

131 47 of the exchange of dialogue until the moment when the door bursts open. Kurth singles out two typical formations:

Ex. 15*a* Sketch

Ex. 15*b* Sketch

Of the first he writes that it occurs very frequently and is governed dynamically by the powerful start and calmer conclusion. Of the second, that it consists of 'a wave reaching down to the depth, then driving vividly zigzagging lines before it up to the height'. One should notice how the great overall surge of the undulating movement throws off fragmentary motives in passing, which are themselves capable of acting as development motives. The process is naturally one of the separate elements proceeding from the greater whole:

> the *complete* two-bar figure is a unified movement of force; as it vibrates it shakes from itself fragmentary movements which detach themselves; indeed the complete two-bar figure itself . . . springs if anything unconsciously from the totality of the whole symphonic wave movement. (Pp. 522f.)

Both these figures, which Kurth quotes from the score, are already in the composition sketch in exactly the same form, confirming their involuntary dynamic origin. Indeed, on looking at these pages in the sketch, one gets the impression that the semiquaver figurations are the channel for the stream of the melos, as in the finales of Beethoven's two 'Tempest' sonatas.

After all the sections of the composition sketch of *Die Walküre* that we have analysed so far, the two pages (sheets 14v and 15r) bearing the most 150 53 familiar melody in the whole work stand out by reason of the abundance of alterations and emendations. Right at the start, the introductory cello figure formed from the Storm motive of the act prelude was subsequently lengthened by the addition of a bar:

Ex. 16 Sketch

Of the voice part, only the first four bars were written out almost without alteration: only the last note, F, on 'Lenz', was crossed out and replaced by the C, a fourth lower, that is now sung, while the text was altered more substantially:

Ex. 17a Sketch

[bracketed words crossed out in ms.]

Then, as the melody continues to unfold, not only are there several instances of whole bars crossed out, but also of alternative versions being written in above and below the original, which enable us to see just how the eventual version gradually crystallized. Obviously these first four bars form the motivic germ of the song, supporting Richard Strauss's observation that an 'idea' is seldom longer than two to four bars.[2]

It so happens that we are in a position to trace the development of the germ of 'Winterstürme'. It was while Wagner was working on the prose draft and verse text of *Die Walküre* that he first conceived the idea of the May night bursting into the hut, which is absent from the prose sketch. He spent several weeks, from the middle of May to the beginning of July, 1852, at the Rinderknecht Pension, on the slopes of the Zürichberg, 'in the open air, with unimpeded views of the lake and the distant Alps', and formed the habit of going for morning walks with the writer Hermann Rollett, to whom he used to read each new instalment of the text. When Rollett expressed the

[2] *Betrachtungen und Erinnerungen* (Zürich, 1949), p. 138. Westphal demonstrates that the same applied to Beethoven (*Vom Einfall zur Symphonie*, pp. 12ff.).

wish that he would now write a 'really fullblown melody' to this 'in every sense, poetic passage', Wagner tore a page out of his notebook, drew a five-line stave in pencil, wrote out the text and its melody and then sang the whole aloud, more or less as he intended it to be.

Ex. 17*b* The sketch written out for Rollett (June 1852)

Win - ter - stür - me wi - chen dem Won - ne - mond   in   lin - den Lüf - ten wiegt sich der Lenz

Wagner had already noted the song's rocking rhythm in the margin of the original manuscript of the verse text.[3] This first version of the melody, later published in facsimile, cries out for the rocking to go on longer, to arch across a wider span; that in turn demanded an extension of the text, such as Wagner wrote out one day in his pocketbook. But he still had to make further alterations to the words and the tune and even to the metre – replacing the 3/4 time with its triplets by 9/8 – before the song reached the score in the form that we know today.

Arnold Schoenberg rightly points out that it is by no means always the simple melodies that are produced easily, nor always the complicated contrapuntal passages which require hard work: what sounds easy is by no means always easy to write.[4]

It is all the more surprising that certain accompanimental features are already there in their final form in the composition sketch: first and foremost, the combination of the dactylic melody – and the dactylic metre altogether – with a trochaic accompaniment on the strings, which is what gives the song its magical lilt, underlined by the long pedal point on the dominant F. Another instance is the wide-arching clarinet part accompanying 'durch Wald und Auen weht sein Atem, weit geöffnet lacht sein Aug'', which is written down in the sketch in tiny notation.

The rest of the song shows numerous other alterations to the melody and the accompaniment, but the combination of the two conflicting rhythms is always maintained. With the thicker scoring that starts after 'trennte von ihm', the sketch's notes of instrumentation also become more detailed: 'wind' against the repeat of the Love motive (woodwind in the score), 'violas' against the demisemiquavers, and, qualified by a question mark, 'harp?', which is then sparingly used from the next bar onwards. Even so delicate a nuance as the broken triad in the clarinets at 'die Liebe lockte...' and the harp's imitation of it as the phrase finishes, '...den Lenz', was part of the original version.

158 55

161 55

[3] Strobel, *Skizzen und Entwürfe zur Ring-Dichtung*, p. 257. Strobel was mistaken in supposing that this first sketch was in C major: it has to be read in the tenor clef. It would otherwise be a unique example of Wagner conceiving a theme in quite the wrong key.

[4] Cf. 'Heart and Brain in Music', *Style and Idea* (London, 1975), pp. 53–76.

Ex. 18 Sketch

169 *58* 174 *59*

At 'Du bist der Lenz' the simple arpeggios are transformed into development motives, which are written into the sketch a few bars later than they appear in the score, at a highly expressive point in fact, where what inspired them immediately leaps to the eye: the sustained middle syllable of 'erblühte'.

Ex. 19 Sketch

From this point the constantly varying development motives take control. It is interesting to watch how clearly defined Leitmotive dissolve into motoric development motives and, on the other hand, how figurations of that type shape themselves back into Leitmotive, so that the flow of the melos, now urged forwards, now restrained, remains in constant motion.

175 *59*   The violin figure that starts after 'Fremdes nur sah ich von je' is formed directly out of the Love motive that has just been used in the voice part.

Ex. 20 Sketch

[with sharp key signature in the score]

It is followed by a development motive in triplets:

Ex. 21 Score

182 61   which is transformed in turn, after 'den Freund ersah', into the rising Freia
motive, though admittedly in the sketch, exceptionally, it is only indicated
by the accompanimental harmonies. Towards the end of the scene, a short,
209 69   urgent figure originating in the Love motive seems to command the form
taken by the vocal line at 'laß' mich dich heißen, wie ich dich liebe', and,
too, to compel this 'exciting violin figure' to enter 'with a sharp cutting
edge' (Porges).

Ex. 22*a* Sketch

Ex. 22*b* Sketch

If one remembers that the twins' Love motive also develops from Freia's
motive, and specifically from its second part, the Flight motive, then one
recognizes the extent to which the 'plastic Nature motives' of *Das Rheingold* have now indeed become 'the vehicles for the promptings of the
passions'.

213 71   As the act reaches its climax with Siegmund triumphantly drawing the
sword from the tree, Wagner modulates from B minor to C minor, so as to
bring the Renunciation motive at 'Heiligster Minne höchste Not' into the
key in which it was originally heard in the first scene of *Das Rheingold*.[5]
'There is a really tragic strain running through my music,' he wrote to
Princess Marie Sayn-Wittgenstein on 28 May 1854; '"Nur wer der Minne
Macht versagt" are the words of a fearfully profound, often heartbreaking
lament.'

216 72   As the fanfare of the Sword motive erupts into C major, the sketch bears
the annotations 'Maestos[o]' and 'arpeggios (throughout)', and, at the
fermata on the final chord, 'or 4 bars'. In the score the six harps are

---

[5] William Ashton Ellis describes it as a stroke of genius, that Woglinde's
'Love-*versus*-power melody', which ends in *Das Rheingold* with the nucleus
of the Ring motive, should now launch the Nothung motive on the same note
(*Life of Richard Wagner*, vol. IV, London, 1904, p. 381).

augmented by all the violins and violas in the arpeggios, so that the motive is wrapped in a brilliant sheen, and the fermata is, in fact, extended across four bars.

220 73   Wagner made three attempts at writing the following passage, 'Sieg-mund, den Wälsung, siehst du Weib!', in the sketch. He did not insert the statements of the Wälsungen motive until the second version. But whereas the eight-bar phrase starts and ends on the chord of E major in the second version, in the third, which is how it appears in the score, there is a surprise modulation to B major, thus preparing the atmospheric move into the G major of 'So freit er sich die seligste Frau'. In all three versions in the sketch, however, the accompaniment, comprising the full orchestra, is marked *pp* throughout (*p* and *pp* in the score), an express enjoinder of restraint in performance, so that the effect should be all the more rapturous.

Ex. 23*a* Sketch (1st version)

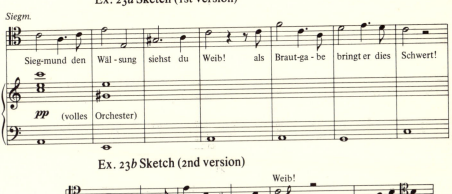

Ex. 23*b* Sketch (2nd version)

Ex. 23c Sketch (3rd version)

238 76   In the coda, which was written down at great speed, with crossings-out and alterations, the Love motive gains the ascendancy once more and in a form note for note the same, though rhythmically altered, as at its first appearance at the beginning of the act, when it was played by the solo cello while the cup of mead was offered. The composition sketch again offers three different versions of the following three bars:

Ex. 24a Sketch (1st version)

Ex. 24b Sketch (2nd version)

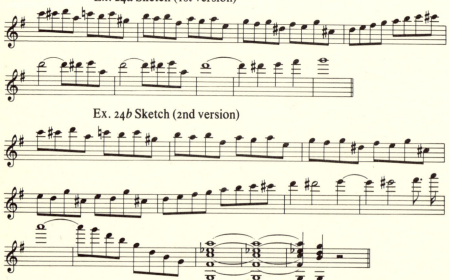

Ex. 24*c* Sketch and Score (3rd version)

1 Sept 54

A born dramatist, Wagner knew that how you begin and, above all, how you end, is everything. His problem here was how to sustain the tension with which the music surges on – 'like a whirlwind' (Porges) – from the emphatic *ff* of the Love motive to the even greater excitement of the final chord. The first version offers a very unsatisfactory solution: the impetus starts to falter after the fourth bar, and the end is particularly unconvincing. In the second version he kept the quaver movement going and added the sharp, sustained dissonance before the closing chord of G major. The third version is hard to find at first, until one discovers it written down on the staves of the voice part, still with a tenor clef! This time Wagner at last succeeded in maintaining a steady, truly inexorable momentum from the Love motive to the syncopated, chromatic climb and on to the sustained tonic chord, Sieglinde's scream. The momentum is sustained by a development motive formed out of the Love motive; the curve it describes, downwards for four bars and then upwards for four bars, enhances the energy of its drive.

The end of the composition sketch is dated '1 Sept 54'. That means that, counting from 3 August, when composition was resumed at 'Friedmund darf ich nicht heißen', the major part of the act was composed within one month.

Act II

'I have finished the first act of the *Walküre*,' Wagner wrote to Hans von Bülow in a letter which, though undated, can be put between 1 and 3 September 1854; 'when I shall get on to the second, God knows – I am in a very bad mood now!' In fact, however, he started sketching the prelude of the second act on 4 September. Then there was a short break, during which he finished the fair copy (the second draft) of the score of *Das Rheingold* on 27 September, but he resumed the composition sketch of the second act on the very same day ('27 September!!!'). 'Let us regard the world with nothing but contempt', he wrote to Liszt in (early?) October. 'It is bad,

bad, fundamentally bad, and only the heart of a friend, only the tears of a woman can redeem it from its curse . . . I have started the second act of the *Walküre*: Wodan and Fricka: as you can see, I'm bound to succeed with it.'

There are no separate sketches of individual motives relating to the composition of the second act, but motives from the Herrmann manuscript and the composition sketch of *Siegfrieds Tod* (both 1850) serve for comparison.

The composition sketch fills twenty-six sheets of manuscript paper on both sides, with fourteen staves on each side (the original notation in pencil, inked over later). Dates noted are '4 Sept. 54' at the beginning of the prelude, '27 September' at the start of the first scene, and '18 Nov. 54' at the end of the act.

Prelude

Looking at the composition sketch, it is amazing to see just how the two motives from the coda of the first act – the Love motive ('Viol.') and the Sword motive ('Tr.') – are reshaped in triplet form to build an orchestral movement which rushes forward with an irresistible rhythmic impetus. This sketch was written down in one burst, without any alterations and, unlike the finale of the first act, in an elegant, fluent hand. Even complicated passages, like the interchange between the first and second violins, were written out exactly as they are in the score.

8 *79*

Ex. 25 Sketch

Scene 1

16 *80*

As the first scene starts, a new motive, that of the Valkyries, is heard for the first time. It is the oldest surviving Leitmotiv of the entire *Ring*, appearing among the 1850 sketches for *Siegfrieds Tod* in two differing versions, once without a text:

Ex. 26*a* Herrmann manuscript (Bailey, p. 465)

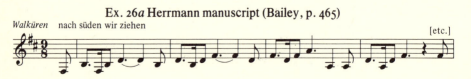

and then, somewhat changed, and with the words of the Valkyries' chorus
from the first act of *Siegfrieds Tod*:

Ex. 26*b* (Bailey, p. 465)

The American Wagnerian scholar, Robert W. Bailey, deduces from this
that Wagner wrote down the theme in association with the Valkyries, but
at first without any specific textual reference. 'Afterwards, he probably
looked through the text of this scene and found that the lines of the
concluding chorus could be adapted to the melody' (p. 465).

This sketch is a good example of how, frequently, Wagner's musical
ideas came to him in quite unrelated contexts: the other sketches on the
sheet are of themes from the Norns' scene and from Siegfried's farewell to
Brünnhilde. It is indeed obvious that the Norns' theme, written on the other
side of the sheet, was the direct musical inspiration of the Valkyries' theme:
although the two differ rhythmically and harmonically, they both have the
characteristic outline of all the motives in the *Ring* formed from the broken
triad: it does not do to have too constricted a notion of motivic relationship
in Wagner. The association of ideas was in any case a close one for him,
since he had gathered from Jacob Grimm the idea of kinship between the
Norns and the Valkyries.[6]

Ex. 26*c* 1850 composition sketch

[Figuration omitted]

[6] Newman, too, finds 'a hint, in the opening words of the first Norn, of the
theme that was afterwards to be associated not with the Norns but with the
Valkyries' (NLRW, II, p. 160).

The sketches on the Herrmann manuscript even include a tentative prototype of the Valkyries' cry:

Ex. 27*a*

23 *82* This is already in its final form when it first appears in the composition sketch of Act II of *Die Walküre*:

Ex. 27*b*

The first three bars of a new, impressive motive, that of Fricka's anger, are crossed out and then rewritten somewhat differently: it is only after two false starts that the first bar acquires its incisive syncopation:

Ex. 28*a* Sketch

Ex. 28*b* Sketch

39 *86* Wotan's 'Der alte Sturm, die alte Müh'!' is notable for its absence from the sketch here. The vocal writing does not start until the eighth bar, with Fricka's 'Wo in Bergen du dich birgst, der Gattin Blick zu entgehn'. Wotan's words were set later on a different system. While he was setting this passage Wagner had a suspicious, complaining letter from Minna, who was in Germany. 'It was really not badly timed', he admitted resignedly.

55 *92* The downward movement of a fifth in the syncopated motive in ex. 28*b*

was reduced to a third and in that form became a development motive, launching Fricka's arioso 'O, was klag' ich' with its urgent rhythm, and sweeping it on to its dynamic climax:

Ex. 29 Sketch

The arioso was originally marked 'A♭ minor' but was then written in 'G♯ minor'; as with Erda's scene in *Das Rheingold* the flat key one really hears here is written out in a sharp key for purely practical reasons. The stretto between voice and first violin at 'Trauernden Sinnes' is already there in the sketch.

59 *94*

77 *99*

As Fricka demands: 'Nimm ihm das Schwert', the Sword motive flashes piano on the C trumpet, its transience stressed by the harmonies remote from C major that immediately precede and follow it. Then, as the motive returns in its familiar, standard form, a curiously impressionistic adaptation of it chimes in, which can be traced right through the *Ring*, up to *Götterdämmerung*, Act II, Scene 3. This can plausibly be related to an experience of Wagner's childhood: the owner of the house where his family lodged, a sword-cutler, had allowed the boy a brief glimpse of a sword intended as his Christmas present. It caught the light momentarily then vanished as the cutler hid it again – 'an impression that was still vivid in Wagner's memory *more than sixty years later*' (GLRW, I, pp. 59f.).

Scene 2

102 *109*

With the second scene we enter a totally new territory of musical and dramatic expression that posed Wagner himself many problems to begin with. 'At times of dispassion and despondency I was frightened most of all of Wodan's long scene, in particular his revelation to Brünnhilde of the whole fateful history', he wrote to Liszt on 3 October 1855, after he had finished the first draft of the score of the second act on 20 September.

> Indeed, there was a moment in London when I was ready to throw the whole scene out: in order to make up my mind, I picked up the [composition] sketch once more and sang the scene through to myself with all the necessary expression; fortunately I found in doing so that my spleen was unjustified and that, on the contrary, the appropriate delivery made it riveting even from the purely musical point of view...It is the most important scene in the whole progression of the

great, four-part drama, and as such it will probably soon arouse the necessary interest and attention.

Wagner wrote about the difficulty of performing the scene in a letter to the singer Franz Betz, dated 8 August 1868:

> To gain a proper sympathy with the role from the start, study the third act of *Die Walküre* first, the second act is where the really great difficulty lies; if you want my advice, you ought only to recite it until you have familiarized yourself with it – although how it could be delivered without the help of the musical modulation – as an actor might do it for instance – is quite inconceivable. *Das Rheingold* is a good stylistic exercise, incidentally, especially for the correct rhythmic and musical inflexion of the words.[7]

It was while he was sketching Act II, Scene 2 of *Die Walküre* that Wagner wrote a highly significant letter, dated 26 October 1854, to Hans von Bülow, about the technical problems of composition that were preoccupying him at the time.[8] In the course of a critical survey of Bülow's compositions, he wrote that he knew from personal experience that there were some things that could not be expressed musically in any other way than by the employment of harmonies which were bound to affront the ear of the musical Philistine:

> Though I have recognized this in my own work, I have at the same time always been guided by a quite positive determination to disguise the difficult nature of the harmony as much as possible and to present it in such a way that in the end it is not even felt to be difficult (so far as my own senses can tell).

The art consisted in

> communicating precisely the strangest, least familiar sensations to the listener in such a way that he is not distracted by the material substance of what he hears but surrenders to my blandishments unresisting, so to speak, and willingly accepts even the most unaccustomed of sounds.

Although Wagner does not expressly mention instrumentation here as a means of disguising difficult harmonies, it is obviously one of the things he meant. Earlier in the letter he had said that, in order to gain a 'clear impression of the matter', he had tried to imagine what it would sound like, first with Bülow himself 'as pianist', and then with 'an orchestra of inconceivable excellence'. In other words, the envisaged orchestral sound was his criterion of the admissibility of difficult harmonies.

[7] *An seine Künstler*, p. 6, note.
[8] On the dating of the letter, see Altmann, *Richard Wagners Briefe nach Zeitfolge und Inhalt* (Leipzig, 1905), p. 180.

A passage in a letter Wagner wrote to Theodor Uhlig on 31 May 1852 is really the last word on the subject: 'Anyone who separates the harmony from the instrumentation when talking about my music is doing me as great an injustice as someone who separates my music from my text, my song from the words!' For him, the inseparability of harmony and instrumentation was so much a matter of course, that he did not mention both expressly every time the subject arose.

This attitude of his is confirmed by something he said to Cosima many years later, which she recorded in her diary: 'With such subjects as his it was essential to use an unconventional palette, "nott' e giorno faticar" was not good enough; but the skill consisted in disguising the unconventionality.' The sentences immediately preceding explain what particular artistic means he had in mind.

> R[ichard] spoke of three pages [of the third act of *Parsifal*] he had been scoring and mentioned how reluctant he was to have jarring effects, and how he always tried to mitigate them, make them assimilable, rather than let the harshness be obtrusive, and he picked out Gurnemanz's line 'kalt und starr', and said how pleased he was with today's idea of accompanying it with muted horns.[9] He said he had been delighted, listening to the 'Nibelungen', by the way the boldest steps he had been driven to take did not force themselves upon the attention purely as such. (13 November 1881; BBL 1938, p. 6.)

In this instance, in fact, he referred to the instrumentation as the *sole* means of mediation.

When Wagner wrote to Bülow, he had already applied his use of orchestration to disguise difficult harmonies several times in Wotan's long scene in Act II.[10] At the start, at Wotan's 'O heilige Schmach!', the instrumentation he noted on the composition sketch combined bass trumpet, bassoon and trombone with tremolo violins (in the score the trombones are replaced by tubas which, according to Richard Strauss, when they reach *ff*, represent the angry swelling of the veins on Wotan's forehead).

113 *112* The bass clarinet solo that leads into Wotan's 'revelation of the whole fateful history' was emended while it was still being written down, as often happened to cantilenas in the sketch; while the first version gets lost in the depths after the first ten bars, the second carries on with the Love motive played sequentially and ends as if depicting Brünnhilde lifting her head:

---

[9] The allusion is to the chord of the ninth after 'tot', which effects the transition to the cantilena of the alto oboe and cellos (study score p. 14, vocal score p. 250).

[10] Breig, in 'Das Schicksalskunde-Motiv' (Dahlhaus, ed., *Das Drama Richard Wagners*, p. 223), relates the letter of 26 October to the sketching of the Annunciation of Death scene, but that is refuted by the reference to that scene in a letter of *November* 1854 to Princess Caroline Sayn-Wittgenstein: 'I am now on the second act, in the scene where Brünnhilde appears to Siegmund to foretell his death' (*An Freunde und Zeitgenossen*, p. 166).

Ex. 30 Sketch

[Bracketed notes and bars crossed out in the sketch]

The early part of the narration is written out without any significant revision. The bass underlying the strictly rhythmical declamation is a pedal point on the cellos and double basses in the sketch, which are relieved for stretches by *pp* contrabass tuba and contrabass trombone in the score.

> For all its simplicity, this passage is to me the rarest miracle of a genius, more richly endowed than any other with the gift of transforming every nuance of feeling, every tremor of passion, into orchestral timbres with an exactness that invincibly captivates and convinces every listener

wrote Richard Strauss in his revision of Berlioz's *Traité de l'Instrumentation* (pp. 106f.). Already in the sketch, too, individual motives rise up from the depths of memory, as if from the remotest primeval past: the Rhinemaidens' cry of 'Rheingold!', the Ring, Valhalla, Erda – the last marked 'Str.' (in the score a combination of violas and clarinets).

137 *121*   It is only at 'Nur Einer könnte, was ich nicht darf', where the motive of Wotan's restless wandering assumes the role of a melodically self-sufficient accompaniment, that alterations to the sketch become more numerous; the composer's concern was to blend the singing voice and the 'deeply passion-

143 *123*   ate and simultaneously elegiac song of the strings, sounding as if coming from the mouths of invisible rhapsodes' (Porges), in such a way that at the same time the two parts are clearly distinct from each other. The accompaniment shows a tendency at this point, even in the sketch, to develop

polyphonically, as the divided cellos and the violas make canonic entries one after the other.

153 *126*   The Allegro, as the scene approaches its climax, once again requires the concealment of difficult harmonies by a well-judged blend of instruments, and Wagner's ideas are already noted down on the sketch: horns, bassoon, bass clarinet for the chord on 'be-*rühr*-te', triangle, two horns, two clarinets, two bassoons, violas, cellos on 'Ring', cymbals, cor anglais, three clarinets, horns, bassoons, bass clarinet, tubas, violas, cellos on 'Gold' – almost the same instrumentation as is found in the score.

160 *127*   The following page, 'Fahre denn hin, herrische Pracht', is written exceptionally clearly and fluently, in a very energetic hand. The semiquaver runs in the strings are notated very precisely, and their impetus seems to seize hold of all the parts. And that Wagner's imagination never ceased to hear what he was writing is demonstrated by the note 'violas, trumpets'
168 *128*   against Erda's rising motive after 'für das Ende sorgt Alberich!' (augmented in the score by bass trumpet and bassoon).

Three times the distorted Valhalla motive and the Gold motive appear in clashing combination: the fact that each time they were written down without a single emendation is another instance of the complicated not necessarily being difficult to do. The second time it is marked 'Maestoso' in
174 *130*   the sketch ('very broad' in the score). This is the example Wagner cites in *Über die Anwendung der Musik auf das Drama* (RWGS, X, pp. 187f.) of a passage where 'the essentially jarring character of musical combinations of that kind' ought to be disguised. In the essay he refers to the role, not of the composer, but of the conductor, whom he enjoins 'to disguise the unaccustomed, whether by appropriate restraining of the beat, or by anticipatory dynamic adjustments...so that it seems to ensue naturally, and our perception willingly assimilates it as another artistic feature of the whole'. 'A slight restraining of the tempo enables this remarkable passage to be shaped perfectly clearly' (Porges).

Ex. 31 Sketch

+ alle Hr. m. d. Bs. Tr.

(There is another note of the instrumentation here, 'all horns with bass trumpet'.)

181 *134*   The closing section of the scene, rising to the climactic orchestral epilogue following Wotan's exit, is again sustained by development motives: a warmly sympathetic triplet motive accompanying Brünnhilde's 'Den du zu lieben stets mich gelehrt', the polyphonic development of which by the violas, second and first violins, is already written out in detail in the

184 *135*   sketch; and Wotan's angrily rumbling semiquaver figure,[11] which is merely suggested in the sketch.

Ex. 32*a* Sketch

Ex. 32*b* Sketch

200 *138*   After the sequence of wind chords the storm dies away with the 'heartbreaking lament' of the Renunciation motive.

204 *140*   The motive of Wotan's restless wandering, which we heard accompanimentally played by the cellos, echoes in Brünnhilde's heart in a short orchestral postlude: 'cor anglais (very expressive)', then 'oboe'. These thirteen bars went through three different versions: the first was crossed out and is totally illegible, the second, written immediately after it on the page, appears to correspond to the eventual form, but comparison with the score reveals yet a third version there: the cor anglais's imitation of the cello melody starts a bar earlier, seeming to lie on top of it, so that the part-writing becomes yet denser – a process we often find in Wagner:

[11] Written as quaver triplets in Klindworth's piano reduction.

Ex. 33*a* Sketch

Ex. 33*b* Score

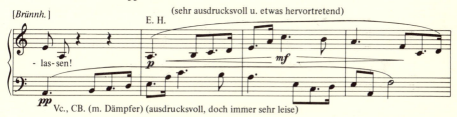

Scene 3

206 *140*   The scene between Siegmund und Sieglinde consists principally of a free
elaboration of their Love motive (which is identical with Freia's Flight
motive); motivically, therefore, it forms an extended reprise of the act
prelude, which is based on the same principle, and the two together serve to
frame the two important Wotan scenes. The development of the Love
motive in the third scene, moving between the utmost emotional extremes,
is written straight down in its final form in the sketch, with only minor
alterations. Only in the case of the four bars at the stage direction 'Then she
throws her arms passionately round his neck and rests on his breast', was it
not until he came to the score that Wagner arrived at the thrilling idea of the
unaccompanied *ff* unison of the first and second violins:

Ex. 34*a* Sketch

Ex. 34*b* Score

209 *141*   It is possible in this scene, too, to trace the way the Leitmotiv repeatedly turns into a development motive, in order to give itself renewed impetus:

Ex. 35 Sketch

Scene 4

The passage quoted above from Wagner's letter of November 1854 to Princess Sayn-Wittgenstein (cf. footnote 10 on p. 87) comes in this context:

> I've been able to continue doing a little work on *Die Walküre* all the time, but it's going much more slowly than I thought at first. What I finally sketch is always the best I can do, but the times when I feel in the mood to work are getting fewer and fewer with the dreary way I spend my life...And then I find the subject of *Die Walküre* too painful by far: there's really not one of the world's sorrows that the work does not express, and in the most painful form; playing artistic games with that pain is taking its revenge on me: it has made me really ill several times already, so that I have had to stop completely. I am

now on the second act, in the scene where Brünnhilde appears to
Siegmund to foretell his death: something like that can hardly be
called composing any more!

The secret of Wagner's 'artistic games' was that the demanding, painful
sharing of his characters' experiences was allied to a very alert capacity for
simultaneous self-criticism. Simple as the theme of the Annunciation of
Death may sound, its genealogy is a complex one. The implications of the
first motive are far from being exhausted by the recognition that its three
notes and rising third reproduce the intonation of a question, and that it is
the familiar formula of an imperfect cadence, used by countless composers
before Wagner. A composer's genius is not demonstrated only by his
invention of new forms of expression, but also, perhaps more cogently, by
his ability to give old, well-worn forms a new content. Kurth devotes eight
crammed pages (pp. 473ff.) to this 'typical primitive phrase', analysing
its changing function in Beethoven, Schubert, Weber, Mendelssohn,
Schumann, Chopin, Liszt and Wagner, pointing the very subtle distinction
between its function in *Tristan* and in the *Ring*, where it is 'more sharply
focused from being, in the stricter sense, a Leitmotiv'. He shows that the
conventional figure could only acquire the metaphysical significance it has
as the Fate motive after a long process of development – part of which took
place in Wagner's own earlier works.

The theme of the Annunciation of Death, eventually twelve bars long, is
clearly divided into three segments by pauses when only the *pp* pulsation of
the drums is heard: the first segment consists of the Fate motive; the second
of the same repeated a whole tone higher – even that is nothing strikingly
'new': the figure is one that invites repetition, preferably sequential; the
decisive innovation is in the final four-bar segment. But we must go back a
little way to trace its evolution.

Ever since Otto Strobel published his essay 'Das Archiv des Hauses
Wahnfried' in 1943,[12] we have known that Wagner made two false starts on
this scene, and only managed to arrive at the form we know today the third
time. There are about twenty-four bars crossed out in the composition
sketch, which are still fairly legible: one can see that in the first
version – which is only six bars long – the Fate motive was repeated *without
transposition*. In the second version, which gives the theme in a complete
a–a–b form, the second 'Stollen' of this miniature 'Bar' is a whole tone
higher,[13] corresponding in that respect to the final version, while the

---

[12] In *Bayreuth, die Stadt Richard Wagners* (Munich, 1943), p. 44.

[13] I am not convinced by Breig's reading ('Das Schicksalskunde-Motiv', p. 230),
according to which the transposed Fate motive in the second version begins
with the chord of E minor: it is not always unambiguously clear in the sketches
whether a note is meant to be on or between the stave lines; a case could even
be made for there being a 𝄪 here, which would mean F double sharp after all.
In any case, the notation would not settle the matter on its own, since it is not
always consistent in the sketches.

eight-bar 'Abgesang' still makes a colourless, inconsequential effect.

247 *154*   Wagner's final resolution of the problem is as simple as it is inspired: at the third attempt at the Abgesang, after a one-bar anacrusis, he again repeated the two statements of the Fate motive, on the same notes but an octave higher, with the whole-tone rise but without the repetition of the first and last notes, so that the two statements are linked together in such a way that the appearance of mere repetition is completely avoided, while the inner tension of the two Stollen is sustained. It is the logic of the construction that makes the Fate motive, which elsewhere carries a somewhat emotional charge, so implacable here in the Annunciation of Death theme.

Ex. 36a Sketch (1st version, crossed out)

Ex. 36b Sketch (2nd version, crossed out)

Ex. 36c Sketch (3rd version)

Two questions remain. First: how is the first chord to be defined? There can be no doubt that it is meant to be understood as dissonant, on reflection. That it is *heard* as such in context is associated with the fact that it follows four statements of the Love motive:[14]

Ex. 37 Sketch

These have prepared the hearer, by suggestion, for a chord of A minor, so that the E♯ or F that comes instead, however it is written, sounds like a dissonance. The impression is strengthened by the doubling of the tenor tuba in this part by the bass tuba. Once this impression has been painlessly absorbed, it continues to hold good whenever the motive is repeated, unless, as at the end of the Magic Fire music, it comes in a totally different context (and with a different resolution).

There are various theoretical ways of analysing the harmonies of the Fate motive. Where Wagner is concerned I always prefer analysis which corresponds most exactly to the impression received by the ear, in this case Kurth's interpretation: 'the first chord is already in the same tonality as the second, and generates tension by behaving as an anticipation of the second, on to which it resolves' (p. 188). Anyone who wants to exercise his wits on a more complex analysis is free to do so; but he will have to face the fact that Wagner would have numbered him among those for whom music is 'a curiously abstract thing, floating somewhere between grammar, arithmetic and gymnastics'.

The second problem concerns the fact that in his first sketch of the

[14] An emendation in the composition sketch suggests that the expansion of the motive was not originally foreseen.

beginning of the Annunciation of Death theme, Wagner contented himself with merely repeating the Fate motive, in spite of the figure's persistent inclination towards sequential development wherever it is found (including *Lohengrin* and the *Siegfrieds Tod* sketch). The explanation is not to be sought in any consideration of compositional technique but simply in the stage direction that comes at this point in Wagner's original text: 'Brünn-hilde, leading her horse by the bridle, has walked slowly and solemnly forward from the cave and now stops a short distance from Siegmund.' The tranquil character of the first version of the theme corresponds to that *tableau vivant*.

But the second version already incorporated the whole-tone rise at the repeat, which urges the motive onwards.[15] And since the Abgesang he then wrote failed to satisfy Wagner – it does not create the effect of organic development, though he extended it to eight bars – he wrote the third and final version, in which the sequential repetition of the Fate motive is not restricted to the two Stollen but, as I have already described, permeates and shapes the Abgesang as well. At the same time as he wrote the music, he also rewrote the stage direction, which appears in a new form here in the sketch, where he can only have written it for his own use: 'Brünnhilde approaches slowly / (she stops) / (approaches again) / (she stops beside him and gazes at him) / (he looks up at her)' and so on. The visual and sound images are now in perfect accord, with the impulse towards further development almost certainly having developed in the music. The process is comparable to the stages in the conception of the Spring Song in the first act, where it was again the melody which insisted on further development.

The genealogy of the theme can be traced back further still. The instances from the first and third acts of *Lohengrin* cited by Breig and Dahlhaus[16] strictly speaking need hardly concern us, since they are confined to the initial figure, whereas the characteristic structure of the theme consists in the elaboration of that figure to form a miniature Bar. (It shares with other Beethovenian and Wagnerian themes the capacity for appearing later divided once more into its separate motivic components, which are then deployed individually.)

---

[15] In the second version the C$\sharp$ on the drum, now dissonant, is replaced by a D$\sharp$ at the repetition of the Fate motive (this is not Breig's reading, however). The retention of the C$\sharp$ only materialized in the third version and the score.

[16] Dahlhaus, ed., *Das Drama Richard Wagners*, p. 228 and p. 34, ex. 9c. The second of their examples, which is quoted from the vocal score and without the words, belongs to King Henry's line 'Was führt ihr her? Was soll ich schaun?' (Act III, Scene 3), and makes a quite different impression in the full score, since the interrogatory intonation (admittedly a literal replica of the Fate motive) belongs solely to the voice part and is overlaid by the chords of the three trombones and the tuba, which are sustained for whole bars. Additionally, the semiquaver triplets, which might appear from the vocal score to be played by the drum, are in fact played by the violas. Finally, no attempt is made to develop the figure any further.

The original, *Ur*-form of this miniature Bar is a four-bar melody written out on the verso of the Herrmann manuscript. After an upbeat, the first bar contains the three notes of the Fate motive, the second the same motive starting a whole tone higher, and the last two consist of a concluding cantilena developed from it.[17]

Ex. 38*a* Herrmann manuscript

By expanding the first two bars of the melody and varying the cantilena each time, Wagner has now obtained an expressive theme for the words of the First and Second Norns[18] (clearly, the working-out of the Abgesang was a problem from the start, until the definitive solution was found four years later, in the third version of the Annunciation of Death theme).

Ex. 38*b* 1850 composition sketch (emended after Bailey)

[17] Cf. Bailey, 'Wagner's musical sketches for *Siegfrieds Tod*', p. 475.
[18] Cf. Westernhagen, *Vom Holländer zum Parsifal*, pp. 43f., where it is cited without the concluding cantilena, whose organic relationship to the theme was not revealed until the publication of the Herrmann manuscript with the above melody.

272 *161* The scene continues in the composition sketch in precisely the form it takes in the full score. In other words, the sketch already gives the outline of the peculiarly regular shaping of its first half (up to 'grüß' auch die holden Wunschesmädchen'), which Lorenz describes as a 'Bar to the power of three' (pp. 179ff.).[19]

286 *165* Of the several instances of Wagner's use of words to indicate keys, the most significant is '(B♭ minor key signature)' written above the word 'Tod' (death), falling here on the dominant. B♭ minor was Alberich's key in *Rheingold*, the key of the threat of destruction.

287 *165* From here on (marked 'faster' in the sketch; 'rather more lively but not too fast' in the score) the melos is driven onwards by triplet development motives, again formed from the Love/Flight motive.

Ex. 39*a* Sketch

293 *168* Also in the form:

Ex. 39*b* Sketch

307 *171* When Siegmund threatens Sieglinde's life with his sword: 'frommt es nicht gegen den Feind, so fromm' es denn wider den Freund!', we can already observe in the composition sketch how the motivic germ of the Siegfried theme emerges quite spontaneously out of the Sword motive (while the note of a stage direction, 'he draws', again illustrates the close relationship of action and music):

Ex. 40 Sketch

[19] Wagner's 'potentiation' of musical forms is one of Lorenz's most brilliant discoveries. It is described in more detail below, on p. 173, in the context of Brünnhilde's awakening in Act III of *Siegfried*.

The further evolution of the motive can be traced in the composition sketch of the third act.

309 *172* From the moment when Brünnhilde decides to help Siegmund: 'Halt ein! Wälsung!', a tempestuous elaboration of the triplet motive in ex. 39*b* takes the initiative until the postlude to the scene, when it is absorbed into the stormy line which is already marked for clarinet in the sketch.

Scene 5

328 *177* The motive changes direction in the few bars of Siegmund's farewell from Sieglinde: 'Leblos scheint sie, die dennoch lebt', and starts to descend in calm crotchets and quavers, a movement which, in the score, is transferred to the vocal line as well and is continued and intensified in the viola figure. (The sketch is marked 'slow', the score 'slower'.)

Ex. 41*a* Sketch

Ex. 41*b* Score

When Wagner told Liszt, during the preliminary rehearsals held in Bayreuth in 1875, 'the next theme is one I got from you', and the latter replied, 'fair enough, then at least somebody will hear it for once', each

knew the other was joking. They were referring to the similarity that the
viola melody introducing Sieglinde's 'Kehrte der Vater nun heim!' bears to
the first theme of Liszt's *Faust* Symphony. The similarity is in fact quite
superficial: the essential feature of the 'Faust' theme is the chromatically
descending sequence of augmented triads which are sometimes replaced by
other harmonies in the development, whereas there are no such triads
whatever in Sieglinde's modest little melody, which obviously evolved out
of the Love motive which dominates the whole act, and to which it soon
returns.[20]

Ex. 42*a* Sketch

Ex. 42*b* Liszt, *Faust* Symphony, 1st movement

The last three pages of the composition sketch of Act II were written out
at great speed. Sieglinde's 'Haltet ein, ihr Männer! Mordet erst mich!' was
inserted later, on a different stave.

The coda, 'Doch Brünnhilde! Weh' der Verbrecherin!' ('Allo', Wagner's
usual contraction, in the sketch; 'fast' in the score), is another of the free
reprises – this time of Wotan's stormy exit at the end of Scene 2 – that help
to convey the sense of the periodic structure in the larger context.

'18 Nov. 54 (that was a bad time!!!)', Wagner wrote underneath the
violent D minor close. It was the time of a severe financial crisis, averted on
that occasion by the intervention of Jakob Sulzer and Otto Wesendonk.

Act III

Wagner began to compose the third act of *Die Walküre* on 20 November
1854, only two days after completing the second.

There is only one surviving sketch of a motive from the third act: the
recto of the sheet in question (written in pencil) has a few bars of Brünnhilde's 'Schützt mich und helft', and two small sketches on the verso turn
out to be studies for the middle section of the second version of the *Faust*

[20] Ashton Ellis drew attention to the possibility that the Lisztian and Wagnerian
motives had a *common* source in the development section of the first movement of Schubert's B♭ major piano sonata: 'Liszt's fondness for Schubert's
music is notorious; this is one of the sonatas he afterwards re-edited: at Zurich
or Paris he *must* have played it in 1853, and thus Wagner might really be said,
in a sense, to "have the theme from" him, i.e. from Liszt's fingers.' (*Life of
Richard Wagner*, vol. IV, p. 409.)

337 *179*

348 *183*

361 *186*

119 *214*

Overture, which was finished on 17 January 1855 (p. 9, bars 7ff. and p. 14, bars 16ff., in Hans von Bülow's piano reduction).

181 *235* Remote prototypes of two motives in the third act of *Die Walküre* can
275 *272* also be detected in the 1850 composition sketch of *Siegfrieds Tod*: Sieg-
linde's 'O hehrstes Wunder' and Brünnhilde's 'War es so schmählich'. I shall discuss these prototypes in context.

The composition sketch of the third act comprises eighteen sheets of manuscript paper, the last used on one side only. The start is dated '(20 Nov. 54)', the finish '27 December 1854'. The orchestral introduction is written out on between two and four staves, all the rest on two or three staves.

Scene 1

The vigour and energy of the handwriting of the first scene is a graphic reflection of the animation and strict rhythm of the music.

Bailey points out that the key of the scene, B minor, was chosen in 1850 for the Valkyrie motive conceived in a totally different context (p. 465). The 'Riding' motive in the accompaniment, merely suggested on the Herrmann manuscript, has gained in energy from the enlargement of the intervals.

Ex. 43*a* Herrmann manuscript   Ex. 43*b* Sketch

5 *188* The accent is now marked over the first quaver of each bar in the principal motive. In rehearsal, Wagner asked that 'chiefly the dactylic figure (and especially the first note, B) should be accented incisively and heavily' (Porges). Similarly, in a note he wrote for the conductor Mancinelli in Bologna (3 December 1880):

Deux mots, mais immédiatement

pas trop vite, la première note bien accentuée, non pas la 4e. Ainsi: ♪ ♪♪♩ ♩, non: ♪ ♪♪♩ ♩, ce qu'on fait d'ordinaire – ne pas accélérer – presque solonnel![21]

1, 3 *188* The demisemiquaver runs which turn into trills (Wagner noted 'tr.' on the sketch) and the sextuplet arpeggios (quintuplets in the score) are written out for one or two bars and then their continuation is indicated by 'etc.' or '·/.'. 'Violins' is noted against the runs in the seventh bar (violins and violas in

[21] Reproduced in facsimile in Karl Ipser, *Richard Wagner in Italien* (Salzburg, 1951), facing p. 170.

the score), and 'violins' and 'violas' against the arpeggios (the same in the score): the characteristic sound of the passage was already in Wagner's mind when he first wrote it. The transition to B major takes place four bars later in the sketch (where it is spelt out) than in the score.

60 199

Wagner's use of a shorthand notation means that the great Allegro of the Valkyries' Ride (up to the entry of C minor), 105 pages in the study score, occupies no more than 6½ pages of fourteen staves each in the composition sketch. The consequent ease with which the first sketch can be read and grasped in its entirety contributed to the fact that Wagner never lost his thread in detail, though there is detail in plenty, but had the overall shape of the whole movement always before his eyes.

The differences between the sketch and the score include a rare instance of an orchestral motive that is missing from the sketch. The statement ('*p*, faint') of the Valhalla motive by the bass trumpet and trombones at 'Nach Walhall brechen wir auf, Wotan zu bringen die Wal' makes its first appearance in the score, whereas the corresponding bars are as follows in the sketch:

98 208

Ex. 44 Sketch

There are other considerable differences due to the fact that only one part of the Valkyries' polyphonic ensembles is written out in the sketch.

When Wagner came to score the following three bars:

Ex. 45 Sketch

120 215

he divided the ensemble of eight voices into two quartets, one of which puts the question 'Wo rittest du her in rasender Hast?' imitatively in 12/8 time, while the other, entering later, interjects the comment 'So fliegt nur, wer auf der Flucht!' in 4/4 time, and their melodies are free adaptations of the line written in the sketch.

Always endeavouring to vary the stage picture and the vocal writing, and at the same time to avoid the danger of monotony lurking in the use of an all-female ensemble, Wagner sends Waltraute and Ortlinde to keep a lookout in the score, so that with their cries of warning these two now act as chorus leaders, while the remainder divide into two trios.

140 *222*

Porges wrote, under the impact of the rehearsals:

> I cannot restrain myself from pointing out the absolute novelty of the style of the Valkyries' singing in every respect. In doing equal justice to the dramatic principle of the greatest freedom in the representation of each individual character, and to the musical principle which insists on the unity of the overall effect, the composer eradicates every trace of merely schematic formalism in his design, and yet prevents the whole from storming away in blind anarchy . . . It is possible that in Aeschylus's *Eumenides* the dread songs . . . of the goddesses of vengeance made an impression stylistically akin to this.

The contrast with Sieglinde, at first withdrawn and then breaking out in despair, is all the more striking. The expression of her emotion is intensified in the score, though not in the sketch, by a reminiscence, played three times by the cellos and basses, of the motive played by the violas in the second act at 'Kehrte der Vater nun heim!':

147 *225*

Ex. 46*a* Sketch   Ex. 46*b* Score

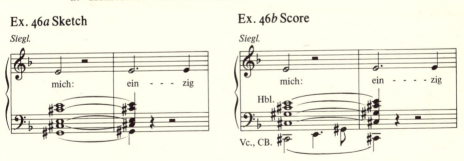

149 *225*   On the other hand, the mournful echo of the woodwind and horns at 'Fern von Siegmund' is already there in the sketch:

Ex. 47 Sketch

II, 307
171
III, 175
233 We all recognize Siegfried's theme, as Brünnhilde prophesies his birth; after the prototype heard developing out of the Sword motive in the second act, it is now stated in full for the first time. But the composition sketch reveals that the apparent spontaneity of the theme is deceptive, and that it only attained to its eventual form after several tries:

Ex. 48*a* Sketch

(The note values, metre and rhythm are indicated only imprecisely in the sketch.) Wagner made two attempts in the sketch at constructing a fully-rounded theme from the idea contained in the first four bars, but he 414 *312* did not accomplish it satisfactorily until he came to set Wotan's final words: 'Wer meines Speeres Spitze fürchtet...' Then, when working on the score he added the two syllables, 'o Weib', to Brünnhilde's prophecy, and so was able to fit it to the Siegfried theme in its new form, with one minor variation.

Ex. 48*b* Score

It is even more surprising to discover that this great G major period does not end in the sketch with the Redemption-through-Love melody, but with a declamatory phrase for the voice. The note added: '4 bars', and the symbol

♯ used to mark each of those bars on the stave, suggest that the idea of the final version came to Wagner before he started work on the score.

Ex. 49*a* Sketch

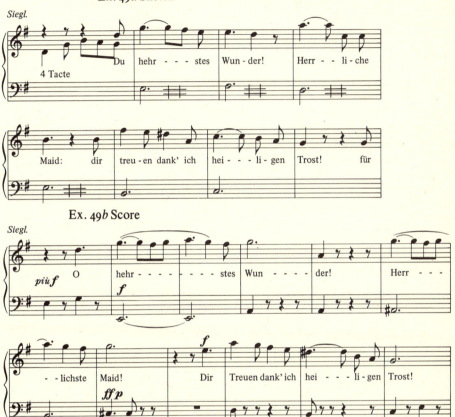

But where did this new motive originate?

In *The perfect Wagnerite*, Bernard Shaw criticizes the 'rapturous passage sung by Sieglinda…of no great musical merit: it might easily be the pet climax of a popular sentimental ballad', and is especially scathing about the reappearance of the motive at the end of *Götterdämmerung*: 'There is no dramatic logic whatever in the recurrence of this theme to express the transport in which Brynhild immolates herself.'[22]

But the motive's absence from the composition sketch of *Die Walküre* supports very strongly the idea that it did not originate there at all, but was conceived in connection with *Götterdämmerung*, or rather with *Siegfrieds Tod*. The existence of the 1850 composition sketch of the first two scenes of the latter, and Wagner's known creative methods, make it virtually certain

[22] *Major critical essays* (London, 1955), pp. 236f.

that he had already thought of other motives besides, and that, above all, he had at least some idea of a melody for Brünnhilde's final scene. That the 'great heroic opera' began to pursue rather different concerns as it evolved does nothing to invalidate the idea of love bringing about the final redemption. Brünnhilde's words

> Das Feuer, das mich verbrennt,
> rein'ge den Ring vom Fluch

are already there in the verse text of *Siegfrieds Tod*, and the 'rapturous passage' would not have been unsuited to them. The sequence of events would, in that case, have been the reverse of what has hitherto been assumed, with Wagner using a theme from *Siegfrieds Tod* in *Die Walküre*, back-projecting in fact, as we know he did with the Valkyries' theme.

There may be some support for this hypothesis in the presence in the 1850 composition sketch of what may be a prototype of the motive, though it is not immediately recognizable. Brünnhilde's 'Zu neuen Taten, teurer Helde' is prefaced there by an eight-bar orchestral introduction, accompanied by the following stage direction: 'Brünnhilde's expressive mime / loving embrace'. While the first two bars unmistakably anticipate the motive (first heard in the F♯ minor Fantasia of 1831) of Brünnhilde's love for the Wälsungen, of which there will be more to say, in the following four bars, if one looks in particular at the inner parts, it is possible to detect the basic outline of her motive of Redemption through Love.

Ex. 49*c* 1850 composition sketch

Ex. 49*d*

[the 'hidden' motive]

Sceptics, who find this interpretation too contrived, may revise their opinion when they come to a similar case in the chapter on *Siegfried*, where the evidence is quite unambiguous and beyond all doubt. The composer's creative imagination sometimes follows stranger paths than are dreamt of in our philosophy.

Scene 2

202 244
207 247
At 'Schrecklich ertost dein Toben!' the Valkyries divide into two four-part groups, then finally coalesce at the thrilling 'Zu uns floh die Verfolgte' in an eight-part polyphonic ensemble, written in a rich, differentiated texture, which is so constructed that Waltraute, who has steadily been emerging as the most important of the eight, now sings the leading part – her part alone bears the direction 'urgently' – while the others provide an accompaniment that rises and falls, passing from voice to voice. The simple melody in the sketch would never have led anyone to foresee such a development, achieved by dint of fragmentation and motivic elaboration.

Ex. 50 Sketch

A comparison of this melody with the ensemble writing in the full score (or the vocal score) tells us much about Wagner's instinct for discovering the latent tensions in a melody and his ability to translate them into polyphony.

240 260
If (departing for once from the normal sequence) we now look at the final large ensemble passage in this scene, 'O Vater! halt' ein!', the climax is achieved by quite different means. In this case the sketch already gives some notion of the part-writing of the score, indicating the separate

counterpoints in the sequences based on the cantilena-like motive that rounds off the Annunciation of Death theme. The twelve bars of the sketch are doubled in the score.

Waltraute begins it with 'Halt' ein! halt' ein!', followed by the other voices entering one after the other in pairs, the two lowest first, then the middle and higher voices, forming a kind of canon on the melody and building up to a torrent of lamentation, until the main theme, reinforced by the trumpet and bass trumpet, swells out again *ff* like a wail of despair:

Ex. 51 Sketch

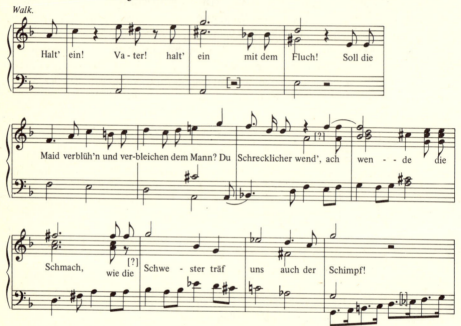

What one might call the improvised character of the first version of the Valkyries' scene allows one to infer that its performance should also have an improvisatory quality about it. This is borne out by a letter from Wagner to the conductor Hans Richter (23 June 1876):

> When Wotan begins: 'Wo ist Brünnhild?'...we must have a tempo here such that almost everything that follows can be taken quite conveniently at two beats in a bar. As soon as the Valkyries come in with 'schrecklich ertost dein Wetter' [sic], beating four in a bar must stop! No more of it! But that doesn't mean it should be at all hurried. 'Zu uns floh die Verfolgte': I would never want four in a bar here, it holds the music back, and restricts its freedom.[23]

[23] Published in the *Bayreuther Festspielbuch 1951*, pp. 59f.

To turn to the scene's two soloists, Brünnhilde is introduced by a
218 *252* fourteen-bar orchestral passage, the restrained character of which is
already outlined in the sketch by the delicate shading of the numerous
instrumental indications: 'drums', 'wind', '4 clar.', 'viola', 'viola', 'cor
anglais', 'Vc.', 'clar.', '3 bassoons'.

[*Wodan*]   Ex. 52 Sketch

Both sketch and score are marked 'slower'. In the same letter to Richter,
Wagner commented:

> 'Slower' – yes, but not too slow, so that when 'somewhat more lively
> again' comes, we get the tempo a *little less moderate* than the
> impassioned tempo primo. Beat four here in the complicated orches-
> tral passages (with the syncopations), if you find it helps you to
> prevent hurrying; but *I* would go on beating two.

The ensuing passage, falling into three periods in which Wotan pro-
nounces judgment and sentence on Brünnhilde – 'furious throughout, never
histrionic' (Porges) – was written down in one great energetic flow, though
not without some emendations and alterations in places. The angry orches-
225 *254* tral interjection after 'gegen mich doch reiztest du Helden' was changed
already in the sketch and lengthened by three bars, the revision being
inserted in tiny notes:

Ex. 53 Sketch

254 267   The following examples illustrate an impressive alteration of the text and melody, and even of the metre, in the score:

Ex. 54a Sketch

Ex. 54b Score

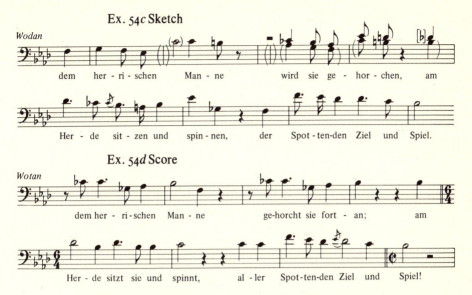

Ex. 54*c* Sketch

Ex. 54*d* Score

The text gains in immediacy, and whereas Wagner was normally intent on avoiding or concealing parallelism in the melodic construction, he here deliberately introduces it in the second version, to emphasize the pitilessness of the sentence. Finally, the scorn of the last words is made more biting by the change from 4/4 to 6/4 time: the singer's part is marked 'harshly and somewhat drawn out' in the score.

229 *255*   The preceding section of Wotan's tirade, the cantabile ('very sustained') 'Nicht send' ich dich mehr aus Walhall', has been advanced, in an essay on Wagner's 'concept of melody', as an example of how the form and elaboration of his vocal melodic writing are determined by 'dramatic speech', that is, by an extra-musical principle; this creates, it is argued, a 'concatenation' of melodic four-bar elements, which positively demands the 'periodicity which is lacking'.[24]

There is no disputing the fact that the form and elaboration of the vocal melodic writing were preconditioned by the verse form of the text. But to limit oneself to that is to overlook the most important thing: that the verses themselves owe their particular cast to a *musical* principle. That is not to say that Wagner had the melody to which he eventually set a line in his mind when he first wrote the words: that seems particularly improbable in this case, since this melody makes its first appearance in the composition sketch in the Annunciation of Death, that is, two years after the text was written. But the impulse that shaped this dramatic period was musical. The significance of that is best illustrated by comparing the pre-musical version of the same passage in the prose sketch, with the musically-inspired verse text:

[24] Cf. Dahlhaus, ed., *Das Drama Richard Wagners*, pp. 127f.

aus Walhall send' ich dich nicht mehr, nicht mehr weis' ich dir helden
zur wal, nicht mehr führst du sieger in meinen saal, das Trinkhorn
nicht reichst du mir mehr; aus der götter schaar bist du verstoßen, aus
meinem angesicht bist du verbannt!

Nicht send' ich dich mehr aus Walhall,
 nicht weis' ich dir mehr
 Helden zur Wal;
 nicht führst du mehr Sieger
 in meinen Saal:
bei der Götter traulichem Mahle
 das Trinkhorn reichst du
 mir traut nicht mehr;
 nicht kos' ich dir mehr
 den kindischen Mund.
 Von göttlicher Schaar
 bist du geschieden,
 ausgestoßen
 aus der Ewigen Stamm:
gebrochen ist unser Bund:
aus meinem Angesicht bist du verbannt!

This does more than predetermine the metre and rhythm of the setting, it
establishes more generous proportions: the tension that steadily mounts as
this poetico-musical period runs its course clearly demands greater expan-
siveness before it reaches its climax in the last six bars.

The result was that two years later Wagner was able to write out the vocal
line in the composition sketch in one straight draft, with only minor
alterations.[25] As he had prophesied to Liszt in 1852, it was only a matter of
'the effectuation of what is already completed'.

I shall explain more fully what I mean by a musical impulse, as opposed
to mere bar-counting, by means of an instrumental example, when we come
to the violin cantilena in the transition to the final scene of *Siegfried*.

The cantabile Abgesang of the Annunciation of Death theme, which we
have just observed in Wotan's 'Nicht send' ich dich mehr aus Walhall' and
in the Valkyries' chorus 'Halt ein!', is now heard again in the transition to
the third scene as a bass clarinet solo, passing to the cor anglais and bassoon
at the change to B major. The composition sketch makes two attempts at
establishing the rhythms of this passage but the proper solution had to wait
until the score:

273 271

[25] The three lines 'bei der Götter traulichem Mahle / das Trinkhorn reichst du /
mir traut nicht mehr' appear thus in the original verse text, and were originally
set thus in the composition sketch, but were soon revised to the eventual form:
'Bei der Götter trautem Mahle / das Trinkhorn nicht reichst du / traulich mir
mehr', which follows the melodic line even more closely than the original
version.

Ex. 55*a* Sketch (1st version)

Ex. 55*b* Sketch (2nd version, written above the first)

Ex. 55*c* Score

The first version wavers between 9/8 and 6/8 tempo; the second is in 9/8 throughout and the rising figure is also more relaxed; but it is not until the score that the rhythm and metre are in sufficient accord to give the melody that freedom from all restraint that now characterizes it, especially with the modulation to B major.

Scene 3

Wagner wrote to Liszt about the style of this scene on 8 May 1857:

> I have been rehearsing the last, great scene of *Die Walküre*... with a
> soprano from the theatre here; Kirchner played the piano; I did
> famously, and this scene that so upsets you fulfilled all my expecta-
> tions. We did it three times at my house and now I am completely
> satisfied with it. The fact is that everything about it is so subtle, so
> profound and so gently stated that it needs the greatest awareness,
> delicacy and perfection in every aspect of the performance, if it is to

be understood; but if that is achieved, then there can be no doubt of the impression it will make. Of course something like this also skirts the edge of total disaster, if any aspect of the performance should fall short in perfection, dedication or awareness.

Appreciation of the style of the scene, with its abundant nuances, is greatly assisted by studying the composition sketch and then comparing it with the score.

Its two principal motives are stated as it starts: the motive of Wotan's discontent from the second act and, advancing against it as if in entreaty, the motive of Brünnhilde's love for the Wälsungen, which had already made its appearance in a significant position in the composition sketch of *Siegfrieds Tod* (see ex. 49*c*, bars 1 and 2):

274 272   Ex. 56 Sketch

              Ex. 57*a* Sketch

The two are the motivic sources of the music of the third scene, the second, cantabile motive being developed principally in the vocal writing, while the first undergoes a series of variations in the orchestra. From a musical point of view, the whole of the final scene is basically a variation movement on these two motives, progressing from their conflict to their reconciliation.

One more specific point should be made here: the form that the motive of Brünnhilde's love for the Wälsungen takes in ex. 57*a* differs in one important respect from the eventual form, shown in ex. 57*b* and in fact anticipated at a repeat of the phrase in the sketch: in the score the rising seventh comes *before* the rising octave. On the face of it, it is a minor matter, but it makes all the difference to the strength of the expression. When Brünnhilde starts to sing the motive and to elaborate it: 'War es so schmählich' –

Ex. 57c Sketch and score

Brünnh.

War es so schmählich, was ich verbrach, daß mein Verbrechen so schmählich du be - strafst?

– the octave interval is saved up, even in the sketch, until the fourth statement of the motive, and when it comes the effect is overwhelming.

Sketch and score are in agreement to begin with, even down to such 278 273 details as the tremolo in the strings at 'dunkle Schuld', but differences soon begin to appear in the melodic writing, as a result of the growing independence of the acompanimental figures.

The motive of Brünnhilde's love for the Wälsungen, which was meant initially to be understood as E minor, according to the note on the sketch, is 'transfigured' with the unexpected change to E major at 'Der diese Liebe mir ins Herz gelegt' ('gehaucht' – 'breathed' – in the sketch). After the first four bars, in which it is introduced in its new form rallentando diminuendo, like the reprise in a symphonic movement, the following twelve bars of sequences in the composition sketch are crossed out, and rewritten slightly differently on the next page – with another short section crossed out; but the sequential writing did not arrive at its final, far more 302 281 expansive form until the score:

Ex. 58 Sketch

Brünnhilde [with textual changes]

langsam   Bl.   Viol.

Der die-se Lie - - - - - - - be mir ins Herz [12 bars ge - -
(ins Herz)   (die - - se) (Lie) deleted]

[drum]

haucht,   dem Wil - len, der mich dem Wäl - sung ge - sellt

ihm - - in - nig ver - [4·bars   traut,
deleted]

Once when Wagner was playing this passage on the piano he complained of the lack of recognition given to his feeling for beauty, which in his view made him the 'successor of Mozart' (GLRW, VI, p. 156).

The composition sketch shows that this beauty did not fall from heaven but had to be worked at. Wagnerian sequential writing, which I mention so often, has nothing in common with the discredited practice of writing sequences when other inspiration fails. According to Kurth it constitutes a breach of the tonal evolution by the 'linear strength' of a melodic fragment (extra-tonal sequence): 'Like the individual notes in a melody, in a sequence whole melodic phrases are swept up and carried forward by a momentum...Wagner's technique of sequential writing became fundamental to the music of all the later Romantics.'[26]

The other principal motive of this scene, introduced in the form of the motive of Wotan's discontent, dissolves into a series of development motives which have in common the feature that they descend stepwise, in quavers, semiquavers, dotted notes and sextuplets, and coil round the vocal line, lamenting, pleading and conciliating, until gradually they re-form in a new, clearly defined Leitmotiv. This is usually called the 'Waberlohe' motive in German, alluding to the 'wavering light' of the newly kindled flames (while in English it is lumped together with the following 'Feuerzauber' as Magic Fire music), but that designation is quite superficial: in reality it is nothing less than the transformation of the Discontent motive into a motive of kindness and goodwill.

In the composition sketch these accompanimental figures begin only one bar before Brünnhilde's 'Weil für dich im Auge das Eine ich hielt':

287 277

Ex. 59*a* Sketch

---

[26] *Romantische Harmonik und ihre Krise in Wagners Tristan*, pp. 302ff. The whole of the chapter entitled 'Melodische Durchbrechungswege' is fundamental to the understanding of Wagner's sequential technique.

They continue in these variant forms:

Ex. 59*b* Sketch   Ex. 59*c* Sketch

335 *293*   Eventually they re-form as the Goodwill motive, first in the minor mode at
354 *298*   'Dies Eine mußt du erhören', and at last in the major at 'Leb' wohl, du
kühnes, herrliches Kind!':

Ex. 59*d* Sketch

Ex. 59*e* Sketch

From the composition sketch alone one might hesitate to name the
Discontent motive (ex. 56) as the source of the series of variants (exx.
59*a–e*). But the score closes the gap between ex. 56 and ex. 59*a*: there the
277 *273*   accompanimental figures begin much sooner, before Brünnhilde's 'O sag',
Vater!', and actually start with the Discontent motive, stated note for note
as it is in ex. 56, played alternately by the first oboe and the cor anglais and
repeated sequentially. The proliferation of crossings-out and alterations in
the sketch serves to coordinate the vocal part with the accompaniment;
to judge by the appearance of the pen strokes they were not made until
Wagner was actually scoring:

Ex. 59*f* Sketch (and score, from the eighth bar)

schwei - ge den [?] Zorn, zäh - me die Wut! deu - te mir

[Greater differences in the score from here on, figuration omitted]

Brünnh.

zäh - me die Wut und deu - te mir

hell die dunk - le Schuld, die mit star - - - rem Trot - ze dich

Trem.

klar die dunk - le Schuld, die mit star - rem Trot - ze dich zwingt, zu ver-

(2 Tacte)?

zwingt, zu ver - stos - sen dein trau - te - stes Kind.

stos - sen dein trau - te - stes Kind.

284 *276*   The first variant of the figure, which is not included in the sketch either, at 'doch wußt' ich das Eine', is characterized by the semiquaver triplet at the end:

Ex. 59*g* Score

287 277   Then follows the form already quoted as ex. 59*a*, which is in both the sketch and the score, with which the dissolution of the Discontent motive into development motives begins.

    The demonstrable development of the Goodwill motive ('Waberlohe') from the Discontent motive is yet another proof of Wagner's assertion, after finishing *Das Rheingold*, that 'there is scarcely a bar in the orchestral writing that does not develop out of preceding motives'.

    When, immediately after the first statement of the new motive in the major mode, ex. 59*e*, Wotan continues it with 'Leb' wohl, du kühnes, herrliches Kind!', he does not take over the fully distilled form straightaway as the accompanimental figure to the voice part, but allows instead one further, more impassioned variant to be heard as the expression of his
354 298   underlying emotions:

Ex. 60 Sketch

    The composition sketch reveals that the figure was originally not included at this point, but entered only at the seventeenth bar; to judge by the handwriting it was a later addition even there. Evidently Wagner was not sure to begin with what character to give the accompaniment. Wotan's catharsis could not be completed until he had composed the subsequent
372 303   'symphonic song of redemption in E major' (Porges). 'The knot of the tempo is untied here', Wagner said of the emergence of the new motive (Porges), but it is not only the knot of the two opposing motives that was tied at the beginning of the scene. It is not until this moment that the
380 304   development of the inner action has advanced far enough for the accompaniment, which in Wagner plays the role of psychological commentator and interpreter of what is sung, to present the new Goodwill motive. This time it is elaborated to its full extent in the sketch, yet again it looks like a later addition.

    The musical significance that Wagner accorded to the individual variants of the development motive is revealed by a specific instruction he gave for the performance of ex. 59*a*: the first figure, while played with all due expression, should not be allowed to drag; in the second phrase, which alternates and intertwines with the first in a kind of duet, the sextuplets should always be played without any particular emphasis, but the dotted notes should be slightly accented (Porges). As Wagner said to Liszt, in the letter already quoted, 'just running through the music, the way we tried to do it, is simply not good enough'.

302 *281*   If the first E major passage of sequences based on the motive of Brünnhilde's love for the Wälsungen needed to be 'worked at', even greater exertion was necessary for the second, more extended passage, the
372 *303*   'symphonic song of redemption': once again the final version does not occur until the score:

Ex. 61 Sketch

To understand the difference between the sketch and the score in this passage, we must take into account that Wagner's sequential technique can be further enriched in one or both of the following ways: 1, the interval of transposition can be changed; 2, the motive can be shortened. In the 'symphonic song of redemption', the two-bar motive is reduced to one bar in the middle segment of the sequence, both in the sketch and in the score, by means of a 'shorter-breathed compression of the waves of intensification' (Kurth). But whereas in the sketch the phrase is transposed by the interval of a fourth at the start, and continues at the same interval in the middle segment too, in the score the transposition is initially only a second, so that when it widens to a fourth in the middle segment it induces a sense of further intensification. The interval is a second in the final segment, in both versions. The intervallic symmetry of the first and last segments gives the version in the score a sublime serenity throughout the whole period, in spite of the intensification in the middle.

The tension that has built up between the two principal motives in their various forms resolves, as I have said, at the dynamic climax of the scene with the amazing combination of the two above the second inversion of the tonic chord. But it was only in the score that Wagner introduced the sudden triplet figure whose upward movement enables the sequences based on the principal melody to arrive at the E, on which the accompanimental motive then enters in what we regard as its ideal, prime form. The simultaneous action on the stage, the embrace of Wotan and Brünnhilde, is the visual expression of the musical development, and it is that which gives the moment its power.

The most important of the other new motives in this scene is the Sleep motive, the chromatically descending chords first heard at Wotan's 'In festen Schlaf verschließ' ich dich' and recurring later, expanded from four bars to eight, as Brünnhilde falls asleep:

332 *292*

387 *306*

Ex. 62*a* Sketch

Kurth's analysis of the evolution of this motive is interesting: according to him the chromatic progression does not extend to all the parts equally, but is restricted 'ideally' to the line of the topmost part. Specifically, the bass diverges from it considerably, often performing a conventionally 'harmonizing' function, so that a progression by thirds underpins the chromatic onward flow. One other feature is remarkable technically: the onward flow is continually seeking out a sure tonal foothold, inasmuch as the chord progressions cadence in every other bar, with diminished sevenths fulfilling a dominant function.

Kurth also points out that the first chords of the first, third, fifth, seventh and ninth bars are major triads, whose bass notes, Ab, E, C, G♯ and E, in themselves present a progression by thirds in every other bar – if, as he adds, Ab and G♯ are enharmonically equated (pp. 202ff.).

Ex. 62*b* Sketch

The composition sketch confirms that Wagner himself intended the enharmonic ambiguity of the first chord to be appreciated. The notation alone is enough to show that he explicitly limited the chromatic progression to the top part and that already at this stage he emphasized the sequential nature of the writing by changing the orchestration (woodwind first, strings for the repeat).

In spite of its theoretical complexity this whole design is written straight out in the sketch exactly as it later appears in the score, except for the A in the inner part in the fourth bar, which is introduced in the sketch as a passing note; evidently he did not want a seventh chord to interrupt the succession of triads opening each bar. But in the score the advantages of the hypnotic effect of a regular rhythmic pattern outweighed the harmonic considerations:

Ex. 62*c* Score

[cf. ex. 62*a*]

There is another instructive observation to be made about the chords of the Sleep motive, which are destined to play an important role in the music of the *Ring*. Apart from the kind of motivic development that spreads out, as it were radially, from a centre, and the *direct* motivic relationships ensuing therefrom, there is also in Wagner a kind of lateral connection linking the different developmental radii: the reciprocal penetration of *indirectly* related motives, which create wholly new musical and conceptual associations. Thus, in the last scene of *Die Walküre*, a relationship is established between the chromatic descent associated with Loge from *Das Rheingold* and that of the Sleep motive, whereby the cold flickering of the former is modified to a gentler light. In the composition sketch at this point Wagner wrote out the Loge figure in full only in the first crotchet, and thereafter wrote out only the top and bottom lines of the Sleep chords:

408 311

Ex. 62*d* Sketch

But whereas he emphasized the cadence recurring at every fourth chord by dotting the rhythm in the sketch, he foregoes it in the score, so that the chord progression breathes a greater solemnity.

Before summoning Loge, Wotan takes his leave of Brünnhilde in 'Der Augen leuchtendes Paar', which is written straight out in the sketch in one flow without any alterations. The handwriting responds expressively to the sound of the music, which continues in the solemnly spaced chords of the Sleep motive as the singer finishes.

380 304

Extraordinarily, Wagner had doubts about the cadence: 'so küßt er die Gottheit von dir!', as a question mark in the sketch betrays:

386 306

Ex. 63 Sketch

Die Walküre, Act III, Scene 3 (composition sketch)

The score retains the A♭ after all, and it is impossible now to imagine anything else.

338 *294*   The Siegfried theme is quoted again at Brünnhilde's plea: 'daß nur ein furchtlos freiester Held hier auf dem Felsen einst mich fänd''; the word 'einst' is omitted in the sketch and the theme appears there in its shorter

370 *302*   form. It is quoted again at Wotan's promise: 'Denn Einer nur freie die Braut', in stretto-like treatment in the sketch as in the score, but still with a very different inflexion; it is only in the score that the melodic and harmonic progression allows the following E major of the 'symphonic song of redemption' to shine out in its full glory:

Ex. 64 Sketch

I have already mentioned that it was not until Wagner came to Wotan's

414 *312*   final words: 'Wer meines Speeres Spitze fürchtet, durchschreitet das Feuer nie' in the sketch that he finally established the Siegfried theme in its full form. Repetition marks in the first two bars are the only means whereby the 'Feuerzauber' accompaniment is intimated, as though the composer could not get to the end of the sketch fast enough. The orchestral quotation of Wotan's Farewell that follows ends with surprising abruptness (the accidental against the C looks like a ♭, but should probably be read as ♮).

Ex. 65 Sketch

On the other hand, the Fate motive, stated twice, is already in the new revised form in the sketch. Whereas in the Annunciation of Death scene in Act II the motive begins with a chord that is heard as a dissonance and

resolves into a chord of the seventh, here it appears as a D minor triad
followed by an E major triad:

Ex. 66*a* Sketch and score   Ex. 66*b* Sketch and score

'The original tension-created element resolves irresistibly into sound',
Kurth comments (p. 188).

Four bars at the end

Ex. 67 Sketch

RW / 27 Dez. 1854

are omitted in the score, where the act ends instead with the chord of E
major dying away *ppp*.

Below, very large, 'RW / 27 Dec. 1854': the composition sketch of this
third act had taken a little over five weeks.

Siegfried

'If only for the sake of *Der junge Siegfried*, the most splendid of all my dreams, I must finish the Nibelungen dramas', Wagner had written to Liszt on 16 December 1854. '*Die Walküre* took too much out of me, for me not to allow myself this relief...My heart feels so pure when I think of it!'

But it was not until September 1856 that he was able to start the composition of *Siegfried*. He confessed to his friend and patroness Julie Ritter on 6 May 1857:

> If you would like some good news of me for a change, I think you will be pleased to learn that I have finished the first act of *Siegfried* this winter (though I was greatly delayed at the start by Liszt's visit and later by my own extreme exhaustion), and although one act is less than I would like to have completed, it has nevertheless turned out more satisfactorily than all my expectations. It was completely new ground for me, and after the dreadful tragedy of *Die Walküre* I entered upon it with a sensation of freshness such as I have never felt before.

The first two acts were composed during an exceptionally fertile period of poetic and musical inspiration, as the following table shows:

1856
20 March
Completion of the first draft of the score of *Die Walküre*
16 May
Sketch of the Buddhist legend, *Die Sieger*
May–June
The titles *Der junge Siegfried* and *Siegfrieds Tod* changed to *Siegfried* and *Götterdämmerung*. Prose sketch of a new ending to the latter with a large-scale choral finale
Before 22 September
Start on the composition sketch of Act I of *Siegfried*
19 December
First music sketches for *Tristan*

1857
10 April
Prose sketch of *Parzival*
16 May
'First motive "im Asyl"'' (*Tristan*, Act I)
Before August
'Sink hernieder...', first version (*Tristan*, Act II)
30 July
Completion of the composition sketch of Act II of *Siegfried*
20 August
Start on the prose sketch of *Tristan*

The file of sketches of individual motives in *Siegfried* in the Wagnerarchiv contains ten sheets and part-sheets, some with several different sketches on them. These include the following relating to the first and second acts:

Act I
1. Mime's complaint (study score p. 60, vocal score p. *21*)
2. Immediately following: 'Als zullendes Kind' (62 *21*)
3. Mime's Sidling motive (205 *70*)
4. The Wanderer's second theme, beginning with the dominant seventh chord of C major (154f. *52f.*)
5. 'Hammering' (382 *127*)
6. 'hoho, hoho, hahei!' (382 *127*)

Act II
7. 'Fafner's sleep' (four sketches or variants, cf. exx. 19*a–d*) (Prelude)
8. 'Siegfried's entry / very moderate (easy)' (81 *170*)
9. 'Horn in F' (142f. *194f.*)
10. 'Blackbird's song'
11. Three sketches of birdsong motives
12. 'Bird: "Lustig im Leid"'' (283 *244*)

Apart from the sketches relating to the third act, which will be enumerated later, other music sketches on the same sheets of paper as the above include some for *Tristan*, for *Die Sieger* and for a revision of Senta's Ballad, and also the lullaby 'Schlaf' Kindchen, schlaf'', a study for the *Siegfried Idyll*.

An item of particular interest from the point of view of Wagner's compositional technique is a melody dated '6 Sept' (no year given) and marked 'Andante':

Ex. 1*a*

6 Sept   Andante

A purely instinctive reaction is that it must be a study for the Young Sailor's song from the first act of *Tristan*. In fact the song is hidden in the melody like a bird in the branches of a tree in a child's picture puzzle. If the reader concentrates on the notes marked in the example, and ignores the others, repeating the first ten bars but finishing with D instead of B♭ the second time, and then continues to the last note, the result is:

Ex. 1*b*

This gives another insight into Wagner's technique of melodic development. Besides expanding the initial idea, as he did in the case of the Spring Song in Act I of *Die Walküre*, an alternative method was to compress it, as we saw with the theme of the Annunciation of Death in Act II. Both methods have Beethovenian affinities. With regard to the evolution of the Young Sailor's song out of the Andante melody, it may be that the briefer, more succinct version hovered before Wagner as an 'ideal' form from the first, but he had to wait for a second creative impulse before he could realize it. That impulse may have been provided by the verse text: he had sketched the melody on 6 September (1857) and completed the text of *Tristan* on 18 September. Thereupon the quintessence of the melody turned into the tune of the song quite spontaneously. The Young Sailor's song 'had come to him, he hadn't ever reflected: "this and this is what you must do"', and that was probably what gave his things their naivety and would keep them fresh' (Cosima's diary, 23 November 1882; BBL 1938, p. 11).

The propinquity of *Siegfried* and *Tristan* which comes to light here is borne out by other evidence, including a letter of August 1857 to Princess Marie Sayn-Wittgenstein: 'While I was working again on *Siegfried*, *Tristan*, once more, would not leave me in peace. Strictly speaking, I was working on both of them at once.'

This is reminiscent of Beethoven, who also worked simultaneously on two similarly complementary works, such as the Fifth and Sixth Symphonies, as the sketches show. 'Stylistic criticism could not hope to establish that as a fact, but it emerges with absolute certainty from the surviving sketches.'[1]

'Often I sat looking at my pencilled pages [the composition sketch] as if they were written in utterly foreign characters, which I could not begin to decipher', Wagner recounts of his work on the score of the second act of *Die Walküre* (ML, pp. 611f.). As a result of that experience, he decided he had better make orchestral sketches for the remaining dramas in the tetralogy, allowing an interval of one to four weeks to elapse after finishing the corresponding part of the composition sketches. The orchestral sketches of *Siegfried* and *Götterdämmerung*, also preserved in the Wagner-archiv, are written out very neatly in ink on three or more staves. The manuscript sheets have twenty-one staves on each side (the full scores have thirty) and were stitched together after completion, so that they can be read as easily as a vocal score. The instrumentation is noted in the margin in pencil: for example, for the Funeral March in *Götterdämmerung*, 'Fl., Hb. [oboe], Cl., Eng[lish horn], BsCl., Hr., Tr., Pos. [trombone], Hrf. [harp], Vl.1, Vl.2, Br. [viola], Vc., CB.' are all listed one beneath the other. Numbers are added to indicate for how many bars that particular combination will continue, and on what page of the score the staves should be reserved for it.

This procedure enabled Wagner to pursue the flight of his imagination as it had come to him while writing out the composition sketches, without needing to pause for thought and without the fear that, when he came to score in full – often a great while later – his 'inner memory' would leave him in the lurch. For us it has a certain disadvantage, in that the composition sketches of these works are incomparably more difficult to decipher and moreover there is an almost complete absence of those revealing, spontaneous, early notes on the instrumentation. Nevertheless we are still able to experience the process of musical gestation.

Act I

The composition sketch for the first act of *Siegfried* consists of twenty-seven half-sheets of manuscript paper, the last of which is used on one side only. No date is given for the start, but it was in any case before 22 September 1856, when the orchestral sketch was started; the end is dated '20 Jan. 1857'.

Scene 1

The composition sketch starts with Mime's monologue 'Zwangvolle Plage!' on the first page. It is written out on two staves, and key signatures are

[1] Cf. Otto Strobel, '"Geschenke des Himmels"': Über die ältesten überlieferten *Tristan*-Themen', *Bayreuther Festspielführer 1938*, p. 157; Walter Riezler, *Beethoven* (Zürich, 1951), p. 173.

given only where the key changes, which remains the rule throughout the sketch. The bars from 'Siegfrieds kindischer Kraft' to 'und ich kann's nicht...' are bracketed, normally a sign that Wagner considered revising something, but no subsequent alteration was made in the sketch. The vocal line varies slightly in the score, where it is a semitone higher on average. As usual with accompanimental figures, the motive of Mime's hammering is written out for the first bar only each time that it recurs.

The first impression is that in other respects the composition sketch already corresponds to the score. Closer comparison reveals, however, that the short instrumental interjections are considerably longer in the later version and that the motive depicting Mime's brooding (two bassoons playing in thirds), already encountered in the third scene of *Das Rheingold*, has been added, lending his complaint an undertone of mystery:

19 *6*

Ex. 2*a* Sketch

Ex. 2*b* Score

23 *8*

In place of the sketch's simple quotation of the Sword motive, the score has a strongly moulded passage launched by a statement of the motive, at the end of the middle section of the smith's song, creating a sense of climax which it is hardly an exaggeration to call breathtaking:

Ex. 3*a* Sketch

Ex. 3*b* Score

The monologue ends in the sketch, as in the score, with a varied reprise of its first section, 'Zwangvolle Plage!' – a true parody of a da capo aria in the grand manner to open the Liederspiel, at once humorous and heroic, that is the first act of *Siegfried*.

31 *10*   A motive suggesting the growl of a bear leads into a variation of Siegfried's Horn call, without any words set to it at this stage. Then the page is turned upside down for a scrawled study trying out sequences based on the motive. It is not until the next sheet that Siegfried's entry up to 'Lauf' Brauner!' is sketched, with both the vocal parts and the accompaniment, written down very quickly on three staves with quite a lot of emendations.

The composition sketch of the act prelude appears at last on the verso of this second sheet. 'My preludes must all be elemental, not dramatic', Wagner once said later (GLRW, VI, p. 152). The preludes to *Das Rheingold* and *Die Walküre*, depicting water and wind respectively, are 'elemental' in the most literal sense. This time, the composer evidently had to rack his brains for the best corresponding way to introduce the dwarf, brooding on his obsession and his fears, until at last he hit on the appropriate 'elemental' character in the vision of the hoard of gold emerging out of the silent depths into the light of day.

The prelude appears in a greatly simplified form in the sketch. It starts approximately at what is now the fortieth bar and consists of no more than the motive of the hoard being brought up, breaking at its climax into the distinctive cry of despair ('Wehe!') and then dissolving into confused, ghostly syncopations of the Ring motive, fluttering pianissimo in B♮ minor, until, in place of a final chord, the C major of the Sword motive suddenly rings out and drives the phantoms away. Even the visual appearance of these four lines of music, on two staves each, written down in one outpouring, is enough to convey an impression of the elemental character of the prelude, and even in the full score, where there are up to twenty staves on a page at times, that impression is not dissipated.

The composition sketch contains more of the prelude than that, however. Two lines of two staves each, headed 'beginning', follow on the same page, with the missing opening bars including the motive of Mime's brooding for the first time. It is quite clear from this that Wagner was first reminded of II, I 4, I the thirds of the Brooding motive by the very act of writing out the related thirds of the Ring motive; it was primarily a musical association, which then evolved into a conceptual one, and it was in the latter function that it later suggested to Wagner the inclusion of the motive in Mime's monologue, when he was working on the score.

Ex. 4a Sketch   Ex. 4b Sketch

Vorspiel: [Ring motive]   *Anfang:* [Brooding motive]

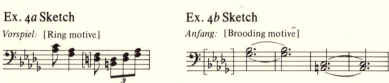

After the sketch of the prelude, sheet 3 of the manuscript continues with
38 *13* Siegfried's 'Nach bess'rem Gesellen sucht' ich'. The first four bars, the motivic germ of the melody, are written down with hardly any alterations. The syncopated pulse in the bass is still absent, but the expressive bass line (cellos, cresc. in the score) already appears in the fourth bar –

Ex. 5 Sketch

– and continues in syncopation. The second four-bar period has some emendations, but there are none in the third which leads into the Horn motive (sketch: 'horn *f* dim.'); after the delicate nuances of the accompaniment to Siegfried's song the D major of the dominant now sounds particularly 'ringing'.

44 *16* Wagner tells of the inspiration of Siegfried's furious outburst, 'Da hast du die Stücken, schändlicher Stümper', in *Mein Leben* (p. 624): the hammering of a tinker had almost driven him to abandon composing altogether for the time being.

> But it was precisely in a moment of rage with the tinker that I
> suddenly had the idea for the motive of Siegfried's anger against
> Mime, the 'bungling smith': at once I played the boisterous theme of
> his childish petulance to my sister [Klara] in G minor and sang the
> words furiously, which made us all laugh so much that I decided to
> carry on this time after all.

The whole passage must have been written down immediately afterwards, to judge by the scrawl in which it is written and the hastiness of the
alterations. But everything is already there: the canonic entries, the rising
counterpoints (set a third higher in the score), the dotted rhythm of the
giants ('Schwatzt mir von Riesen'), and even the formal structure of the
period, which Lorenz has shown to be a rondo (three principal sections
and two episodes) (p. 99).

With the 'boisterous theme' with its descending fourths added to Mime's
Hammering motive and Siegfried's Horn call, Wagner now had three
motives possessing an inherent motoric drive and lending themselves to
transformation, to be 'lines of force in the great sustaining current of the
infinite melody' (Kurth).

60 *21*

The twelve bars of Mime's complaint, 'Das ist nun der Liebe schlimmer
Lohn!', with their strong sustained dissonances, were first sketched hastily
in pencil on a separate sheet (no. 1 in the list of sketches on p. 129), and then
copied in the composition sketch without change. The same was the case
with the 'Starling's Song' ('dem alten Starenlied'), 'Als zullendes Kind',
that immediately follows it, except for a few changes in the superficially
simple harmonization, which is in fact far from simple. The acciaccaturas in
the vocal part show that Wagner already had in mind the sobs that Mime
produces here.

As the scene advances one can trace how the 'boisterous theme' turns
into a 'development motive' in Kurth's sense: peaceable, legato at Sieg-

70 *24*
73 *25*
89 *31*

fried's 'Vieles lehrtest du Mime'; accelerando, staccato in a climbing
sequence at 'Seh' ich dir erst mit den Augen zu'; as a flute obbligato 'with
gentle tone quality' (Porges) accompanying the charming idyll 'da flatterte
junges Geflügel auf' (notated on an additional, fourth stave in the sketch);

101 *35*

or as a restless semiquaver figure at Siegfried's impatient 'Siehst du, nun
fällt auch selbst mir ein' – carrying the many different motives of the period
along in the current of the melody.

81 *28*

One of these motives, that of Siegfried's love of nature, stands out by
reason of a new note of tender sentiment:

Ex. 6 Sketch

Wagner directed that it should be played 'as if emerging from a dream...as if coming from a remote distance, without any emotion' (Porges). Its own origin is certainly remote: Lorenz draws attention to its affinity with the cor anglais melody in the second act of *Die Walküre*, at the moment when Brünnhilde is resigning herself to abandoning Siegmund (*Walküre*, exx. 33*a* and *b*). 'The feeling it conveys is one of a...mother forced to abandon her child, and this is...what Siegfried, too, recognizes in *mother-love* in his observation of wild life' (p. 84, footnote). The harmonic colouring is already there in the composition sketch, but there is not the slightest hint of 86 *30* the instrumental refinement – the cello melody, the viola accompaniment.

97 *34*   The idyll's conclusion, 'Wie die Jungen den Alten gleichen', is already distinguished in the sketch by an effect of light and shade, wherein the 'flat' key of the shadows of the forest turns into a 'sharp' key when Siegfried comes to describe how he saw his reflection in the stream – 'impressionism with the simplicity of genius,' Kurth writes, 'the nature poetry of the *Ring* is full of such effects' (p. 137).

Of the various emendations Wagner made while he was in the act of 99 *34* sketching, the one after 'Da sah ich denn auch mein eigen Bild' is interesting inasmuch as it shows that his original intention was to return to B♭ major, after the modulation to D major mentioned above, as early as 'Bild', which would have made nonsense of the final chord of the Siegfried motive. Accordingly he crossed out eight bars, rounded off the motive with the correct chord of D major, and returned to the principal key of B♭ via D minor.

Ex. 7 Sketch

104 *36*   This main section of the dialogue between Siegfried and Mime ends, at 'So muß ich dich fassen', with a twenty-six-bar reprise of the 'boisterous theme' in its original form and with its original connotations, after all its transformations as an 'anonymous' development motive.

111 *39*   After Mime's whining reproach, 'Was verhofft' ich mir Tor auch Dank!', the sketch bears the note '(*1st December*)'. This was the date on which Wagner resumed work after a six-week break occasioned by a visit from Liszt (13 October to 27 November 1856). 'This very day I shall finish the first scene', he wrote to Liszt on 6 December.

It's strange! It's only now that I am composing that the true nature of my text is revealing itself to me: everywhere I am discovering secrets which until now have remained hidden even from me. Consequently everything is turning out more violent and more urgent. But on the whole it's going to take a great deal of perseverance if I am ever to finish it all. I'm afraid that you weren't completely successful, after all, in making me want to do it. But I think I shall do it just for myself, anyway, as a way of spending my life. So be it!

Up to this point the *Siegfried* sketch has lacked any indications of instrumentation but with the quotation of the Wälsungen motive that now follows, Wagner makes the following note: 'bass clarinet – horns – clarinet'. This reminder of Siegfried's parentage ushers in a passage in which tragedy and comedy are unusually mixed: something which German dramatists learned from Shakespeare. The musical risk involved is met with such skill that the hearer is not even aware of it: the motives associated with the Wälsungen mingle with the isolated lines from the Starling's Song to form a continuous melodic line, the articulation of which is further under- lined by the alternation of 6/8 and 3/8 time.[2] 'The *reflective* passages concern Siegfried alone', Wagner commented (Porges).

At Siegfried's impatient 'Soll ich der Kunde glauben', nine impassioned bars of sequences formed from the motive of his love of nature are deleted (before the voice part had been added) and rewritten in a new, rapidly ascending form:

III *39*

116 *41*

128 *45*

Ex. 8*a* Sketch I

[breaks off here, crossed out]'

[2] Not written out consistently in the sketch.

Ex. 8*b* Sketch II

Lebhaft *(Siegfr.)*

(Kun-de glau - - - ben, hast du mir nicht ge -

lo - gen, so laß mich Zeichen)

It cannot have escaped Wagner's notice that there were six consecutive fifths in bars two to five of ex. 8*b*, which were particularly obvious in the simplified notation of the sketch. While he was writing *Parsifal* he confessed that he was very pedantic and always gave the matter a great deal of thought before writing fifths; but when he did decide to use them he threw the rule-book out of the window. Bach had been just the same; his attitude had been: 'Everyone knows what kind of musician I am, and that, if I write something of that sort, then I do it deliberately, for the sake of expression.'

Wagner was referring to the unique obtrusiveness of successions of fifths, though in this case it was moderated by the fact that the fifths were the result only of notes alien to the harmony.

Five bars accompanying Mime's pause for thought after Siegfried's question 'Welch' Zeichen zeugt für dich?' were also crossed out and rewritten at greater length. The original tempo marking, 'lento', was dropped for the second version and the retardation expressed only by increased note values: as always, Wagner was concerned not to break up the overall line by too many details of tempo.

From now on everything does become 'more violent and more urgent'. The eight-bar period containing Siegfried's exclamation 'Und diese Stücken sollst du mir schmieden', introduced by the Sword-motive fanfare, was performed 'like a whirlwind, rushing towards a target', Porges reports, while the following passage, in which the motive is playfully repeated sequentially with an altogether lighter tone quality, should be played 'almost in the style of comic opera', in Wagner's own words. But the fact that the whole of the finale of the first scene was written out in one burst in the composition sketch does not by any means signify that its conception was equally spontaneous. By chance we know how much thought, and for how long, preceded the actual notation.

In the first version of the poem of *Der junge Siegfried*, begun on 3 June

1851, Wagner sketched metrical patterns in three places in the margin against Siegfried's Roving Song

> Aus dem Wald fort
> in die Welt ziehn!

The one sketched against those first two lines is revealing in that it is the Ionic metre used by Goethe in *Pandora*:

> *Epimeleia*:
> Meinen Angstrúf
> Um mich sélbst nícht...

'Discussed ...choriambics and ionics *a minori*', Goethe wrote in his notebook on 17 May 1808. And Adlatus Riemer records that work on *Pandora* was delayed, among other reasons, 'by the classical metres that Goethe felt at liberty to try out in his own way, without being so conversant with them as the beauty of the poem demanded'.[3]

But the impression of a certain artificiality is not due to any lack of familiarity with classical metres on Goethe's part but to their *musical* origins. Droysen's translations of Aeschylus and August Apel's book on metre had long acquainted Wagner with the difficulties involved in imitating Greek metres, and he wrote in 1851, in *Oper und Drama*, that we can understand the reason for the superabundance of rhythmic variety in classical choruses only if we grasp that they are 'governed by their melodic origin' (RWGS, IV, p. 144). And his own ionics sound so natural precisely because they are meant to be *sung*.

At all events the marginal note on the manuscript of the text of *Der junge Siegfried* proves that Wagner's musical fantasy was already occupied with the Roving Song five years before he came to set it. And this allows us to assume that other passages, where there is no such direct proof of it, also went through a similar period of incubation. 'He must have done an immense amount of thinking and sketching for the music of the *Ring* during all the years since 1848. He must have seen and heard it all, with his inner eye and ear, very much as it would be at the finish.' (NLRW, II, p. 389.)

The Roving Song, with which the first part of the 'Liederspiel' attains its climax, has another distinctive feature in that it alludes motivically to something that has preceded it – Mime's Starling's Song, of all things; the melody of

Ex. 9*a* Sketch and score

[3] *Goethes Werke*, Sophienausgabe, Section I, vol. 50, pp. 450f.

recurs, with its rhythm changed, in the choriambic

142 *49*   Ex. 9*b* Sketch and score

Siegfr.

flieg' ich von hier,   flu - te da-von,

This was another of the places where Wagner sketched the metrical pattern
in the margin of the manuscript of the text. After once sketching the
magnificent orchestral postlude, with the concentrated counterpoint of its
accompaniment, Wagner went back to it and extended it, so that its
fortissimo finish now repeats the Starling's Song melody note for note, in
the choriambic rhythm:

          Ex. 9*c* Sketch

The outcome is such that, as Lorenz remarks, in this scene 'the parody is
given precedence over the original theme' (p. 225, footnote 1).

Scene 2

The second scene springs a surprise with the Wanderer's entrance: it starts
on the verso of sheet 11 of the composition sketch with the colourless
cadence

          Ex. 10*a* Sketch

Mime

ganz

Wanderer

Heil   dir!   wei - - ser   Schmied! [breaks off here]

then suddenly breaks off. Wagner makes a fresh start on the recto of sheet
12, rewriting the heading 'Second scene' and only now writing down 'the
154 *52*   Wanderer's marvellously luminous chords' (Kurth) for the first time.[4]

----

[4] The motivic germ of the Wanderer's chords in ex. 10*b* can be detected in the
two first inversions on 'Heil' and 'dir' in ex. 10*a*, if one ignores the
intervening harmony. It is another case where we directly experience the
origination of a motive.

Ex. 10b Sketch

The chords were also missing from the previous sketch that Wagner had made (no. 4 in the list on p. 129), which began straightaway with the second theme (played by the woodwind, horns and strings), so we must conclude that the Wanderer's chords were born of the wish to replace the original dull cadence with a more 'luminous' harmonic succession.

Kurth points out that, simple though they may sound, the Wanderer's chords are quite complex, structurally and harmonically. He analyses them as a sequence, disguised by harmonic shifts. The basis of the sequence is provided by the first chords of the first, third and fifth bars, which form a succession of major chords descending at whole-tone intervals. The intervening chord progressions must be related tonally to whichever one of these basic chords follows, being in each case in the relationship to it of, respectively, subdominant, Neapolitan sixth and dominant. 'What distracts attention most powerfully from the underlying sequential progression is the solemn glow shed by the many successions of chords a third apart, brilliant harmonic effects that conceal the melodic element.' Kurth compares this with the manner in which the harmonies merge into each other in the Magic Sleep music in the third act of *Die Walküre*, which is also close to the sequential principle (pp. 316f.).

We notice at once, from exx. 10a and b, that the orchestral chords relating to the Wanderer begin two bars earlier in the second version – as in the score – than they do in the first version in the sketch, so that they overlap the end of Mime's singing. Interleaving of the orchestral and vocal periods and of the verbal exchanges – except during Mime's pauses for thought – is one of the characteristics of the ensuing conversation, and we find it already there in the sketch: evidence that it was conceived from the first as a vivid dialogue, each statement or question of one speaker prompting the other's reply.

During the preliminary rehearsals held in 1875, Wagner had this to say of the style of this encounter:

> Didn't Mozart himself bequeath us the basic form of German bel canto in *Die Zauberflöte*? The dialogue between Tamino and the Speaker will stand as the model for all time. What else do you suppose I am trying to achieve in the dialogue between the Wanderer and Mime in the first act of Siegfried?[5]

205 *70*   Almost imperceptibly a cadential figure attaches itself to Mime's Hammering motive, after Wotan's challenge 'Drum frische dir, Mime, den Mut!' Although the instrumentation is not actually stated in words, it is already notated in the viola clef in the sketch: in fact, just as trumpets are always associated with the Sword motive, so the timbre of violas, occasionally reinforced by flutes or oboes, is characteristic of this figure, sometimes known as the Sidling motive. It is called upon to play an important role as long as Mime is on stage in *Siegfried* – not least because it adds to the number of motoric development motives which are so characteristic of this score.

Ex. 11*a* Sketch

409 *135*   Ex. 11*b* Sketch

[5] Julius Hey, *Richard Wagner als Vortragsmeister*, p. 149.

Scene 3

237 *83* The forty bars that Mime's terrified vision of Fafner – 'a piece of orchestral painting of extraordinary power' (Newman) – occupies in the sketch are extended to forty-six bars in the score. One can make out, from the recto of sheet 17 of the sketch, that the period was originally articulated in two-bar groups; then later the bars were numbered off in groups of three instead, or supplemented as appropriate by repetition marks, ·/., and redivided by moving the bar lines. Wagner decided on this alteration, as so often, while he was still writing down this first draft, for the last twelve bars, on the back of the sheet, are written straight out in three-bar groups with appropriate phrasing. The triple grouping (i.e. three bars of 2/4 time) is not merely visible to the eye but heard as well, thanks to the Dragon motive, played by the bass tuba. This combination of duple time with triple grouping adds to the bizarre fantasy of the orchestral writing.

The use made of Loge's motive is very easy to read in the concentrated notation of the sketch: the harmonic progressions – in quavers – are written out exactly, while the semiquavers of the figure at first appear in mirrored form:

Ex. 12*a* Sketch

Ex. 12*b* Score

239 *84* The forte in the accompaniment at the F major modulation of Loge's motive is distinguished by one of the rare notes of instrumentation in the sketch: 'horns (muted)', which are retained in the score; they relieve a low F (on the bass tuba) in order to enable the crescendo that has been building up until this point to drop back again to pianissimo: 'Dort glimmert's und glitzt's in der Sonne...'

270 *94* Mime's attempt to instruct Siegfried in the meaning of fear, motivically related to his own terrors, has the appearance of having been sketched very rapidly, but a closer inspection reveals that all the essentials are already there. The demisemiquavers[6] (played by the violas and cellos) starting on 'braust', and breaking out into arpeggios (on the violins, divided into three) at 'Flackern', are written out meticulously in microscopic notation: this impressionistic painting of the fire was so important to Wagner that he could

6 Semiquaver triplets in Klindworth's vocal score.

282 *98*

not postpone its precise notation until the orchestral sketch. On the other hand the arpeggios that accompany Siegfried's unruffled reply are not sketched: they are the same as those of the Magic Fire music ('Feuerzauber') from the third act of *Die Walküre*.

Another rare note of instrumentation is the 'Cl.' marked against the Dragon's motive at Mime's 'Fühltest du nie im finst'ren Wald'. Wagner wanted to establish on the spot that he was going to use the clarinets' 'menacing' low register (Richard Strauss's description) at this point, instead of the contrabass tuba which is used for this motive elsewhere.

'The scene with the Wanderer has turned out splendidly, and now I'm in the act of forging the sword', Wagner wrote to Princess Marie Sayn-Wittgenstein in a letter that can be dated at the beginning of January 1857:

> Today – in the midst of my anguish – Mime exclaimed
>> Nun ward ich so alt
>> wie Höhl' und Wald
>> und hab' nicht sowas gesehn!
>
> which made me laugh so much that my wife came into the room in amazement, since she had last seen me on the sofa with my head buzzing.

This letter helps to calculate the speed of his progress; he had resumed work on 1 December 1856 with Mime's 'Einst lag wimmernd ein Weib', so it took him approximately five weeks to reach the point he mentions here.

A letter to Otto Wesendonk refers directly to the start of the finale:

> Des Vaters Stahl
>> fügt sich wohl mir:
>> ich selbst schweiße das Schwert!
>
> I had got as far as that, and I was just pondering the motive which is going to convey the sudden change in Siegfried's fortune, the beginning of his prodigious forging, when your letter interrupted me, with *the* news

– the news, that is, of the purchase of the plot of land on the Grüner Hügel in Zürich, which was to be Wagner's 'Asyl'.[7]

The motive in question is a reshaping of a fragment of the Horn motive, the sequential continuation of which ushers in the Forging Song. Even so

314 *109*

small a detail as the change of time-signature from 6/8 to 3/4 for a single bar in Mime's part is already noted in the sketch.

---

[7] The letter is undated, but its date can be inferred from Mathilde Wesendonk's reference to it in a letter to Minna Wagner, from Paris, of 11 January 1857.

Ex. 13 Sketch

At the same time that Wagner was handling the rhythms and contrapuntal and fugal textures of this passage with an enjoyment and a dexterity that seem to mark material of this kind out as his natural element, the first languorous themes of *Tristan* were flooding in on him: there could be no clearer proof of the futility of trying to reduce his creative activity to a single formula.

The Forging and Hammer Songs form the brilliant finale to the 'Lieder-spiel' that the dialogue of the Riddle scene interrupted. 'They are quite remarkable songs', Wagner wrote to Mathilde Maier on 15 January 1865:

> I remember something that happened when I was setting the first, the Forging Song. The spring of 1857 saw the realization of my long-cherished wish to live in a country cottage with a garden...One morning, as I sat at the open window, playing and singing the Forging Song loud and clear, my neighbour Wesendonk was outside listening, and he called across to ask me what that fearfully majestic music was.

The letter goes on to say how he explained to Wesendonk what the song was about and then makes this comment about Siegfried: 'You see, a terrible kind of artist, so his singing, too, sounds almost like a majestic lament.'

327 *112* Five years later, in Vienna, when he heard the Forging Song with an orchestra for the first time, he was struck once again by its 'remarkable' quality: while the other song-like passages remained within the accustomed framework, the Forging and Hammer Songs stood out, creating a monu-mental al-fresco style. In addition, the former is motivically related to Mime's Starling Song and Siegfried's Roving Song, so that it has the effect of being the culmination of a series of variations:

Ex. 14*a*

Ex. 14*b*

flieg' ich von hier, flu - te da- von,

Ex. 14*c*

[zu] Spreu nun schuf ich die schar - fe Pracht

The composition sketch shows how the inner tension of the melody of the Forging Song increases from verse to verse. In the first stanza, 'Zu Spreu nun schuf ich', the bass is the only other part to begin with, until, at 'Wild im Walde', an additional inner part enters, rising in contrary motion (written on the same stave as the voice part in the sketch, but transcribed on a separate stave in the following example).

Ex. 15*a* Sketch

Wild im Wal - - de wuchs ein Baum, den

hab' ich im Forst ge - - - fällt,

In the second stanza, 'Des Baumes Kohle', not only is there a variation in the voice part, but another accompanimental figure is added:

Ex 15*b* Sketch

des . . .

The semiquaver sextuplets are meticulously notated in full on the second beat of each bar even in the sketch, which shows that they are not mere ornaments but a structural element, whose rhythmic function is emphasized even more clearly in the score by the sharp articulation and bright timbre of the high woodwind. There is also a new quaver figure, spanning a whole bar, which makes its first entrance in the sketch before 'zerschmilzt mir des Stahles Spreu'.

Ex. 15c Sketch

Its springy rhythm becomes even more buoyant in the score, thanks to the unusual orchestration: three unison harps, *ff*, reinforced by a trumpet in the first instance.

It is necessary to appreciate how these different lines of force increasingly engage with, or work against, each other if one is to understand the rhythmic means whereby, in this case, Wagner raises the music to a monumental level. At the same time he avoids the monotony that always threatens monumental art by interweaving Mime's grotesque scherzandi into Siegfried's song, sometimes in alternation, sometimes in duet.

The same obtains in the Hammer Song which follows. The Hammering motive was first sketched separately in pencil – even the stave lines were drawn in pencil (no. 5 in the list on p. 129).

Ex. 16 Initial sketch

The change from the 3/4 beat of the Forging Song to the mighty 4/4 of the Hammer Song intensifies the rising sense of the approaching climax, which is interrupted only by the 2/4 rhythm of Mime's self-apotheosis. There is still one final surprise in store, as the monumental style unfurls, in that this 2/4 time is retained in the last verse of the Hammer Song in the following manner: every three bars – every two bars in the case of Mime's interruptions – combine to form one unit. The sketch shows that Wagner originally wanted to revert to the 3/4 metre of the Forging Song:

Ex. 17*a* Sketch   Ex. 17*b* Score

He did not hit on the device of compounding larger units as above until he was in the act of writing the passage out. Thereafter he moved the bar-lines accordingly, used phrase marks to link the sets of three (or two) bars together, and indicated the frequent alternation of these larger units by marking them '3/2' or '2/2' as appropriate, with the result that the penultimate side of the composition sketch has an unusually large number of deletions and alterations.

Another alteration is that, as ex. 17*a* shows, he crossed out the A in the penultimate cry of 'Nothung' and substituted the usual F, reserving the A for the final 'Nothung', where the higher note is enhanced by being heard in combination with the leading-note effect of the third.

It is only in the coda, 'Schau, Mime, du Schmied', that 3/4 time is restored, though the bars are now grouped in fours: 'più Allo – molto Allo – Presto'.

Finally the date: '20 Jan. 57'.

Act II

Wagner moved into the house he called 'Asyl' (refuge) in Zürich on 28 April 1857, and he began the composition sketch of the second act on 22 May, his forty-fourth birthday, at a time when he had good cause to be worried about the future of his work. His offer of it to Breitkopf & Härtel for publication had elicited a reply on 16 May which expressed doubts as to its appeal to the public and its money-making potential.[8] 'This tough slice of old Härtel is a distinctly unpleasant morsel that I am having to chew in my new "refuge"', he wrote to Liszt on 19 May. However, on 30 May he was able to send him a brief musical 'letter', comprising his sketch of Fafner's 'Ich lieg' – und besitze: laßt mich schlafen!', to show that he was nevertheless getting on with the work.

[8] A letter from Liszt of 9 June, recounting a conversation with Dr Härtel, says 'the publication of the *Ring* in full score and in vocal score requires a capital outlay of at least 10,000 thalers'.

The sketches of individual motives in the second act (nos. 7–12 in the list on p. 129) reveal, in particular, the trouble Wagner took with the parts of the Dragon and the Woodbird, the two animal beings.

On the back of the sheet bearing the sketch of Siegfried's horn solo and the beginning of the Dragon's stirring (no. 9), there is a study for the third section of Brangäne's attempt to calm Isolde, 'Wo lebte der Mann, der dich nicht liebe? Der Isolde säh', und in Isolden selig nicht ganz verging'?' (pp. 42f. in the Bülow vocal score). It is headed by the note 'In Asyl / first motive / 16 May' and there is also Wagner's own approving 'good'.

Ex. 18

The composition sketch of Act II consists of seventeen half-sheets of manuscript paper, all used on both sides. The start is dated '22 May 1857', the end '30 July 57 / RW'.

Prelude and Scene 1

I *143*
This truly 'elemental' prelude was written out in one continuous flow without alterations – a particularly striking feature in view of the motivic complexity of the passage. Indications of the instrumentation are noticeably more frequent than in the composition sketch of the first act: the differentiation of the dark instrumental timbres are an integral factor in the setting of the gloomy scene. Fafner's motive is marked 'bass tuba' in the sketch, whereas in the score it is assigned to the contrabass tuba; in rehearsal Wagner asked the player for a 'cantabile phrasing' (Porges). It is only when the melody is repeated that it is brightened by the addition of the bass tuba. The note 'not to be hurried' against the tritone on the drums at the prelude's climax is absent from the sketch. The following musical examples transcribe the separate studies for the Fafner theme (the first marked 'very lethargic and slow').

Ex. 19*a*

Ex. 19*b*

Ex. 19c

Ex. 19d

Ex. 20a Sketch

There are also very few differences between the sketch and the score in the first scene: those there are are characteristic. In the sketch Wotan's 'Deinen Sinn kenne ich wohl' follows Alberich's 'der Welt walte dann ich' without a pause, but the note '3 bars' was later inserted between them. In the score the hectic motive of Alberich's Triumph – a combination of the Valhalla motive and Loge's motive – is inserted here, an impressive coda to the dwarf's outburst of hatred.

50 *157*

In the Wanderer's reply, on the other hand, the sketch has a bar rest between 'des Ringes waltet' and 'wer ihn gewinnt', and the query '(1 bar?)' above it:

52 *158* In the score the rest is incorporated in the following bar, rendering it less emphatic:

Ex. 20*b* Score

The score also has a melodic and rhythmic change at 'dein Bruder bringt dir Gefahr', and the additional direction 'lightly'.

Ex. 21*a* Sketch   Ex. 21*b* Score

While the dwarf's vehemence is even more emphatic in the score, the Wanderer's replies are correspondingly relaxed: 'The words here must be spoken quite casually, thrown off' (Porges).

The last part of the scene was written down without any alterations, like the prelude, which is all the more remarkable here because of the great dissimilarity of the motives, which nevertheless combine effortlessly in an integrated melodic line.

Scene 2

81 *170*

Wagner made a preliminary sketch (no. 8 in the list on p. 129) of the orchestral introduction to this scene, with its contrapuntal combination of Siegfried's Forging Song, his 'boisterous' motive and Mime's Hammering motive, heading it 'Siegfried's entry' and marking the tempo 'very moderate (easy)'. This marking is omitted from the composition sketch and the score has 'somewhat more lively' instead.

84 *171*

Like the Wanderer in the first scene, it is now Siegfried's turn to have his part modified in the score in the interest of 'light', parlando rhythms. The changes, while not particularly important in themselves, are significant for what they reveal of Wagner's stylistic intentions:

Ex. 22*a* Sketch   Ex. 22*b* Score

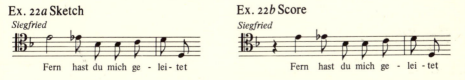

The orchestra's depiction, in its accompaniment to 'eine volle Nacht im Walde selbander wanderten wir', of the comic disparity between the two figures as they made their way through the forest together is already anticipated in the sketch, in the limping syncopation of the woodwind (marked 'wind').

After Mime's 'oh, brächten beide sich um!', the sketch has eight bars of Forest Murmurs, then a date: '26 June 1857 RW'.

'I shall have no more trouble with Härtel's now', Wagner wrote to Liszt on 28 June. 'I have brought my young Siegfried as far as the beautiful solitude of the forest; there I have left him under the linden tree and have bidden him farewell with heartfelt tears.' And on 4 July he confessed to Frau Julie Ritter, whose guarantee of a regular financial allowance had emboldened him to embark on the tetralogy:

> Please accept for the time being the intimation that I am on the point
> – with great self-control – of leaving Siegfried alone in the forest
> for a year, in order to give myself some relief in writing a *Tristan
> und Isolde*...The text is still dormant within me: I shall shortly start
> to rouse it.

In *Mein Leben* we read, however:

> In order to prove to myself, all the same, that I was not just turning
> my back on the earlier work because I had had a surfeit of it, I
> decided that I would nevertheless first complete the composition
> [sketch] of the second act of *Siegfried*, which I had hardly
> started...On the sunny afternoons of that summer I took my daily
> walk in the direction of the peaceful Sihltal. In the woods there I often
> listened with great attention to the singing of the birds, and was
> amazed at the totally new songs I learned from singers I could not see
> and of whose names I was even more in ignorance. What I took home
> with me of their songs I imitated artistically in the forest scene in
> *Siegfried*. (ML, pp. 638, 640.)

The next thing in the composition sketch, after the dated interruption, is, unusually, a scribbled sketch of an isolated motive, one of the birdsong motives.

Ex. 23 Sketch

Siegfried   26 Juni 1857. R. W.

It then continues in the proper sequence with 'Daß der mein Vater nicht ist'. In the ensuing Forest Murmurs, not only are the string figures written out exactly, but also the sustained lines of the horns and double basses and the interwoven clarinet and cello melodies, so that in some places – at

116 *184* 'Aber wie sah meine Mutter wohl aus?' for instance – the pattern made
by the notes on the page has the intricacy of filigree.

There is a significant alteration in the score at the end of the episode, once
again at a place where one would least have expected it: in the sketch
Freia's motive enters in combination with the voice part as early as 'Ein
Menschenweib', whereas in the score it is only three bars later that it is
heard, on a solo violin, with a change to C major, while the voice is silent. It
is now, so to speak, highlighted, raised up into a brighter sphere.

Ex. 24*a* Sketch

Ex. 24*b* Score

In the event the mediant progression from the C major of Freia's motive to
the E major of the Forest Murmurs makes an entrancing effect!

There are further sketches of birdsong motives among the undated
individual sketches (nos. 10–12 in the list on p. 129), the first of which (ex.
25*a*) is more likely to be a preliminary study for the birdcall (clarinet/flute)
in the *Siegfried Idyll.*

Ex. 25*a*

Ex. 25*b*

Ex. 25c

„*Waldvogel*" [on the back of the draft of a letter in French]

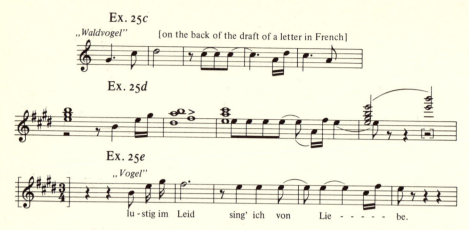

Ex. 25d

Ex. 25e

„*Vogel*"

lu - stig im Leid   sing' ich von   Lie - - - - - be.

A 'scientifico-musical study' of the different birds and their songs was published by Bernhard Hoffmann in 1906,[9] though he did not have the benefit either of Wagner's account in *Mein Leben* or of the sketches. He found in the music reminiscences of the songs of the nightingale, the oriole, the yellow-hammer, the tree-pipit and, above all, the blackbird. Hoffmann explains Wagner's preference for the blackbird, and his choice of it as the prototype of the talking bird, by pointing out its song's capacity for subtle inflexion: its construction from different, usually wide intervals; the free, swift, parlando-like delivery in 'verses' that often vary considerably from each other; the freedom from rhythmic or melodic restraints; the variational capacity of the motives, leaving the composer complete freedom; the similarity of some of the bird's sounds to sounds made by the human voice; and finally the unique and ethereal qualities of the song.[10]

123 187   In the ensuing orchestral passage, the Forest Murmurs, the songs of the various birds appear in the sketch in an order slightly different from that in the score:

Ex. 26 Sketch

[Nightingale]   [2 bars]

[Blackbird]

[9] 'Die Waldvögel-Motive in Wagners *Siegfried*' (with musical examples), BBL 1906, pp. 137ff.
[10] The talking bird is identified as a nightingale in the prose sketch of *Der junge Siegfried*, but it is already called a 'woodbird' in the verse text.

[Oriole]   [Blackbird]

The yellow-hammer and tree-pipit are conspicuous for their absence;[11] they were not added until the score, where their effect is rather bracing and astringent.

Ex. 27a Score
[Yellow-hammer and tree-pipit]

Ex. 27b Score

142 *194* Siegfried's horn solo is another of the motives first sketched on a separate sheet (no. 9 in the list on p. 129), but even there it has the Dragon's motive making its low entry at the end. The exchange of insults as the two prepare to fight undergoes slight rhythmic and melodic changes in the score, resulting, as usual, in an improvement in the pacing. The change in the
177 *206* rhythm in the following example, after Fafner is dead, intensifies the expression of breathless surprise:

Ex. 28a Sketch   Ex. 28b Score
Siegfried   *Siegfried*

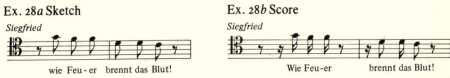

wie Feu-er brennt das Blut!   Wie Feu-er   brennt das Blut!

182 *207* After the Woodbird's first verse, ending 'der macht ihn zum Walter der Welt!', Siegfried cries, in the prose sketch of *Der junge Siegfried*, 'mich dünkt meine mutter hör' ich singen!' ('I think I hear my mother singing'), and in the verse text, 'Mich dünkt, meine mutter singt zu mir!' ('I think my mother is singing to me'). This exclamation is omitted in the verse text of *Siegfried* itself, but in the composition sketch it is restored – on second

---

[11] The yellow-hammer's motive is briefly suggested once in the composition sketch, but without the grace note and with an interval of a third at the end, not the characteristic second. In the orchestral sketch the motive appears three bars after the change to E major, with the interval of the second at the end but still without the grace note.

thoughts and on a different stave – and placed a little earlier, after the
Woodbird's 'O fänd' in der Höhle den Hort er jetzt!'

Ex. 29 Sketch

Then in the score Wagner finally decided to omit it after all, although he
once later called the Woodbird 'Sieglinde's maternal soul'.[12] This may have
been because, according to the score, the part was originally intended for
a boy's voice, though that has never in fact been tried in performance,
probably in view of its rhythmic difficulty.[13]

Scene 3

188 *210* The 'quite singular dialogue between Alberich and Mime' (Porges) is one of
the rare episodes which are relatively incomplete in the composition sketch:
while the two vocal parts are written out straightaway in their eventual
forms (apart from two cuts, of six and three bars respectively, already made
in the sketch), the accompaniment differs quite considerably from the score
in places. The semiquaver figure in 2/4 time (in an otherwise 3/4 context)
accompanying the slithering motion of the brothers as they rush in to
confront each other –

[12] According to Hans von Wolzogen, BBL 1930, note on p. 139.
[13] In the sketch Wagner confines himself to combining the 4/4 time of the bird
with the 3/4 time of the orchestra. Only in the score did he give the bird's part
its free, improvisatory rhythm, with only the first and last notes in each phrase
fixed precisely. (Cf. the footnote on p. 183 of the study score.)

Ex. 30*a* Score

is completely absent. In its place the sketch has a very hastily scribbled triplet figure, approximately as follows:

Ex. 30*b* Sketch

But it is precisely the combination of the three-bar groupings of the vocal parts and the four-bar groupings of the accompaniment that makes the scene so grotesque.

202 *216*   At the scherzo motive of Mime's furious outburst, 'Selbst nicht tauschen? Auch nicht teilen?', the introductory semiquaver figure on the woodwind is not yet fully developed:

Ex. 31*a* Sketch   Ex. 31*b* Score

Obviously, in this exchange the delivery of the words was Wagner's primary concern, and he worked out the orchestral accompaniment later, taking a great deal of pleasure in embellishing the details. 'The two squabbling dwarves are incapable of...developing a large-scale, noble form', Lorenz comments. 'They converse in a scurry of tiny, short-breathed sentences, which hardly qualify as stanzas, but which must nevertheless be called stanzaic because of their formal similarity' (p. 257).

210 *218*   As Siegfried emerges from the cave, gazing at the ring and the Tarnhelm, six horns quote, *pp*, the Rhinemaidens' lament: 'Gebt uns das Gold, gebt uns das Gold! O gebt uns das Reine zurück!' The sketch shows that originally Siegfried started to sing three bars earlier than he does now, though the alteration was already made in the sketch: the Rhinemaidens' song was not inserted for its own sake but as a reminder, a reflection on the

immensity of the tragic background to this scene, like a chorus in Greek tragedy. The process is the exact reverse of the 'highlighting' of the Freia motive, when Siegfried was thinking about his mother. When Wagner reached this passage while working on the final draft of the score twelve years later, he wrote to King Ludwig: 'As we take in the full significance of it, our emotion is overwhelming' (23 February 1869).

221 *221* By contrast with the scene between the two dwarves, the scene between Mime and Siegfried is sketched almost entirely in its final form, and complete with all the accompanimental parts – an example of Wagner's gift for thinking polyphonically from the outset. Only at the end were a few changes made. Originally the accompaniment to Mime's 'hätt' ich des 247 *232* Schimpfs und der schändlichen Mühe' was envisaged as consisting merely of repetitions of the 2/4 phrase with which he has been trying to ingratiate himself with Siegfried. This version was crossed out before it was even finished and a fresh start made, so that the phrase now begins with the fourth quaver a whole tone lower and continues in chromatically rising sequence:

Ex. 32*a* Sketch I

[deleted, lacks vocal line]

Ex. 32*b* Sketch II

(Mime) (hätt' ich des Schimpfs . . .)

There is an alteration to the text here, too. The line 'haßte ich dich auch nicht so hell' ('if I did not hate you so intensely'), which appears in the published verse text and in the composition sketch, was changed in the score to 'haßte ich dich auch nicht so sehr' ('if I did not hate you so much'). This was probably done for the sake of the enunciation, because normally Wagner was fond of using the word 'hell' so as to suggest its original sense, when applied to sounds, of 'clear, ringing'.[14]

252 *234* Finally, the sketch still lacks a stroke of genius present in the score, when, after Alberich's mocking laughter, the motive of Mime's brooding plunges down, *ff*, through four octaves: at his last instant his useless wisdom, on which he so prided himself, flashes in front of him before death envelops him in darkness.[15]

[14] Cf. 'den . . . im tiefsten Herzen hell ich haßte!' (*Tristan*, Act II).
[15] The four overlapping statements of the motive do not emerge clearly in the vocal score.

Siegfried's valediction, 'Neides Zoll zahlt Nothung', begins a fourth higher in the sketch than in the score; the later version is more restrained in its effect. The most notable difference in the orchestral passage accompanying the removal of Mime's body to the cave is that the sketch has ten bars of Forest Murmurs with two birdcalls, blackbird and oriole: idyllic allusions which the score dispenses with. Consequently the transition to G major, at 'Linde Kühlung erkies ich', with the shy return of the birdsong (solo horn in the score), is all the more instrumental in clearing the atmosphere. From here on 'the tempo becomes a little quicker, and everything is to be lighter in expression. Even the cellos' eloquent melody must not cause any slowing' (Porges).

The initiative now passes to some vivid development motives, rapidly descending in semiquavers, of a type that has already made its appearance in *Die Walküre* and reaches its fullest potential in the third act of *Siegfried*. There is a study on a separate sheet, which relates to the third act, to judge by the form of the motive. There is also another sketch of the Woodbird's song on a separate sheet (cf. ex. 25*d*).

Although there are no notes of the instrumentation here, a figure in the sketch preceding 'Noch einmal sage mir, holder Sänger' is already so flautistic in character (and is given to a flute *f* in the score) as to be a reminder that Wagner always had the colour of the sound in mind even when he was still thinking out his melodies.

245

Ex. 33*a* Sketch

Ex. 33*b* Score

The last four sides of the composition sketch (from 'Mein einz'ger Gesell' on) are written in a light, elegant hand, with hardly any alterations, so that even the eye gains an impression of the steady brightening of the orchestral sound, which dissolves into runs and high-pitched tremolos and trills, similar to those in Beethoven's op. III sonata that Wagner admired so much.

Then comes the note '30 July 57 RW'. If we do not count the sixteen-day break from 26 June to 13 July, this second act was composed in fifty-four days. The orchestral sketch was finished on 9 August.

'I have taken *Siegfried* up to the end of the second act, which has turned out rather strange and novel, but has given me a great deal of joy', Wagner wrote to Julie Ritter on 8 October. 'Now the Nibelungen have been locked away for a year: I only hope they will not lose any of their vitality for me in that time.'

The compositional technique of *Siegfried*, departing ever further from the conventional relationship of 'singing and accompaniment', could certainly be called 'strange and novel', but perhaps the description is even more appropriate to the extension of music's capacity for speech that took place in the setting of this act:

> He has given a language to everything in nature that until now did not want to speak; he does not believe that some things must inevitably be dumb...If the philosopher says there is one will that thirsts for existence in animate and inanimate nature, the musician adds that that will desires its existence, on every level, to have a voice.[16]

Act III

The *Ring* did not stay locked away for the one year that Wagner had predicted: he wrote the first draft of the score of the second act of *Siegfried* in Munich between 22 December 1864 and 2 December 1865, and finished the second draft on 23 February 1869 in Tribschen. Only then, enriched by the experience gained in the composition of *Tristan* and *Die Meistersinger*, did he start the composition of Act III in Tribschen, on 1 March 1869, after a break of twelve years.

In spite of that the work had lost none of its vitality for him – quite the reverse! 'I am wonderfully in the mood for the third act of *Siegfried*,' he had written to Hans von Bülow from Starnberg on 30 September 1864, 'and particularly for the first scene with Wotan: it shall be a prelude, short but – significant.' And when he had at last sketched the scene in 1869 he wrote to the king, not without satisfaction:

> A break of twelve years in a work must be without precedent in the history of art, and if it transpires that this break has in no way impaired the vitality of my conception, than I can probably cite it as proof that these conceptions have an everlasting life, they are not yesterday's and not for tomorrow. (23 February 1869.)

Some of these sketches are very early in date:

337 *338*   1. The E major 'Peace melody': 'Gracefully / 14 Nov. 64'. It was originally intended for the 'Starnberg' Quartet.[17]

---

[16] Friedrich Nietzsche, *Richard Wagner in Bayreuth*, chapter 9.
[17] Westernhagen, *Wagner* (Zürich and Freiburg i. Br., 1968), p. 313.

94 *271*   2. The page was turned upside down for a sketch of the World Inheritance motive in a form rather different from the eventual version.[18]

Ex. 34

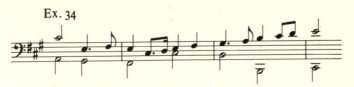

3. A theme with the note 'Act III or *Tristan*'. Converted from 3/4 to 4/4 time, it was eventually used in the third act of *Siegfried*, just before 304 *327*   Brünnhilde's 'Dort seh' ich Grane, mein selig Roß'.[19]

Ex. 35

[etc.]

306 *328*   4. Siegfried's 'Auf wonnigem Munde weidet mein Auge' is sketched below the preceding theme, in a somewhat variant form.

Ex. 36

auf   won - ni - gem Mun-de   wei-det mein Au - - - ge

396 *355*   5. The melody to which Wagner set 'Sie ist mir ewig, ist mir immer'. When he was working out the 'Shepherd's merry tune', 'die neue Weise', in the third act of *Tristan*, in Lucerne in 1859, he thought of an alternative version of the melody, 'which is much more jubilant still, almost heroically jubilant, and yet completely like folk music. I came very close to changing everything I had written, then finally realized that this melody did not belong to Tristan's shepherd but to Siegfried himself.' (Letter to Mathilde Wesendonk, 9 July 1859.)

Ex. 37

[etc.]

[18] According to Glasenapp Wagner conceived this motive in 1856, in association with *Die Sieger*. 'This origin is quite literally true . . . the author had it from the master's own lips.' (GLRW, III, p. 119.) Both themes were reproduced in facsimile in *Bayreuth* (Munich, 1943), p. 43.
[19] Reproduced in facsimile in the *Bayreuther Festspielbuch 1951*, p. 90.

351 *342*   6. A study for the development motive used for 'Ein herrlich Gewässer'.

Ex. 38

7. Another study for development motives in Act III, Scene 3.

Ex. 39

8. What is probably a study for the bars leading into the transformation in Act I of *Tannhäuser*, made when Wagner was working on the Paris version (1860) but not used in this form.

Ex. 40

If we add the 'Hort der Welt' motive, which immediately follows the 'Peace' motive in the setting of the text, but was probably originally intended for the 'Starnberg' Quartet, to the list of sketches conceived in advance of the composition of Act III of *Siegfried*, then we can see that a relatively large number of new motives used in the act originated in a separate context, a departure from the process of motivic development that had hitherto obtained in the composition of the *Ring*. But by now the motivic material of the work as a whole had developed such richness that these 'alien' motives could easily be assimilated and form new motivic germs in their turn. Only the 'Peace' melody is found in this one scene alone, and was only used again in the *Siegfried Idyll*.

338 *338*

The composition sketch for the third act comprises twenty-two half-sheets of manuscript paper, used on both sides. The start is dated '1 March 69', the end 'Safely delivered / 14 June 1869'.

The lapse of time since the completion of the second act is reflected, at the very first glance, by the handwriting: compared with the graceful calligraphy of the close of the earlier act, the beginning of the third looks almost lapidary: the difference is as great as between the music of the Forest Murmurs and that of the introduction to the Wanderer/Erda scene.

Prelude and Scene 1

Wagner called the prelude 'Wotan's last ride, as he descends once more to the underworld' (Porges). It fills less than a half-side in the composition sketch, including four deleted bars. Nevertheless, as usual with the passages where the notation makes use of abbreviated forms, every detail is already as it later appears in the score, with one minor exception: in the sketch the Spear motive is stated for the first time beginning on E in the fifteenth bar, whereafter it is repeated twice more in overlapping statements, beginning on F and then on A, while in the score the climax mounts more slowly and more powerfully, and the motive is stated four times in all, starting on D, E, F and A.

5 *251*

There is also one significant change, made in the sketch itself: the succession of the Wanderer's chords, beginning in the twenty-third bar, originally started only with the first inversion C major chord and also lacked the accompaniment of Erda's motive rising and falling in four-bar phrases. But a footnote symbol directs us to the last system on the page, where the six bars beginning with the first inversion D major chord appear as they do in the score, with the undulations of Erda's motive also sketched in, giving a very marked impression that the idea had only just occurred to Wagner, for normally accompanimental figures and motives are indicated for at least one bar's duration in the first sketch.

Ever since his return to Munich after visiting the king at Hohenschwangau in 1865, the theme that greets us at the very beginning of the act had haunted him, Wagner told King Ludwig, in a letter dated 23–4 February 1869:

Ex. 41 Sketch[20]

---

[20] In the sketch: 'Wache! Wache! Wala! erwach'!'; in the score: 'Wache, Wala! Wala! Erwach'!'

Siegfried, Act III, prelude (composition sketch)

'Awe has prevented me until now from writing down what has often flared up in me as brightly as lightning, when I have been walking alone in a storm.'

But in all probability the musical daring of this scene will also have been one reason for his hesitation.

Prior knowledge of the motivic wealth of this 'heart of the great cosmic tragedy' from performance or the score, makes one eager to know how it was assembled: spontaneously or by passing through stages of reflection. The very appearance of the composition sketch gives the answer: written in a continuous flow, rarely interrupted by emendations, it makes the impression of complete spontaneity. The motivic reminiscences, often dashed in in the tiniest notation, seem to drop into place involuntarily. Apparently invoked by textual association alone, at a deeper level they follow the bidding of a characteristic of their musical nature: ultimately all akin to each other, they exult in new combinations and new transformations.

The statement of the theme of the call to Erda to awake, the third and fourth bars of which are the same as the final cadence of the Valhalla theme from the second scene of *Das Rheingold*,[21] is followed by more prolonged developments of Erda's motive, of the chord progressions associated with the Magic Sleep and with the Wanderer, and of the Ring motive, which is transformed, one might say right before our eyes, into the Valhalla theme. Even such minor details as the triplet motive accompanying 'die Welt durchzog ich, wanderte viel', or the suggestion of the Valkyries' motive at 'Kühn ist sie, und weise auch' are not forgotten in the sketch. The whole manner of the sketching is such as to demonstrate that the vocal and orchestral parts were conceived together, as a unified 'melos', whose flow sweeps on 'inexhaustibly', as Wagner said of Beethoven. The onward flow was so important to him, in this scene in particular, that he actually cut in the score two lines of Erda's that he had set in the sketch – 'Friedloser, laß mich frei! Löse des Zaubers Zwang!' ('Man without peace, set me free. Lift the spell of your magic') – because they retarded the flow, and instead goes straight on, after 'zu stören der Wala Schlaf', with Wotan's 'Du bist nicht, was du dich wähnst!'

86 *269*

Apart from this cut, there are only two places in the great dialogue where Wagner subsequently made changes.

82 *268*

The accompaniment to Wotan's 'mit Furcht vor schmachvoll feindlichem Ende füllt' ihn dein Wissen' consists merely of separate chords in the sketch, but in the score it is a statement of the Gods' Downfall motive, which entails alterations to the harmony and to the vocal line and also furthers the onward flow of the melos.

[21] It also recurs as Freia's Flight motive, as the Wälsungen's Love motive, as the expression of Wotan's despair, *et al.*; Richard Sternfeld calls it 'Wotan's life-urge'.

Ex. 42*a* Sketch

Ex. 42*b* Score

An even more significant change was made at the scene's climax, Wotan's joyful renunciation, revised already in the sketch in the interests of greater emphasis. In the first version in the sketch the new motive of the World Inheritance is stated for the first time, merely as the accompaniment to the voice:

94 *271*

Ex. 43*a* Sketch I (deleted)

Wanderer

froh und freu - dig

füh - - - re ich frei - - - - - es nun aus.

[breaks off here]

Ex. 43*b* Sketch II

Wanderer

frei ich nun aus.

Ex. 43*c* Score

Wanderer

frei ich nun aus.

In the second version in the sketch, it is 'highlighted' like Freia's motive in the second act, in that it does not now enter until the last note of the voice part and is then played *ff* on its own. The upward transposition by a semitone, from G major to A♭ major, too, imbues it with a brighter, warmer radiance. It ought to be taken 'just a little faster' than what has gone before it, and be 'very clearly projected', Wagner remarked in rehearsal: 'it must sound like the proclamation of a new religion'. The slight increase in tempo ought to have the effect of the sudden illumination that has just burst upon Wotan himself (Porges).

105 *273*   The World Inheritance motive appears later in this scene in the sketch, as in the score, in its original G major version, with a repetition in the dominant, as the accompaniment to the words 'wachend wirkt dein wissendes Kind erlösende Weltentat'.[22]

Scene 2

Wagner made two starts on the transition to the second scene in the composition sketch: common to both versions is the fact that after his last words to Erda – 'Hinab zum ew'gen Schlaf' in the first version and 'Zum ew'gen Schlaf hinab' in the second ('Hinab zu ew'gem Schlaf' in the score) – Wotan continues immediately with 'Dort seh' ich Siegfried nah'n',

113 *275*   whereas six bars of purely orchestral music are inserted between the two lines in the score, with *pp* chords on the tubas and trombones illustrating the total darkness enveloping the cave into which Erda has disappeared.

The second scene is another that was sketched in a single outpouring. Fleeting motivic reminiscences, such as a bar of the Woodbird's song or Fafner's tritone, are written with tiny notes. The spontaneity is the more astonishing because Wagner suddenly struck a completely new note 'without any sense of passionate intensity'. The vivacity of expression must be linked with clear delineation of character, Porges adds. The undertones of deeper emotion that break through in the Wanderer's case are to be presented with good humour, while Siegfried's outbursts of boyish arrogance must never be at variance with the nobility of his nature.

127 *280*   A new motive, heard for the first time at Wotan's 'Ein Vöglein schwatzt wohl manches' springs a surprise, both for its tone and in its technique. It is repeated another four times, like a rondo theme, and is never heard again after this scene; it is one of those chord themes with the strong, clear

---

[22] An entry in Cosima's diary has some bearing on the symphonic style of this scene: Wagner 'thinks that if he set the words "Um der Götter Ende grämt mich die Angst nicht, seit mein Wunsch es will" as recitative he would achieve an extraordinary theatrical effect. "But then", he adds gravely, "it would cease to be art."' (DMCW, I, p. 442.) As usual Du Moulin does not give the date of the extract; the nearest date is 8 April 1869, so the utterance must date from some time during his work on the composition sketch started on 1 March. Wagner meant that the means would not be justified artistically in a symphonically through-composed scene like this.

outlines of a woodcut, like the Kareol motive in *Tristan*, the Gibichungen motive in *Götterdämmerung* and Parsifal's motive, but typical, above all, of the style of *Die Meistersinger*. Each time the motive appears in the composition sketch it is at once written out in full in three or four parts. Wagner wanted 'the rhythms sharply defined' in performance, with a short caesura at the quaver rest in the first bar.

156 *288*

Two phrases in the vocal writing illustrate how naturalness and the depiction of character already found completely spontaneous expression in the sketch. Wotan's imploring warning, 'Heut' nicht wecke mir Neid: er vernichtete dich und mich!', immediately exposes the full stress of his internal conflict:

Ex. 44 Sketch and score

179 *296*

Similarly, Siegfried's astonished exclamation, when the Wanderer, defeated, is suddenly swallowed up in the darkness:

Ex. 45 Sketch and score

Wagner tried to help the tenor to understand the state of mind expressed here by speaking the words to him in a tone of naively curious surprise, which demonstrated 'how the spoken line, illuminated, given life by the spirit, is already on the threshold of musical form' (Porges). The rise of a fifth and the descent by the same interval after the semitone lift is nothing other than the crystallization of the line inflected according to the meaning of the words.

184ff.
298

After the first six bars of the transition to the third scene, a whole system in the sketch is crossed out. It is still clear enough to see that Wagner had started Siegfried's motive (on the trombones) on A, with the result that in the third bar of it he necessarily arrived at the triad of B♭ major, which made it awkward for him to modulate to F major for the next statement of the Horn Call. He quickly made up his mind to start the statement of Siegfried's motive on E instead, and so reached the triad of F major without any trouble. The change is interesting for demonstrating that formal considerations played a decisive part: the third statement of the Horn Call, its last triplet repeated sequentially, forms the Abgesang to a small Bar, constructed as follows: the Horn Call in F major (three bars); the same with a changed ending ('Ihr schlosset nicht im gleichen Ton'); a bar's rest, then the same with sequential elaboration ('den Stollen ähnlich, doch nicht gleich') (three bars).

Scene 3

214 *303*   The harp solo at the end of the transition is merely hinted at in the sketch, but already marked 'harp': the timbre was essential to Wagner as the 'sound analogue of the light'.[23]

215 *303*   The melody played by all the first violins, based on Freia's motive and rising through nearly four octaves, is full of deletions and emendations in the sketch, the great majority relating to the durations. The first version, apart from the first four bars, proceeds evenly, written entirely in regular quavers, but the second corresponds to the score, with the insertion of three points of repose: two with the duration of a minim plus a quaver, and the third a dotted crotchet.

Ex. 46 Sketch with alterations

It is a process comparable to the development in the working out of the cantilena for solo cello in the first act of *Die Walküre* (exx. 4a and b), except that the present case, in addition to lending the articulation of the period greater plasticity, puts a slight check in the way of the energy driving the melody which, when released, proceeds each time with renewed impetus.

The sketches enable us to observe the development of purely orchestral melodies in the process of creation, so providing a unique opportunity of ascertaining the fundamental structural principle of Wagnerian melody. The purely arithmetical approach, with its search for divisions four, eight and sixteen bars long with concluding cadences, is soon found wanting in this context, and leads to lame conclusions about a kind of 'chain structure', allegedly governed, so far as the vocal writing is concerned, by the metre of the text.[24]

Talking to Liszt about the one-movement symphonies that he wanted to write after *Parsifal*, Wagner remarked 'only not thematic contrast, Beethoven exhausted the possibilities of that, but spinning a melodic thread out to its furthest extent' (17 December 1882, BBL 1938, p. 12). The inference is that he was thinking, not of observing any particular formal scheme, but of

[23] Egon Voss, *Studien zur Instrumentation Richard Wagners* (Regensburg, 1970), p. 218.

[24] Cf. Stefan Kunze, 'Über Melodiebegriff und musikalischen Bau im Wagnerschen Musikdrama', in Dahlhaus, ed., *Das Drama Richard Wagners*, pp. 111f.

releasing the flow of dynamic tensions latent in the motivic germ of the melody: drawing a melodic line as the 'outcome of psychic energy', an 'impulse' generated by tension, a 'shape which represents the unity of a motivic process' (Kurth, pp. 4ff.). This dynamic approach to the structure of Wagnerian melody comes closer, at all events, to uncovering the psychology and the technique of his creative methods than a purely arithmetical or architectonic approach. The arithmetical or architectonic articulations that are revealed in the process are of secondary importance.

The process is the same one that we have been able to observe at work in the construction of development motives, above all at the end of the first act of *Die Walküre*.[25]

Like the first-violin tutti, the three bars of violin cantilena that follow, marked 'longer' on the sketch, are extended to four bars in the score.

Ex. 47*a* Sketch

Ex. 47*b* Score

244 314   The two variants of Freia's motive – one on bass clarinet, one on cello – played immediately before Brünnhilde opens her eyes were similarly expanded, already in the sketch:

Ex. 48*a* Sketch   Ex. 48*b* Sketch

Once again the purpose is to release the melody's latent tension.

From Siegfried's cry 'Das ist kein Mann!' to Brünnhilde's awakening, the music consists predominantly of quavers, triplets and semiquaver figurations. This is particularly obvious in the composition sketch, which confines itself to the principal parts. These motoric development motives, some of which proceed from, and re-form as, Leitmotive, constitute the musical substance at this juncture. Brünnhilde's awakening changes the

[25] In the case of the Nature motive in the prelude to *Das Rheingold* we saw that the potential energy was created only when the motive was revised, with the enlargement of an interval from a third to a fifth. As it now is the motive is the release of the energy stored up in the first interval (cf. *Das Rheingold*, exx. 5*a*, *b*).

248 *315* situation, as an expansive melos that has been taking shape in the figurations at last emerges fully formed to occupy the foreground.

The published verse text has here:

> (Brünnhilde has opened her eyes. He looks at her in amazement.
> Both remain for a while, rapt in the sight of each other.)
> *Brünnhilde*
> (slowly and ceremonially sitting upright)
>   Heil dir, Sonne!
>   Heil dir, Licht! [etc.]

In the score the stage directions are slightly different: 'Brünnhilde opens
her eyes...Slowly she sits up...She raises her arms in ceremonial greeting
of her return to consciousness of the earth and sky.' The published text
gives no hint of this mime, which is accompanied by the chords greeting the
sunlight. Obviously, as in the similar case at the beginning of the Annunciation of Death scene in Act II of *Die Walküre*, the stage direction was
suggested directly by the music, in particular by the musical form: the first
twenty-one bars perceptibly make a Bar (a–a_1–b), which is repeated,
slightly varied and enriched by the vocal part, to give a second Bar; the two
together make up the Stollen of a larger Bar, the Abgesang of which
consists of the succeeding thirty-nine bars. The unprecedented degree of
intensification in this episode is not merely a matter of perceptible dynamic
heightening; it is due, in the first place, to the thrilling assertion of Siegfried's key of C major, but above all to a process, to describe which Alfred
Lorenz employed the analogy of potentiation: the raising of a form to a
higher power (p. 177).

It is clear from the composition sketch that the musical form was not the
result of revision, but was fully constructed straightaway in the first hasty
sketch. The second and fourth chords of the theme are sustained for only
one bar in the sketch, instead of five as in the score. But the diminuendo
caused by withdrawing sections of the orchestra is already expressed in the
notation of the second and fourth chords with the indication of a quaver
rest:

Ex. 49 Sketch

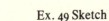

The E minor one-sharp key signature, which is kept only for the greeting of the sun even in the sketch, is dispensed with altogether in the score, so that the eye, too, perceives the C major.

273 *319*   The sketch is dated '(1 May 1869)' at 'O Heil der Mutter, die mich gebar', which shows that Wagner had got so far in the third act in exactly two months. A letter to King Ludwig proves that by 18 May he had got as

334 *337*   far as Brünnhilde's 'Sonnenhell leuchtet der Tag meiner Not!' (distress: the score has 'Schmach', disgrace). 'But the work is dour and very exhausting: I find the sorrowful passages, expressing the most painful emotions, particularly tiring.'

The expression of painful emotions begins with the theme for which a separate sketch exists, marked 'Act III or *Tristan*' (no. 3 in the list on p.

304 *327*   161; ex. 35), heard just before Brünnhilde's 'Dort seh' ich Grane, mein selig Roß'. Everything since her greeting of the sun has been in triple time, and this theme, 3/4 in the separate sketch, is made the means of introducing a change to quadruple time: there can be no doubt that the cantilena assigned to cor anglais in the score gains greatly in emotional expression from the broader tempo.

Ex. 50 Sketch

    The attractive melody sketched separately for Siegfried's line 'Auf

306 *328*   wonnigem Munde weidet mein Auge' (no. 4 on p. 161; ex. 36) is slightly changed on its appearance in the composition sketch. For a few bars it interrupts the anguished development which continues to intensify up to the

328 *335*   terror of Brünnhilde's 'Trauriges Dunkel trübt meinen Blick'. There is heard in the orchestra at this point the peroration of Alberich's curse from the fourth scene of *Das Rheingold* ('Dem Tode verfallen, feßle den Feigen[26] die Furcht'), in the very form that Brünnhilde herself heard it at Wotan's despairing outburst in the second act of *Die Walküre*, 'O heilige Schmach!': a musical reminiscence which lifts the present situation above its purely personal implications and places it in the wider context of the tragedy of Wotan.

The music on this page of the composition sketch (sheet 17, verso) is scribbled in great haste, on three staves. None of the subsidiary parts are included; even the syncopated Anger motive from *Die Walküre*, Act II, Scene 1, which is played twice, *ff*, in the score, is only indicated once:

[26] 'Feige', as usual in the *Ring*, does not have here its modern German meaning of 'coward', but the meaning of the Middle High German 'veige', 'doomed to die'.

331 *336*   Ex. 51 Sketch

Eight bars were crossed out after Siegfried's 'Nacht umfängt gebund'ne
Augen'. They sketched the orchestral part alone and reappear on the next
sheet, with some minor revisions and extended to twelve bars.

337 *338*   After this disturbed episode what is sometimes called the 'Peace melody'
('Friedensmelodie') enters, played by the strings in four parts *pp*. This was
originally intended for a quartet that Wagner planned in 1864, to be
dedicated to Cosima (see no. 1 in the list on p. 160), and was later adopted as
the main theme of the *Siegfried Idyll* of 1870. In both the original 1864
sketch and the composition sketch for *Siegfried* there are signs that Wagner
was thinking of adding another high part, probably for woodwind, as
actually happens in the *Idyll*. The reason why the idea was abandoned in the
score of *Siegfried* at this juncture, for the first thirty bars, is that he wanted
to preserve the pure sound of the strings, so as to achieve that 'transcen-
dental ideality' that seems to come from another world (Porges).

Ex. 52*a* The original sketch

Ex. 52*b* Composition sketch

338 *338*   The succeeding melody, to the words 'O Siegfried, Herrlicher! Hort der Welt!', was also conceived for the abortive Starnberg Quartet, as Ernest Newman shrewdly deduced: why else, he asks, would Wagner have constructed it in such a form that it can combine with the Peace melody in *double* counterpoint, when that rare and valuable attribute is not exploited at all in *Siegfried* but only in the later *Idyll*? The obvious inference is that it was originally intended for a composition in which that attribute would have been an advantage – that is, for the quartet, of which nothing is known, however, except what Cosima recorded in her diary (NLRW, III, pp. 271ff.). In other words, Wagner reserved contrapuntal games of that kind for chamber music, and did not consider them appropriate to his music dramas.

    The adoption of the two instrumental melodies by the voice part leads to awkwardness in the 'declamation' as Newman goes on to remark. Thus the original lines of the text as published:

> ewig licht
> lachst du aus mir
> dann selig selbst dir entgegen

had to be recast, not altogether happily, as:

344 *340*   ewig licht
> lachst du selig
> dann aus mir dir entgegen

in order to fit them to the vocal melody created by combining the two themes (the meaning of the words is not affected). Another instance of how Wagner was always swayed by the musical considerations is provided here: the introductory sustained chord is held a bar longer in the score than in the sketch, which gives the ensuing melody emphasis.

Ex. 53*a* Sketch

Ex. 53*b* Score

348 *341*   As the dramatic dialogue becomes more animated (score: very lively), development motives once again come to the fore, with some rich variations of the two types, 'run' and 'wave', tried out in separate sketches (exx. 38 and 39 on p. 162).

350 *342*   Ex. 54*a* Sketch and score

352 *343*   Ex. 54*b* Sketch and score

The latter figure, which enters on unison violins at the word 'Welle' ('wave'), at once sweeps all the string parts into a kind of whirlpool, which is already adumbrated in the sketch; after the transition from the flat key to
354 *343* the sharp key, the writing is in six parts at the word 'Wogen' ('billows').

      Ex. 54*c* Sketch

Isolated wind entries are noted down as the briefest of hints, leading Wagner to describe his composition sketch as 'wild jottings that only I can understand', which he would have to transcribe presently in a 'more respectable notational language' – i.e. the orchestral sketch. (Letter to King Ludwig, 1 July 1869.)

      Ex. 55*a* Sketch

371 *348*　　　Ex. 55*b* Score

The last ten sides of the composition sketch, from the Peace melody onwards, were written down in a single sustained burst, with a total of only ten bars deleted and rewritten. 'Not a day's interruption, no distractions!' he wrote to King Ludwig on 18 May. 'For I am at the most tender and the most excited point of my work: the crystallization of the jewel that is intended to be the cornerstone!'

There was one interruption that Wagner was glad to admit: Cosima had sent for the Maurin Quartet to come from Paris, in order to celebrate his birthday on 22 May by playing him the works of his 'great master', Beethoven, which he had loved 'earliest and most deeply'. We know the significance they had for his own work, and on this occasion too they put him into a 'cheerful, exuberant frame of mind, ready to begin life anew' (letter to King Ludwig, 26 May 1869).

390ff.　The 'cornerstone' is the combination of the theme that he had originally
353ff.　thought of giving to the Shepherd in *Tristan* (no. 5 on p. 161; ex. 37), with the motive 'Heil der Mutter, die mich gebar'; how wonderfully appropriate it was, he said to Cosima, that the theme of rejoicing made such a perfect accompaniment to the latter, 'so that the rejoicing goes on sounding in the orchestra without interruption. He will probably finish the sketch tomorrow.' (DMCW, I, p. 452.)

The last two-and-a-half sides, consisting almost entirely of four-stave systems, are written out in a very clear, energetic hand, with few alterations.

'Safely delivered. / 14 June 1869', he noted at the end, alluding to the birth of his son, Siegfried, on 6 June 1869.

Götterdämmerung

Wagner started the composition sketch of *Götterdämmerung* on 2 October 1869, before he had finished scoring *Siegfried*. 'Come...to Tribschen,' he wrote to Karl Klindworth on 26 April 1870,

> and I will show you a lot of new work, and I will probably give you a sizeable part of the score of the third act of *Siegfried* to take away with you as well [so that Klindworth could make the vocal score]. I have had to put the orchestration of it on one side, in fact, because I am writing *Götterdämmerung* now, and it is quite impossible to concentrate on both at once.

He was in no hurry to finish the score of *Siegfried*, in any case, since he hoped to spare the work the fate of an unsatisfactory first performance in Munich.

No sketches of individual motives for the Prelude of *Götterdämmerung* have survived, but there are eleven sheets of sketches for the three acts, several with more than one sketch on them. For the most part these consist less of separate ideas noted down in isolation than of studies of quite lengthy passages of motivic combinations.

Act I
Fragments of a composition sketch of Scene 1: 'Sitz ich herrlich am Rhein...' (with the Gibichungen motive); '....den wünsch' ich Gutrun zum Mann'; 'Welche Tat schuf er so tapfer, daß als herr-lichster Held...' (with Gutrune's motive); from 'Jagt er auf Taten wonnig umher' (with Siegfried's Horn Call in the accompaniment) to 'Willkommen hieß ich ihn gern'. Obviously these were all passages that Wagner wanted to try out before getting down to the composition sketch proper: contrapuntal studies and the introduction of new motives as they occur in the course of the dialogue.

Scene 2. 'Was nahmst du am Eide nicht Teil?' – 'Mein Blut verdürb' euch den Trank.' Here Wagner was experimenting with the combination of different, contrasting motives.

On the same sheet there are six bars from Scene 3: 'Als dem Gott entgegen Siegmund ich schützte...' Also from Scene 3, on a small mildewed sheet, the accompaniment to a section of Waltraute's narration, from 'da brach sich sein Blick' to 'erlöst wär' Gott und Welt'. Wagner's concern here was to amalgamate different motives or motivic fragments to create a continuous melodic line: Wotan's farewell to Brünnhilde, the 'Rheingold!' cry, the Ring motive, the Renunciation of Love, Alberich's Curse, Valhalla. I shall compare this very early sketch with the composition sketch and the score in context.

Act II

Scene 1. The dialogue between Alberich and Hagen: 'früh alt, fahl und bleich...' This is on a sheet used on both sides, partly written in pencil, partly in ink, which otherwise bears studies for the third scene, Hagen and the Vassals, starting with 'Groß Glück und Heil', then, over the page, 'zum Hochzeitsrufer ward er bestellt' and 'wie halten wir es dann?' the last a contrapuntal study of the part writing.

A study for the accompaniment to Hagen's 'Nun laßt das Lachen' follows on another sheet.

A study of harmonic progressions at the end of the Vassals' chorus, not used in that form.

Scene 4. A few bars of Siegfried's 'Achtest du so der eignen Ehre?...Mich trennte seine Schärfe von diesem traur'gen Weib' and two versions of Brünnhilde's 'Wohl kenn' ich seine Schärfe', the second being as the passage appears in the score.

Scene 5. Only the final bars, the combination of the wedding procession with the Murder motive, still somewhat different from the score.

Act III

The separate sketches for this act are particularly substantial.

Scene 1. A sketch of the opening of the scene: the Horn Call, the canon for eight horns, the new, chromatic Wave motive, 'Frau Sonne', and the motive of the Rhinemaidens' sudden alertness at 'Ich höre sein Horn'. One sheet, used only on one side, has eight bars of 'Frau Sonne' sketched in pencil. Another such has the introductory Wave figure and the entry of the voices, followed by this note:

Die deutsche Kunstempfänglichkeit
hat etwas vom russischen Soldaten:
es genügt nicht, diesen totgeschossen
zu haben, man muß ihn erst noch umstoßen.

('German receptivity to art / is rather like a Russian soldier: / shooting him dead is not enough, / you have to bowl him over as well.')

Scene 3. A longer, continuous period, beginning at 'Der Wassertiefe weise Schwestern ', and the most significant sketch of all, the first draft of the symphonic finale, employing almost the same motivic material as the eventual version, but still differing widely in the development and final details.

This résumé of the separate sketches ought to suffice to show why Wagner wrote special studies of particular, isolated passages. Obviously, he wanted to work out the elaboration of new themes, motivic combinations and contrapuntal passages, but a more profound reason was the density of the symphonic texture of *Götterdämmerung*.

Exhaustive evaluation of these separate sketches demands a special study of its own. In the context of this book, the closest attention will be given to the sketch of the symphonic finale, as a preliminary study for the composition sketch.

Prelude and Act I

The composition sketch of the Prelude and Act I consists of thirty-one half-sheets of manuscript paper, the first of which, bearing the sketch of the orchestral introduction, is used on one side only.

From sheet 22 onwards the notation is not inked over, and is very hard to read in places.

The start of the orchestral introduction is dated '9 Jan. 1870' and that of the prelude and first act '2 Oct. 69'; the end of the act is dated '5 June 70'.

Prelude

The 'Prelude' of *Götterdämmerung* is something more than the usual orchestral introduction: it consists of the Norns' scene, Siegfried's leavetaking from Brünnhilde and his journey to the Rhine. 'J'ai fini la grande Ouverture (*Vorspiel*) de la *Götterdämmerung*, formant, pour ainsi dire, une Ouverture tout extraordinaire...', Wagner wrote to Catulle Mendès on 1 March 1870; '(l'ouverture vous fera plaisir)' (TWLF, p. 312).

Wagner began the composition sketch on 2 October 1869 with the first line of the First Norn, 'Welch Licht leuchtet dort?', not with the brief orchestral introduction. The way it is written and the heading ' *Götterdämmerung* / I. / Prelude' suggest that originally no orchestral introduction was planned. At all events, none was written until more than three months later, when it went on to a separate sheet of paper, which was numbered '1', necessitating the renumbering of all the other sheets.

There is no hint of an instrumental introduction to precede the Norns' scene in the sketches of *Siegfrieds Tod*, either. Marked though the textual and musical differences between it and *Götterdämmerung* are, both versions have the following features in common:

1. the key of E♭ minor;
2. the principal 6/4 metre;
3. the rondo form of the exchange of questions and answers.

Obviously the introduction had posed special problems, requiring prolonged deliberation. In the Norns' scene

> the fates of the primeval world entwine to make the threads of the
> rope which we must see the sombre sisters passing from one to
> another when the curtain rises, in order to understand its significance.
> For that reason, this introduction had to be brief, its purpose being to
> create tension; the use in it of motives whose significance had been
> established in earlier parts of the work made possible a richer har-
> monic and thematic treatment. (*Über die Anwendung der Musik auf
> das Drama*, RWGS, X, p. 187.)

In the composition sketch the introduction occupies three systems of
three staves each, and already corresponds exactly to the version in the
score, except for two bars, sketched lower down on the page and intended
to be inserted after the statement of the Fate motive, but which were after
all omitted from the score, because they would have disrupted the flow of
the melos.

Ex. 1 Sketch

The full harmonization of the accompanimental figure is already indicated
in the sketch: the first bar of the new motive of the Norns' Rope is written
straight out in three parts.

The choice of the two principal motives – Brünnhilde's greeting of the
sun (transposed from C major to Cb major,[1] and darkened by the use of
tubas) and the Fate motive – fulfilled Wagner's requirements of brevity and
the creation of tension, and also shows that in certain circumstances the
musical function of a motive can be more decisive than the poetic.

In the first part of the Norns' scene the discrepancies between the
composition sketch and the score are slight: the four bars of the First
Norn's 'An der Weltesche wob ich einst' are contracted to three:

---

[1] According to the key signature the introduction is in Eb minor, but the
consistent writing of Fb for F means that the first sixteen bars are in fact in Cb
major. There was a similar tonal ambiguity when Brünnhilde greeted the sun in
Siegfried: E minor in the sketch, C major in the score.

Ex. 2*a* Sketch

An der Welt - e - - - sche wob — — ich einst

Ex. 2*b* Score

An der Welt- e - sche wob ich einst

35 9

Wagner held the greater breadth in reserve, so that when it is eventually deployed at the Third Norn's 'Die Weltesche war dies einst!' it is an effective means of enhancing the climax.

The setting of the lines that immediately follow, from 'Brennt das Holz' to 'den glänzenden Saal', provide a rare instance of the accompaniment being richer motivically in the sketch than in the score. The Magic Fire motive crackles in the composition sketch:

Ex. 3 Sketch

Brennt das Holz hei - - - - lig brünstig und hell, sengt die Glut

In the score, on the other hand, Wagner refrains from any motivic allusions and instead has violin and viola arpeggios climbing chromatically from one bar to the next, against a background of sustained wind chords: the impression of rising flames is still there, but the voice is now able to soar freely above, dominating them.

Minor changes on sheet 4, beginning with 'Dämmert der Tag?', are due to Wagner's practice of sketching such passages with a melodically independent accompaniment. In this case he found he could not sustain the chromatic progression contained in Loge's motive long enough to serve as the accompaniment to the voice part when the latter was subsequently woven in, so he had to insert extra bars.

The following six bars were crossed out for a different reason: Wagner's original idea for the words 'bannte ihn Wotan, Brünnhildes Fels zu umbrennen' was a rather tame variant of Loge's motive, but he replaced that by the present eery form while he was still sketching it, and when he came to score

WFR

48 *13*   it he intensified the effect by adding the leaping sextuplets of the high woodwind.

The spontaneity of the sketching is further underlined by the sudden break after 'in der Weltesche zuhauf geschichtete Scheite' for eight bars
74 *22*   anticipating the next scene.[2]

Ex. 4 Sketch

Brünnh.

ein ein - - - zig Sor - - - - - gen macht mich säu - - men, daß dir zu we - nig mein Wert ge - wann

60 *18*   The Sword motive and the Horn Call intrude on the last moments of the Norns' scene in the sketch as in the score. Motivic quotation of that kind might seem premeditated, but the improvisatory character of the sketch as a whole argues against it. As the web of motives grows more confused and anxious the spontaneous flash of the Sword fanfare is needed for purely musical reasons: 'Nothung zerhaut es den Nornen'.

The question of the metre of the Norns' scene has been mentioned briefly. It preoccupied Wagner from the first. On the Herrmann manuscript of sketches for *Siegfrieds Tod*, the scene starts in 12/8; on the 1850 composition sketch it starts in 6/4, as it does in both the composition sketch and the score of *Götterdämmerung*. The sextuple metre is suggested by the rhythm of the spinning. But a 6/4 beat maintained for any length of time when the tempo is slow is inclined to drag, and to avoid that Wagner had already introduced an alternating 4/4 beat in the *Siegfrieds Tod* composition sketch. The same alternation is tacitly assumed in the *Götterdämmerung* composition sketch, although it is not expressly indicated. In the score Wagner goes further and uses a 3/4 metre as well and even, on two occasions when the recurrent question 'Weißt du, wie das wird?' (or 'ward?') makes its rondo-like reappearance, has recourse to a majestic 3/2. Altogether the beat is changed sixteen times in the one scene. The retention of a single overall tempo, 'moderately slow', shaded only by small

[2] Written very hastily and differing somewhat from the later version!

accelerandi and ritardandi, and the reliance on the variations of beat to modify that tempo, enabled Wagner to achieve the 'fundamental expressive character of a sublime stillness' (Porges), which is the predominant feature of the Norns' scene.

65 *19*   The orchestral interlude leading to the Leavetaking scene: 'First light – dawn – broad daylight' is eight bars longer in the score, with the sequences based on the new motive of Brünnhilde's love for Siegfried prolonged and made denser by overlapping statements.

Ex. 5*a* Sketch

Ex. 5*b* Score

The words of the scene that follows are identical in *Götterdämmerung* to the text that Wagner had set twenty years earlier in the *Siegfrieds Tod* sketches, thus creating a unique opportunity for studying his stylistic evolution.

The following versions are available for comparison:

Siegfrieds Tod:
the Herrmann manuscript (1850)
the composition sketch (1850)

Götterdämmerung:
the composition sketch (1869–70)
the orchestral sketch (1870)
the score (1873)

The stylistic differences can be illustrated quite readily by the juxtaposition of just a few bars in the various versions (the orchestral sketch can be ignored).

Ex. 6*a* Herrmann manuscript (1850)

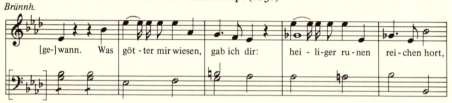

Ex. 6*b* Composition sketch (1850)

Ex. 6*c* Composition sketch (1869–70)

(In ex. 6*d* the orchestral part is reduced to the basic harmonies.) It is uncertain whether Wagner already had it in mind to provide a similar motivic accompaniment in the score of *Siegfrieds Tod*: it is unlikely that at that date he envisaged an accompaniment richer than is found in comparable lyrical passages in *Lohengrin*.

The essential stylistic differences are these: in *Götterdämmerung* note values are doubled, so that the singing is further removed from recitative and elevated to a kind of German bel canto; as a result the number of bars in ex. 6 grows from four to eight, offset somewhat by a brisker tempo. Syncopation and wide intervals enhance the vigour of the melody; isolated notes are changed, an ordinary triad is replaced by the *Tristan* chord; a repeated phrase is raised by a third on repetition, so that it undergoes sequential intensification and gains mediant colouring. The later version is in every way more plastic and more colourful. Above all the inner tension, which keeps the flow of the infinite melody in motion, has become far stronger.

That inner tension is reinforced in the score by the accompaniment, indicated only in the first few bars in the sketch, though its latent presence can be assumed in the rest. In the score it takes the shape of a fragment of a Leitmotiv:

76 *22*

Ex. 7*a* Sketch   Ex. 7*b* Score

This is played in turn by clarinet, violas, cor anglais, horns and oboe during the course of eight bars; the triplet recurring on the last crotchet of every bar impels the movement on to a climax.

The heightening of the inner tension of the vocal part and the accompaniment, and their reciprocal interpenetration as illustrated by ex. 6, are the secret of Wagner's style in maturity. The basic elements of the musical form, on the other hand, which were already prefigured in the verse text, are the same in both versions.

It should not be overlooked, however, that some of the melodic elements and motivic germs are already present in the earlier version, although Wagner no longer had those sketches to hand when he started to compose *Götterdämmerung*. They must therefore have sprung up again directly out of the text after the twenty-year interval, even though in a more fully developed, riper form. For instance, what in *Siegfrieds Tod* is a vocal phrase preceded by a triplet instrumental anacrusis, reappears in *Götterdämmerung* as a major orchestral motive.

Ex. 8*a* Composition sketch (1850)

Ex. 8*b* Composition sketch (1869–70)

124 *35*   In the score Wagner gave up the attempt to incorporate the motive in the voice part in this more highly developed form, evidently for reasons of vocal technique:

Ex. 9*a* Composition sketch (1869–70)   Ex. 9*b* Score (1873)

By dint of minimizing the resemblances between the two settings of the Leavetaking scene and magnifying the differences, it has been represented that Wagner was capable of setting one and the same text in two different ways, in other words that the most that was prefigured in the text were the most general formal elements of the composition and that therefore there can be no question of 'simultaneous' poetic and musical conception, divided into two stages for purely technical reasons. Apart from the fact that this opinion does not make sufficient allowance for the similarities between the two versions, which are still astonishing by any standards after an interval of twenty years, it also ignores one major question: whether the circumstance that the words are the same really amounts to the text being the same. In *Siegfrieds Tod* the Siegfried and Brünnhilde in this scene are little more than two names, about whom we have just learned a little from the Norns' scene. The situation is completely different in *Götterdämmerung*. We have already shared in their story and the story before they were even born, in the action and the music of two, really three, previous dramas, and now their words, though the same as those they utter in *Siegfrieds Tod*, have a totally different resonance. Wagner experienced the same difference too, returning to the words after twenty years. The words were the same, but it was not the same text: against the far greater depth of the background, in the greatly expanded framework of the whole tetralogy, it had become a different, virtually new text. It is that 'newness', and not the greater maturity of the compositional technique alone, that can now be heard in the music.

The idea of Siegfried's Journey to the Rhine, the orchestral interlude leading into the first act, was already there in the text of *Siegfrieds Tod*: 'the orchestra takes up the tune played by the horn and develops it in a vigorous interlude'. Naturally, as it now stands, enriched by the chromatic progressions of Loge's motive and the Rhinemaidens' song, the movement came into existence only in the context of the composition of *Götterdämmerung*. The original intention, revealed in the composition sketch, was that the on-stage Horn Call (6/8) should lead directly into the orchestral scherzo on the Horn motive (3/4). The twenty-nine bars in 3/4 marked 'fast' are written out separately, at the bottom of the same page, with an omission mark to show where they were meant to go in the sketch. Just how spontaneously this afterthought occurred to the composer is demonstrated by the fact that the five bottom staves on the page, where he wrote it out, had already been partly used for some separate sketches of individual motives, written with the page the other way up.[3]

Ex. 10 Sketch

This insertion is the passage referred to by Cosima in her diary on 15 April 1874:

> Richard was working (scoring *Götterdämmerung*), but he says he would need at least a second full orchestra to express his ideas exactly as he would like to. He says of the theme that represents the state of Brünnhilde's feelings as Siegfried hurries away in impatient exuberance: 'with me it's not a matter of seeking to make effects for their own sake, but of enabling different instruments to enter, in order to alternate constantly with each other; not playing virtuoso games. Added to that, I'm a pedant, and I want to produce a score that will look good in print.' (BBL 1936, p. 1.)

In other respects the composition sketch already contains every feature of the Journey to the Rhine just as it was to be in the score, although the accompanimental figures are written out only in the first bar of each phrase. That every detail of the eventual sound was present in Wagner's mind from the first is again proved by the high B♭ above the descending motive of the Gods' Downfall, which foreshadows the unearthly *ff* trills on flutes and piccolos in the score.

---

[3] There are four of these sketches, one a setting of Siegfried's 'Durch deine Tugend allein soll ich Taten noch wirken', but the melody is a little different from the eventual version.

Ex. 11 Sketch

Es-dur

On 6 February 1870 Cosima wrote to Nietzsche, after she and Wagner had been reading his *Sokrates und die Tragödie*:

> The pilgrimage that you made us take to the finest age of human history had such a beneficial effect on us that this morning the master has got his Siegfried as far as the Rhine, where he is blowing his highspirited theme accompanied by the boldest and most exuberant violin figure; hearing it, the Rhinemaidens are filled with joy and hope and let their own motive be heard, broad and strong.[4]

Act I

Scenes 1 and 2

The beginning of the sketch is dated '7 Febr. 70', then, on the line below, 'Family council'. Even this marginal note indicates that Wagner regarded the ensuing scene more objectively. By contrast with the Leavetaking scene and the Rhine Journey, the handwriting is small and clear and the new motives and their elaboration, which had already been sketched separately (see above, p. 179), are written out fully harmonized. The ten bars beginning with Gutrune's 'Welche Tat schuf er so tapfer' are especially impressive, in the combination of her oboe melody with the dotted rhythm of the Gibichungen motive and, when repeated in F major, with Freia's Love motive as well (solo violin and cello in the score).

Following Gunther's surly 'danach zu verlangen machst du mir Lust?', two systems, each of three staves, are crossed out. Originally there were only two bars of instrumental music at this point, and Hagen entered in the third with 'Brächte Siegfried die Braut dir heim'. But it occurred to Wagner at the moment of composition to extend the two bars to the present ten, and to introduce here the new motive of the Potion of Forgetfulness.

After Hagen's greeting of Siegfried, to the accompaniment of the Curse motive, the motive of Enticement (horns, 'expressive and soft', in the score) is also found already in the sketch, lacking only its repeat on the solo oboe.

217 53

231 57

263 66

---

[4] *Die Briefe Cosima Wagners an Friedrich Nietzsche*, ed. Erhart Thierbach, part 1 (Weimar, 1938), p. 27.

Ex. 12 Score

According to Porges, this refers to 'Gutrune's gaze, uncontrollably expressing her longing'.

285 74   The melody of the greeting she gives Siegfried: 'Willkommen, Gast',
differs in the sketch from the score; the entry on the first beat of a bar gives
the later version something of a cajoling but completely naive persuasive-
ness.

Ex. 13*a* Sketch

Ex. 13*b* Score

289 75   The double statement, *pp*, of the Forgetfulness motive, after Siegfried has
drunk the potion, occupies only one bar in the sketch, but in the score it is
extended over two bars (muted horns) and additionally bears the marking
'very slow'. 'Pondering and forgetting', Wagner observed; the curious
harmonization ought to sound as if coming 'out of the void into a void'
(Porges).

Ex. 14*a* Sketch   Ex. 14*b* Score

The impassioned violin figurations at Siegfried's outburst, 'Ha schönstes
Weib!', are so marked in character that they are already indicated in the
sketch. Wagner commented that the transformation that has just taken
place within him is like nothing so much as the effect of his having taken a
poison, which produces a first reaction of immense force (Porges).

    In a letter to Judith and Catulle Mendès of 25 March 1870, Wagner wrote:
'Siegfried a bu hier le boisson fatal de Gutrune; je gage que cela portera

quelque malheur que je dois encore mettre en musique'.[5] Siegfried sets off
on his fateful path accompanied by music that is almost scherzo-like: after
Gunther's confession, 'Nun darf ich den Fels nicht erklimmen', Loge's
motive assumes, at Siegfried's 'Ich fürchte kein Feuer', a dominance as a
shaping force that even extends to the vocal part (cf. Loge's own coloratura
in *Das Rheingold*, Scene 3):

306 *81*

Ex. 15 Sketch and score

In the instrumental introduction to the oath of bloodbrotherhood, the
note values of the Spear motive are halved in the score, so as not to check
the livelier momentum that is now released. The whole oath is written out
on six systems in the sketch, with just the briefest intimation of the
figurations of Loge's motive, as they dissolve into development motives. At
Siegfried's 'So – trink ich dir Treu'!', after 'So' has been held for a bar, the
score adds a two-bar rest for the voice (with a fermata), and then, again
differing from the sketch, the descending octave leap of the Brotherhood
motive strikes like lightning on the word 'Treu'' ('loyalty').

There is an omission mark in the sketch after the statement of the Spear
motive that follows immediately after 'Treu'', but no corresponding addition is sketched anywhere else. The score inserts six bars here to round off
the oathtaking, beginning with the deeply felt phrase

330 *86*

Ex. 16 Score

Siegfried's question, 'Was nahmst du am Eide nicht teil?' and Hagen's
answer is one of the passages for which Wagner wrote a preliminary sketch:
his problem here was how to get seven motives to fuse in a freely flowing
melodic line in the space of twenty-eight bars, which he managed to solve in
the composition sketch.

351 *92*

By contrast with what goes before it, where the accompaniment is merely
intimated in the sketch, all the parts are written out in the instrumental
passage which leads on to Hagen's Watch.

---

[5] *Lettres à Judith Gautier*, ed. Léon Guichard (Paris, 1964), p. 49.

Ex. 17 Sketch

The allusion to the Rhinemaidens' cry of 'Rheingold', which is first heard after 'ich...wehre die Halle dem Feind' and repeated in several variant forms, was cited by Wagner in *Über die Anwendung der Musik auf das Drama* as an example of 'the kind of variation that is capable of shaping the drama' (RWGS, X, pp. 189f.). It is already there in the composition sketch:

Ex. 18 Sketch

The interlude before the third scene falls into two distinct parts, the first a postlude to Hagen's Watch, the second a prelude to Brünnhilde's scene. After sketching the first part as far as the first four bars of the D major period, on the recto of sheet 22, Wagner suddenly broke off, crossed the whole page out, and then, without making good the gap so caused, continued on the verso with the sixth bar before the beginning of the third scene, going as far as Brünnhilde's 'Kommst du, Schwester?' on the same page. Having got so far, he turned his attention to the interrupted interlude again, decided the section he had crossed out was not so bad after all, and went on, on sheet 23, from the point he had reached in it, completing the second part, too, which differs in only minor respects from the score.

Evidently he found it particularly difficult to effect the transition from Hagen and the great world outside to Brünnhilde and the completely personal, intimate world she now inhabits, and expressed musically in the 'incomparable solo writing for two clarinets' (Richard Strauss). Brünnhilde's dreamy mood is emphasized even more in the score by the playful clarinet flourish, which is reminiscent of a similar figure in the scene between Evchen and her father in Act II of *Die Meistersinger*.

372 97

373 97

Ex. 19 Score

Scene 3

426 *112*   Six bars in Waltraute's narration, following 'Der Götter Rat ließ er beru-
fen', were crossed out in the composition sketch before the voice part had
been added. The passage in question comprises sequences based on the
Valhalla motive: after an initial statement in C major, the continuation
appears to have started on the tonic C again (it is not easy to read) instead of
with the chord of A major as now. The revised version which follows
immediately in the sketch corresponds exactly to the score: the same
sequences, spaced at the same intervals and displaying the same fragmentation of the motive in the middle section, as later at the end of the third act.

The amalgamation of several different motives, initially sketched separately on a small sheet speckled with mildew, as the accompaniment – though the sketch lacks the words – to the passage beginning 'Da
brach sich sein Blick', as far as 'erlöst wär' Gott und Welt!', differs at both
the beginning and end from the same period in the composition sketch and
even more markedly from the score. It is not until the last that the eloquent
439 *115*   portamento of the first violins (on the G string) appears:

Ex. 20*a* The initial sketch (opening)

Ex. 20*b* Composition sketch

In the separate sketch the period ends with the Valhalla motive (three bars,
B♮ minor), while the composition sketch and the score substitute the
five-fold perfect cadence in D♭ major.

Ex. 21*a* The initial sketch (close)

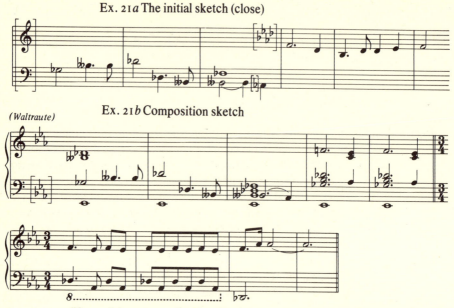

Ex. 21*b* Composition sketch

(*Waltraute*)

The revision means that the close of this period is consciously assimilated to that of the previous one, 'die Hall' erfüllten die Helden', which ends with three repetitions of the perfect cadence in G♭ major. The endings emphasize the symmetry of the two periods and bear out Lorenz's view of their function as the Stollen of a large Bar.[6]

While the orchestral writing in the epic part of this scene, Waltraute's narration, is rich in motivic elaboration, the ensuing dialogue, marked 'very lively' ('Allo' in the composition sketch) to begin with, is dominated by the voice parts, whose expressive power is reinforced in places in the score by a broadening and enrichment of the orchestral part-writing:

Ex. 22*a* Sketch

Brünnhilde

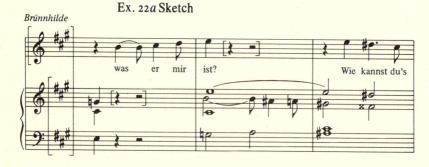

was   er   mir   ist?   Wie kannst du's

---

[6] *Das Geheimnis der Form bei Richard Wagner*, vol. I, pp. 249f. Correspondence between the final bars alone of two musical periods is enough to satisfy the ear that the two are alike or related in some degree.

460 *121* Ex. 22*b* Score

Ex. 23*a* Sketch

470 *123* Ex. 23*b* Score

482 *125* The flaring-up of the Magic Fire ('Waberlohe') in the passage preceding Siegfried's entrance, 'Blitzend Gewölk vom Winde geblasen' ('blown': thus in the sketch; the score has 'getragen', 'carried'), is indicated in a few light pencil strokes, which nevertheless reproduce exactly the overall line followed by the music and the details of the motivic writing.

The final scene, in which Siegfried, in Gunther's shape, overpowers Brünnhilde, is another where the composition sketch corresponds to the score in every respect. The four bars following Brünnhilde's scream, in which the 'Hort der Welt' motive from the third act of *Siegfried* suddenly glints in the clarinet and bass clarinet, and to which Wagner gives the direction in the score 'As she collapses...in his arms, her eyes unconsciously meet Siegfried's', are already there in the sketch, but in triple time, where the score has 4/4. There is an allusion to this at a significant point in the second act.

539 *139* The only important change to this scene in the score is at the close:

Ex. 24 Sketch

Siegfr.

von sei - nem Weib!

5 Juni 70.
(Fidi lacht dazu!)

What a difference from the score! Brünnhilde's motive, now stated twice in the orchestra (*ff*, first violins, then all the woodwind and the horns), is a far more eloquent reflection on her fate, without in the least diminishing the cruelty of the last six bars.

Shortly after finishing the act, Wagner played the last scene through to Cosima. 'His inhuman apostrophe to his wife is dreadful in its effect, and through the great weft of the themes a language has been created of which the world has no conception', she commented in her diary (DMCW, I, p. 495). Wagner wrote a teasing rejoinder below the closing bars: 'Fidi [their infant son] thinks it's funny!'

Act II

Having finished the orchestral sketch of the first act on 2 July 1870, Wagner broke off the composition of *Götterdämmerung* for a whole year, resuming it with the composition sketch of the second act on 24 June 1871. In the interim, among other things, he wrote his Beethoven essay (RWGS, IX, pp. 61ff.), which is relevant here for its clarification of the change that had taken place in his view of the relationship between music and text in his drama. Whereas the emphasis in *Oper und Drama* had been on the role of the text, he now acknowledged that music enshrined 'man's *a priori* ability to create dramatic forms at all' (p. 106). His newer concept also entailed a distinction between the 'perceptible world' of the poet and the 'dream world' of the musician, based on Schopenhauer's metaphysics of music.

Wagner made his first notes for the essay on the back of the last sheet of the composition sketch of Act I, writing in pencil, which is now almost completely obliterated:

> The nation / day aspect: (Schiller) Goethe / night aspect; Beethoven
> the face it presents   what it is at heart
> The nation's vigour, of which they themselves were not fully aware,
> which they merely sensed, produced the poets, and they can be
> explained only in terms of it; but in Beethoven it is expressed directly.
> Solar   Tellurian[7]

Below this there are two music sketches:

1. Waltraute's 'Teilen den Taumel, der dich Törin erfaßt? Ein andres bewog mich in Angst, zu brechen Wotans Gebot.' (On three staves, including the voice part, but without the words.)

2. Waltraute's 'den verfluchten wirf in die Flut!' (Including the words.)

The most significant event to take place during the break in the composition was Wagner's announcement in Leipzig, his birthplace, on 12 May 1871, of the first complete performance of the *Ring* at the first Bayreuth Festival (RWGS, XVI, pp. 131f.). At the time, only the composition sketch and orchestral sketch of the first act of *Götterdämmerung* existed, he had not even begun to sketch the second and third acts and had not written a single bar of the full score. He must have been able to hear, even see, the composition so clearly in his imagination that setting it down on paper was

---

[7] He developed these ideas further in his 'Brown Book': see Richard Wagner, *Das Braune Buch* (Zürich, 1975), pp. 210f., where he refers in particular to Schopenhauer's *Die Welt als Wille und Vorstellung*, vol. II, chapter 29, 'Von der Erkenntnis der Ideen'.

for him only a question of time and opportunity. He miscalculated in announcing that the festival would take place in 1873, but that was mainly due to the unforeseen organizational and financial difficulties that the project ran into, and that constantly distracted him from his work.[8]

The composition sketch of the second act comprises twenty-two sheets, the last used on one side only. The start is dated '24 June 71. *Midsummer Day* [Johannistag]!!!', the finish, '25 Oct. 71'.

Prelude and Scene 1

Both are sketched in considerable detail and with hardly any changes. The sketch of the prelude includes the bright woodwind chords on the top stave, the syncopations of the Hate motive played by the violins and violas on the middle stave, and the low wind and string melody on the bottom stave. From the fifteenth bar on, the top stave serves for the notation of the fragmentary, syncopated triplets on the flutes, oboes and clarinets that now enter. Unlike other parts of the composition sketch, the dynamic markings and phrasing slurs are given here in full detail: the cantabile quality of the unusual melodic writing, which should emerge in performance, and the demonic crescendi and decrescendi are integral characteristics of this nocturnal vision in sound.

11 *142*   Even the lighting console is called upon to play a part: stage directions are extremely rare in the composition sketch of *Götterdämmerung*, but the totally unprepared, impressionistic, *ff* dissonance of the woodwind and muted horns as the curtain rises (the instrumentation is not noted in the sketch) are accompanied by the direction: 'Moonlight'.

23 *146*   Punctuated, like the earlier nocturnal scene, the Norns' scene, by the recurrence of a refrain-like question, the dialogue between Hagen and Alberich hardly differs in the sketch from the score, apart from a one-crotchet rest after Hagen's 'Der Ewigen Macht', which was later extended to eight crotchets.

The motivic references heard fleetingly in the orchestra, which are intended to be played 'as distinctly as possible, but at a volume which is never more than moderately loud, subordinate to the words and notes of the singers' (Porges), are all written out meticulously in the composition sketch.

In *Rückblick auf die Bühnenfestspiele* Wagner described the impression that the scene made on him when performed in the proper style: 'I confess for my part that I regard the ghostly, dreamlike duologue between Alberich and Hagen...as one of the most successfully accomplished parts of our whole endeavour' (RWGS, X, p. 114). As the composition sketch shows, it is an impression that is due not least to the seemingly improvised conception of the scene.

[8] Cf. Westernhagen, *Wagner*, chapter 27, 'Von Tribschen nach Bayreuth'.

Scene 2

Wagner avoided the danger of the second Dawn in the work being a mere pendant to the first by confining himself to creating a general impression of the natural world stirring and waking, rather than depicting, for a second time, the relationship between the scene and his protagonists' frame of mind.

43 *152*   The rhythm of the bass clarinet's cantilena at the close of the first scene was revised in the sketch, as we have observed in the case of other cantilenas. It was originally followed by four bars, written only in pencil and then crossed out, and marked 'E major / horns'. Gutrune's motive is still legible:

Ex. 25 Sketch (deleted)

The intention may perhaps have been that this would greet the break of day, like the fanfares in Act II of *Lohengrin*. At all events it was abandoned in the act of committal to paper and replaced by the canon for eight horns that develops out of the preceding cantilena:

Ex. 26 Sketch

Wagner described the scene between Gutrune, Hagen and Siegfried as a 'very detailed dialogue', 'a kind of animated conversation on the stage, to be performed wholly in the style of comic opera' (Porges). The coloratura-like figures in the vocal writing are in accordance with this notion: for

56 *156*
79 *163*   instance, Siegfried's 'Frei und hold sei nun mir Frohem', which was slightly altered in the sketch, or Gutrune's 'Frohe Frauen ruf' ich zum Fest', which still lacks the exuberant turn in the sketch:

Ex. 27*a* Sketch

Ex. 27*b* Score

Gutrune

Fro - - - - he Frau - - - en ruf' ich zum Fest,

But the exuberance is all on the surface, in the vocal writing, while a deceitful twilight prevails in the depths, in the form of the Loge and Tarnhelm motives. For the most part these figurations, development motives proceeding out of Leitmotive, are written out in full in the sketch, but even where only their beginning is sketched the harmonic alteration of the accompaniment is indicated.

Scene 3

The summer of 1871, when Wagner was composing this act, was an anxious time for him; in addition to the continuing uncertainty as to whether the king would give Bayreuth his blessing, there was the sudden death of Tausig, the prospective business manager of the festival undertaking. Though inwardly tense, Wagner went on working, 'admittedly not with the complete calm and assurance that he had before', as Cosima recorded in her diary. 'He has discarded the setting of Hagen's summoning of the Vassals. He thinks it was over-composed, and attributes that to the external circumstances.' (DMCW, I, p. 578.)

85 *164*

The discarded sketch has survived, on the verso of sheet 36. It is interesting to see what Wagner meant by 'over-composed'.

Ex. 28 Sketch

[bass line only approximate]

[sic!]

bis

[1st version breaks off here]

Wagner did not delete this first version but simply stopped halfway through the descent of the Gods' Downfall motive. The second version, which starts on the recto of sheet 37, corresponds to the score apart from one minor change to which I shall refer in due course.

Hagen's part was more freely declaimed in the first version. In the second sketch and in the score it is restricted almost entirely to C with an occasional Db or D.

Alterations make the bass line illegible in places, but it was worked out in some detail. The string tremolo sketched on the middle stave consisted of a rising chromatic chord progression, which is replaced in the second version and the score by forte Cs (in octaves) sustained by the violins and violas for twenty-four bars, creating a churning effect reminiscent of the tremolo on D in the prelude to *Die Walküre*.

In the first version the accompaniment at the cry 'Waffen! Waffen!' introduced a new motive (with a partly illegible mirrored counter-theme), in which it is not hard to read an exact anticipation of the Vassals' 'da Hagen, der Grimme, so lustig mag sein!' This was dropped in the second version and the score, which have the horn blast of the summons to the wedding entering here instead.

148 *180*

The second version thus meant considerable melodic, harmonic, contrapuntal and motivic simplification. Its elemental effect is strengthened by greater metrical variety throughout the whole period, the original consistent 3/4 now being alternated with bars in 4/4 time. The outcome sounds improvised rather than 'composed'.

The only difference between the second sketch and the score is that the chord of the Neapolitan sixth, on which the Gods' Downfall motive enters, first on Db major and then on D major, is held a whole bar longer each time in the score:

Ex. 29*a* Sketch

Ex. 29*b* Score

After the last six bars of Hagen's horn on C and the Vassals' horns sounding in acute dissonance on Db and D, there are four more bars in the sketch with the new motive depicting the Vassals running to the scene; these were crossed out and 'verte' written against them. The back of the sheet is covered with scribbled music sketches, without the words, for the following choral scene, including the chorus 'Hagen! Hoiho! Hoiho!', with the woodwind climbing from Eb to Ab above the voices and the overlapping entries of 'Welche Not ist da?', and the instrumental accompaniment to

100 *168*

115 *172*   'Drohet ihm Not? Drängt ihn der Feind?', in which the string quavers are combined with the dotted rhythm of the horns.

      Lower on the same page there are a few scrawled notes for the first of these two choruses. If we also take into account the separate sketches listed on p. 180, it must be admitted that the Vassals' chorus, for all the impression it makes of a magnificent improvisation, demanded an unusually large number of compositional studies. Deeply impressed by what he had heard at the rehearsals, Porges wrote of the creation of 'a new style of free counterpoint'; if ever anything deserved the description 'never before heard!', it was this passage.

      On 25 August, the first anniversary of their wedding, Wagner played Cosima the revised version of the summoning of the Vassals. He dated the chorus's running entrance (sheet 38, recto) '*27 Aug*'. It had taken him exactly two months to do that much of the second act.

114 *171*   On the next sheet there is a verbal reminder of the scene's continually asserted principal key, 'C major', written just before Hagen's 'Rüstet euch wohl!'. It is a C major which is somehow menaced, however, by the underlying F♯ of Hagen.

128 *176*   The voice part here undergoes a number of small but characteristic changes in the score, for instance:

Ex. 30*a* Sketch

Ex. 30*b* Score

      The last line of the immediately following exhortation to sacrifice to Fricka appears in two versions in the sketch, the first the one used in the score, the second a more extended alternative, which Wagner then used for the
136 *179* repetition of the words a little later:

Ex. 31 Sketch

Ex. 32 Emendation not used here

      The bleating trill mocking Fricka – reinforced by a low trill on a clarinet in the score – is already there in the sketch.

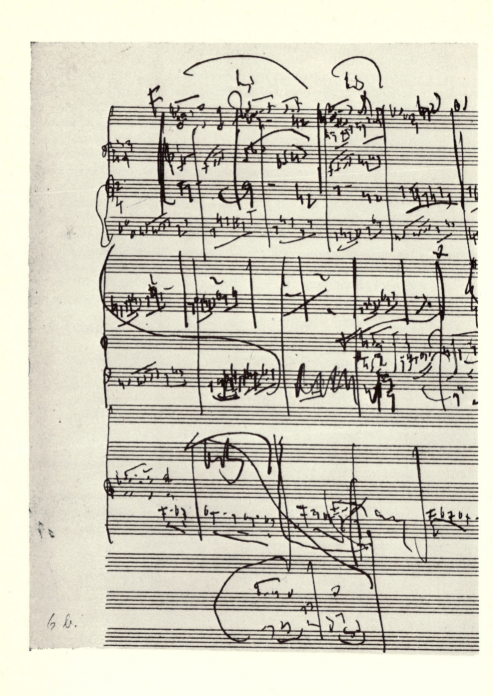

Götterdämmerung, Act II, Scene 3 (preliminary study for the composition sketch of the Vassals' chorus)

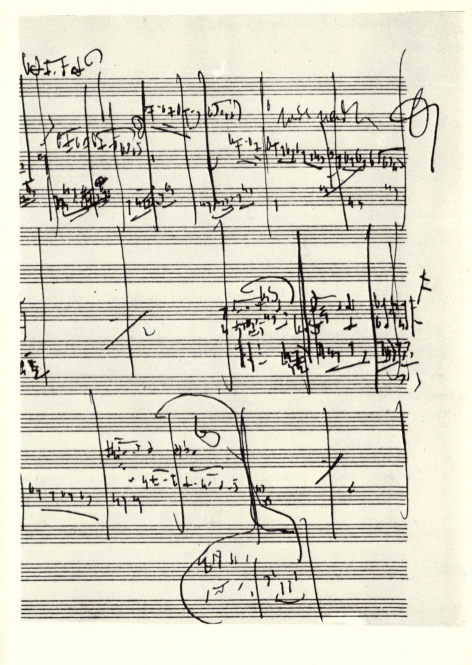

142 *180*   One of the most successful effects in the Vassals' chorus was not fully worked out until it had reached a third version:

Ex. 33*a* Sketch

Ex. 33*b* Revised sketch

Ex. 33*c* Score

Wagner clutched his brow as he pondered this passage: 'My thoughts are itching'. And when Cosima went into his room the next morning he greeted her by playing the line 'der Hagedorn sticht nun nicht mehr' (DMCW, I, p. 581). There is a particularly important melodic alteration already made in the sketch:

158 *185*   Ex. 34 Sketch, and emendation

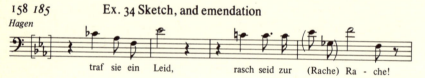

It could be said actually to provoke the subsequent harmonic shifts.

Scene 4

168 *187*   The chorus of welcome is scribbled down in the sketch. The following passage, Gunther's 'Gegrüßt sei, teurer Held!', illustrates Wagner's skill in
180 *191*   modulation: the introduction of G major, noted in words in the sketch, is an even more gradual process in the score –

Ex. 35*a* Sketch

Ex. 35*b* Score

- where it is prepared for by the descending sequence in the clarinet part.

189 *193*   Originally in the sketch, after 'Du lügst', Brünnhilde went straight on in the next bar, on A♭, with 'Mir schwindet das Licht'; but this was already deleted in the sketch, the progression extended over three bars and the diminuendo from *ff* to *p* effected by means of a string figure, precipitously descending and turning into a tremolo, whereupon the voice now enters a whole tone lower, on G♭.

210–36
200–6   Brünnhilde's passionate outcry, from 'Betrug! Betrug! Schändlichster Betrug!' to 'Er zwang mir Lust und Liebe ab', interrupted only by brief interjections from the bystanders, was written down in the composition sketch in a single burst, and once again the isolated minor discrepancies from the final version are all the more informative. At the very start, Brünnhilde's struggle 'to control her gasping breath' is underlined in the score by alterations to the rhythm of the vocal part, in the form of lengthening rests and transferring accentuated syllables to weaker parts of the bar.

Ex. 36*a* Sketch

The three bars of 'Wie noch nie er ge[rächt]' are marked 3/4 (after the preceding 4/4) in the sketch as in the score; the change obviously occurred to Wagner after he had written the phrase out, and the voice part and accompaniment were also adjusted accordingly. The grandeur of Brünn-

218 *202*   hilde's invocation of the gods, 'Heilige Götter, himmlische Walter!' ('Lenker' in the score), sung to a harmonically distorted version of the Valhalla motive (2/2 time), is enhanced in the score by the expansion of the syllable 'Göt-' by a whole bar. On the other hand, in the sequential phrases that follow, 'Lehrt ihr mich Leiden, wie keiner sie litt? / Schuft ihr mir Schmach, wie nie sie geschmerzt?', chords accompanying 'Lehrt' and 'Schuft' in the sketch were crossed out again, so that the unaccompanied entry of the voice at the beginning of each of the phrases provides the greatest possible contrast after the fortissimo of the full orchestra. The final

229 *205*   phrase, again, was altered rhythmically to depict her struggle for breath:

Ex. 37*a* Sketch

Ex. 37*b* Score

Gunther's interjection, 'Brünnhild', Ge-' is broken off in the middle of the word 'Gemahlin' in the sketch, which then goes on with 'Weich' fern, Verräter!' The end of his sentence is filled in on the next system. This is obviously a mistake and an unusual one, and suggests that Wagner was copying the whole passage from a separate, preliminary sketch which has not survived.

All in all, the version of this passage in the score appears in musico-dramatic high relief by comparison with the composition sketch. The comparison is of practical, not merely theoretical, interest, since it shows the trend of the composer's stylistic intention: the singing was to be more than beautiful, more even than passionate, it was meant to express the state of complete emotional and *physical* shock, almost annihilation, that Brünnhilde is in when she determines to seek boundless vengeance.

242 *208*   Her ironic reply to Siegfried's disclaimer is written out three times in the sketch:

Ex. 38*a* Sketch I (deleted)

Ex. 38*b* Sketch II

Although the second version is the same as the third, and as the score, it too is crossed out. The note 'verte' directs us to the back of the sheet, where it is written out again, with a more detailed accompaniment: at all events Wagner wanted to have it on the same side of the page as the following phrase, so as to be able to take in the whole melodic flow at once. He had indeed already sketched the motivic combination on a separate sheet:

Ex. 39*a* Preliminary sketch

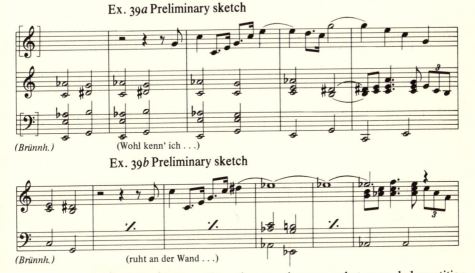

(Brünnh.)   (Wohl kenn' ich . . .)

Ex. 39*b* Preliminary sketch

(Brünnh.)   (ruht an der Wand . . .)

While Brünnhilde's oath on the spear is a somewhat expanded repetition of Siegfried's oath in the sketch, in the score it has become a magnificent variation movement, due to the echoing of each vocal phrase by a solo trumpet:

264 214

Ex. 40*a* Sketch

Brünnh.

Hel - le Wehr, — hei - li - ge Waf - - - fe!   Hilf mei - -

- - nem e - wi - gen Ei - de!   bei des   [etc.]

Ex. 40*b* Score

(Ex. 40*a* reduces the sketch to the vocal and bass lines, but notates the durations, rests etc. in full, rather than reproduce Wagner's shorthand. Ex. 40*b* is even more reduced than the vocal score.)

The fourth bar of ex. 40*a*, where the voice is still heard, shows that no thought of expanding the period in this way had occurred to Wagner while he was writing the sketch.

With the change to the 'wedding' key of C major, the two following pages of the sketch contain numerous emendations. Wagner made two false starts on Siegfried's 'daß ich dir es gewann, dankt dir gewiß noch das Weib', before reaching the eventual version the third time. His invitation to the Vassals to come to the feast contains three instances where, in the revision, two bars are compressed into one to quicken the rousing tempo. The high C added to his highspirited coloratura was another later addition.

286 *218*

293 *220*

Ex. 41 Sketch (emended)

The cheerful whoop in the first violins in the orchestral passage at the end of the scene was likewise added later:

297 *221*

Ex. 42 Sketch (emended)

Scene 5

304 *222*   Brünnhilde's monologue, 'Welches Unholds List liegt hier verhohlen?', is the same in the sketch as in the score, apart from some changes in the rhythm bringing more syncopation to the vocal part.

Ex. 43*a* Sketch

Ex. 43*b* Score

Ex. 44*a* Sketch

Ex. 44*b* Score

Ex. 45*a* Sketch

Ex. 45*b* Score

When she tells Hagen that a single glance from Siegfried's eyes, 'which shone on me brightly even through his disguise', would daunt him at his most courageous, the sketch too quotes quite spontaneously the 'Hort der Welt' motive, first heard in Act III of *Siegfried* and again in that pregnant moment at the end of Act I of *Götterdämmerung*, fitfully gleaming on the clarinets before subsiding into the shadows of the Tarnhelm motive, 'as she collapses in his arms, her eyes unconsciously meet Siegfried's'.[9]

There is a gap in the composition sketch after her 'O Undank! schänd-lichster Lohn!'. The period to fill it is sketched on the next system –

[9] Schopenhauer observed that however much external appearances might have changed, the identity of a personality was retained in the gaze.

Ex. 46 Sketch

(Brünnh.)

(Nicht eine Kunst . . .)

320 *227* – 'accompanied', Newman writes, 'by one of the most expressive strains in the whole *Ring*, which Wagner, however, has no occasion to employ later as a regular motive'.[10]

The sketch of the continuation, 'die zum Heil nicht half seinem Leib! Unwissend zähmt ihn mein Zauberspiel', deserves close attention, because of the way it unites several different motives in a completely self-sufficient polyphonic structure, in which at the same time the characteristic elements of each motive still make their separate mark. This is a feature frequently found in Wagner's music from the composition of the third act of *Tristan* onwards. Richard Strauss commented that the contrapuntal theory of the old school had never interested him much, but the yoking together of themes which were 'intractably' opposed and had to be forced to accommodate each other – that was quite something! This modern 'psychological' counterpoint originated in the third act of *Tristan*.[11] In this particular instance in Act II of *Götterdämmerung*, the only change Wagner made when he came to score the 'yoking together' was to smooth down a slight roughness – replacing dotted semiquaver figures by semiquaver triplets – which shows that the 'accommodation' of the motives had been completely spontaneous in conception and execution, not the product of contrivance and deliberation.

336 *232* There are occasional alterations to the vocal writing, of which Gunther's self-recrimination provides a typical example:

[10] *The Wagner Operas* (2nd printing, New York, 1959), p. 618.
[11] Willi Schuh, ' *Tristan und Isolde* im Leben und Wirken Richard Strauss'', *Bayreuther Festspielbuch 1952*.

Ex. 47*a* Sketch

Gunther

Be - trü - - - ger ich und be - tro - gen!

Ex. 47*b* Score

Ver - rä - - - - ter ich und ver - ra - ten!

The second version is not only more vehement, but also the more expressive for its closer alignment to the accompaniment.

348 235   A complete three-line system is crossed out, following Brünnhilde's 'Wär' ich gerecht, alles Blut der...'; what was sketched on it had not even been completed, but as far as it can be deciphered Wagner's first thought was to prolong the continuation, '...Welt büßte mir nicht eure Schuld', over four bars, whereas in the second version, on the next system, it is limited to three bars, as in the score. The emphasis gained by drawing the declamation out is now reserved for the end of the phrase: '...Tod taugt mir für alle, Siegfried falle...'

358 238   The first syllable of 'Gut-rune' in Brünnhilde's passionate outburst was extended to five beats in the sketch, having originally been written down as three:

Ex. 48 Sketch

Brünnh.   Gut - - - - - ru - ne   heißt der Zau - - - - - - - - - ber,

Another change made already in the sketch is the emphasizing of the word 'Zauber' ('spell'), held for nearly three bars, by the first violins' unison (the instrumentation is not specified in the sketch).

    In the sketch it was originally Brünnhilde who began the vengeance trio, 'So soll es sein! Siegfried falle!' That version was deleted, and the trio starts again on the next sheet, led this time by Gunther, as in the score, singing exactly the same notes as Brünnhilde in the first draft but an octave lower; but whereas in the sketch a whole bar elapses after Gunther's 'falle' before Brünnhilde's entry, in the score she enters with 'So soll...' *on* his last beat.

362 *240*

Were these changes prompted by psychological considerations, or musical ones alone? Both, I believe.

As for the rest of the trio, it is noticeable that the separate parts are pressed more closely together and intercut more in the score than in the sketch, and the inner part, Gunther's, is also woven in continuously in the score, so as to make the texture as dense as possible.

378 *244*

The sketch of the orchestral finale is peppered with an unusual number of stage directions, obviously for the composer's own reference: 'Bridal procession: men carrying Siegfried – Gutrune (to the altar on the hill) / Women approach Brünnhilde to escort her / Brünnh. looks at Gutr.[12] / Gunther yields her to the women and follows.'

The finale is thus completely inseparable from the stage action it depicts; writing it, Wagner had the 'choreography' of the scene in his head, and it becomes meaningless if the stage directions in the score are ignored.

386 *245*

The final bars, like those of the first act, were altered in the sketch:

Ex. 49*a* Sketch

25 Oct: 71

Ex. 49*b* Score

'It was only by concentrating my somewhat depleted resources to the utmost that it was possible to finish the music of this eventful and exciting

[12] This is against the sequences based on Gutrune's motive, which crescendo up to the entry of the Murder motive.

act a few days ago', Wagner wrote to King Ludwig on 4 December 1871, as
he sent him a copy of the orchestral sketch completed on 19 November.

Act III

Having completed the orchestral sketch of Act II on 19 November 1871
Wagner began the composition sketch of the third act on 4 January 1872 and
the orchestral sketch on 9 February.

> Here, restored to the bosom of my dear ones, I am now at last
> collecting myself, in order to embark on the completion of my work
> in the new year, with the composition of the last act of *Götter-
> dämmerung*: Easter's sun shall hail the 'Finis'

he wrote to King Ludwig on 27 December 1871. On 4 January 1872 he told
Karl Klindworth,

> I started the composition of the *last* act today and hope to have it
> finished by Easter. Perhaps I shall also find the time to start scoring
> the whole as I go along as well; at all events the score will be finished
> before the year is out. You will be amazed: once again, there are all
> sorts of things in it!

On the same day he also wrote a rapturous letter of thanks to Nietzsche for
sending him *Die Geburt der Tragödie*: 'Your book is the finest I have ever
read!' Six days later:

> We [he and Cosima] keep quarrelling over the one copy. I need it still,
> to put me in the right mood between breakfast and starting work;
> since reading it I have been working again, composing my last act.[13]

Preparations for Bayreuth and ill health made inroads on the three
months set aside for writing the composition sketch of the third act. 'Our
master is still not completely well, but his work has made a little progress',
Cosima told Nietzsche on 26 March. And on 24 April: 'The pencil sketches
were finished on 10 April, but the master needs a good two months to write
them out in ink, when I think about it I want to cry like a child.' Still in this
anxious mood she wrote to Judith Gautier on 22 April:

> Wagner a terminé l'esquisse au crayon du troisième acte du Crépus-
> cule: il a moins travaillé que nous le souhaitions, car il a été souffrant
> et fort dérangé. Je ne sais pas quand il retrouvera le loisir de se
> remettre à sa tâche, car il y a la mer à boire d'affaires, de pourparlers,
> de voyages etc....devant nous.

There is no way of knowing whether Wagner had already made the

---

[13] He did not omit to express his concern about Nietzsche's health: 'we have
often been alarmed at your bouts of illness, which have caused us serious
fears, not about your physical but your psychic condition'.

preliminary sketches for the first and last scenes of the act (cf. p. 180) when he started the composition sketch on 4 January. We do know, however, from Cosima's diary, that he must have made a sketch for the Funeral March before 28 September 1871 (DMCW, I, pp. 583f.). That may justify the assumption that he had made rough sketches of the other principal features by then, too, and if that was the case it would explain why he was so exact in predicting how long the composition as a whole would take.

The composition sketch comprises nineteen half-sheets of manuscript paper, all used on both sides. The first side, headed 'Third Act – (Prelude)' is not dated. The next side, headed '*Götterdämmerung III*' is dated '4 Jan. 72'. On the recto of the last sheet we read 'So enacted and accomplished, 7 years from the date on which my Loldchen [Isolde] was born / 10 April 1872 / RW.' He wrote yet another variant form of the final bars on the verso.
    Wagner did not ink over the notation of the composition sketch of the third act, and the pencil strokes have faded in places, so that they are often very hard to decipher.

Prelude and Scene 1

The composition sketch of the prelude is undated and was written out after Wagner had made a start on the following scenes. Apart from two changes made while he was in the act of writing it down, it corresponds to the version in the score. The composer's original intention in the eight-part horn canon was to have a new part enter in each of the first four bars, but he then crossed out the entries in the second and fourth bars. The repeat of the horn calls on the stage, just before the new chromatic wave motive is heard, was also a later insertion in the sketch: the effect of the sound of horns both in the distance and close at hand is that this prelude, too, has something elemental about it, the atmosphere of the forest where the hunt is up.
    The Rhinemaidens' song was to have been heard at once as the wave motive died away: the first word, 'Frau', was already written, but then there is a sign directing one to the last system on the following side, where there is a sketch of an *instrumental* version of the trio, 'Frau Sonne sendet lichte Strahlen'. This duly appears in the score, on three clarinets, in advance of the vocal trio.
    Several separate sketches of this song of the Rhinemaidens have survived, one of which, evidently of early date, is interesting for an elaboration of the melodic line which Wagner dropped in the later versions, but which resembles a turn of phrase in the Flower Maidens' chorus (cf. also ex. 10 on p. 190):

Ex. 50*a* Preliminary sketch

Ex. 50*b Parsifal*, Act II

Blumenmädchen

dir zur Wonn' und La - - be gilt mein minni - ges

The second verse of the song, 'Frau Sonne, sende uns den Helden', differs from the score, in that in the sketch it unexpectedly modulates to A major in the fourth bar, as a consequence of which there are other divergences in the following bars:

Ex. 51*a* Sketch

[Rheintöchter]

Frau Son - - - ne, sen - - - de uns den Hel - - den,

Ex. 51*b* Score

Rheintöchter

Frau Son - - - - ne, sen - - - de uns den Hel - den,

cresc. - - - - - - - *f* *dim.*

This surprise is avoided in the score.

The most significant difference between the composition sketch and the score in this scene is found in Siegfried's answer to the Rhinemaidens' warning prophecy, the changes affecting the text as well as the music. In the following quotation the words substituted in the score are given in brackets after the original words.

> des Urgesetzes
> ewiges Seil,
> flochten sie wilde
> Flüche hinein,
> Nothung zerhaut es den Nornen!
> Wohl warnte mich einst
> vor dem Fluch' ein Wurm,
> doch das Fürchten lehrt er mich nicht;–
> der Welt Erbe

gewann (gewänne)[14] mir ein Ring:
für der Minne Gunst
miss' ich ihn gern;
ich geb' ihn euch, gönnt ihr mir Lust (Gunst).[15]
Doch bedroht ihr (ihr mir)[16] Leben und Leib:
    faßte er nicht
    eines Fingers Wert –
den Reif entringt ihr mir nicht!
    Denn Leben und Leib
    – sollt' ohne Lieb'
    in der Furcht Bande
    bang ich sie fesseln –   } (omitted in the score)[17]
    Leben und Leib –
    seht! – so
werf' ich sie weit von mir!

The first of the divergences in the setting occurs in the first two lines: while the words 'des Urgesetzes ewiges Seil' are accompanied by the entwined motives of the Ring and the Norns' Rope in the sketch, in the score they are sung unaccompanied and the phrase is also slightly longer:

Ex. 52*a* Sketch

Siegfried

[14] The mood of the verb is changed from the indicative to the subjunctive; instead of 'a ring won me the inheritance of the world', the second version has the force of 'even though a ring may have won me...' The alteration adds one unaccented syllable.

[15] 'favour' instead of 'pleasure'; perhaps for the sake of the alliteration.

[16] The insertion of the first person pronoun, in an ethical dative, leaves no doubt as to whose life and limb are being threatened, and adds another syllable.

[17] 'If I am meant, terrified, to chain them – my life and my limbs – in the bonds of fear, without love...' The final sentence makes a stronger impact without this parenthesis.

Ex. 52*b* Score

'Der Welt Er-be gewann mir ein Ring' is accompanied in the sketch by the Valhalla motive, rhythmically and harmonically distorted, as it is in the score at the same juncture, but in the sketch the motive does not enter until the second bar of the vocal line, from which it diverges melodically; the orchestral part was written down first and the vocal part was added in counterpoint, undergoing some emendations in the process. In the score the motive enters first, with the two forte chords by the full orchestra; the voice does not enter until the second beat and then moves in unison with the orchestra. This is yet another example of the highlighting of a melody in the orchestra.

These changes serve only to throw the music into more pronounced relief, but the alteration that begins after 'den Reif entringt ihr mir nicht!' is altogether more significant, in that it gives the passage a new background.

In the sketch Siegfried's 'Denn Leben und Leib' is accompanied by the World Inheritance motive, played in full over four bars:

Ex. 53 Sketch

The following words, 'sollt' ohne Lieb' in der Furcht Bande bang ich sie fesseln', are accompanied by the 'Delight' motive, which was first heard in the final scene of *Siegfried* at 'Heil der Mutter, die mich gebar!' (Act III, pp. 368, *347*).

Ex. 54 Sketch

Perhaps Wagner had second thoughts about the desirability of allowing a motive associated with Siegfried and Brünnhilde's love to be heard in the Rhinemaidens' scene: even if the reminiscence were understood to be purely in his subconscious it would still, in view of the Potion of Forgetfulness, be psychologically unmotivated at this stage in the action. Instead, as the passage appears in the score, not only have the words been pruned, but the accompaniment is based on a quotation from the peroration of Alberich's curse: 'Dem Tode verfallen feßle den Feigen die Furcht: so lang' er lebt, sterb' er lechzend dahin, des Ringes Herr als des Ringes Knecht!' (*Das Rheingold*, Scene 4, pp. 196, *185*).

Ex. 55 Score

The reader will remember that the same motive was quoted in the third act of *Siegfried* as the accompaniment to Brünnhilde's moment of terror, 'Trauriges Dunkel trübt meinen Blick' (pp. 328, *335*).

The tragic contrast the reminiscence makes to Siegfried's insouciant response to the Rhinemaidens' warning: 'Leben und Leib, seht! – so werf' ich sie weit von mir!' is overpowering in the revised form, even if the listener makes the connection intuitively rather than consciously. It is one of those places where the orchestra's function is not to express the protagonists' inner feelings, but to act as the chorus in the tragedy.

In other respects the composition sketch of this scene, though hastily executed in places, corresponds to the version in the score, apart from minor rhythmic or verbal differences. The three-part writing for the Rhinemaidens is often merely suggested, especially in the later, contrapuntal passages:

105 *280*   Ex. 56 Sketch

Sometimes it is ignored altogether, as was the case when Wagner was sketching the Valkyries' ensemble.

Scene 2

Wagner wanted the entry of the huntsmen 'to make the impression of a tumult, gradually subsiding' (Porges). The musical depiction of the tumult, with the two horn motives heard in combination –

140 *294*   Ex. 57 Sketch

– and then dying away, was sketched very carefully, with various changes made in the process.

Wagner moved the bar lines of the orchestral introduction to Siegfried's 157 *299* 'Trink, Gunther, trink!' about so much, that it is impossible to tell what conclusion he reached in the sketch; in the end he simply wrote '3½' in the margin. This corresponds to the score, where the passage is three bars long, plus a half-bar rest (not in the sketch at all) before Siegfried's entry.

The sketch already takes into account the alternation of 3/4 and 4/4 time in Siegfried's narration, but some of the various vocal entries are placed differently, coming one or two beats earlier or later than in the score. The

Forest Murmurs in the accompaniment are merely intimated in the shifting harmonies.

188 *311*   An emendation in the sketch at the scene's turning-point, as Hagen gives Siegfried the antidote to the Potion of Forgetfulness, betrays that Wagner had written the orchestral part first, and then found that he could not fit in all Hagen's words, beginning 'Trink erst, Held'. He therefore repeated the first two bars of the orchestral part and added them, with the voice part, on the bottom system on the page:

Ex. 58 Sketch

The alteration in the sketch of D♯ to E♯ and of F♯ to G in the 'long' sustained chord of the three clarinets, in the bar ushering in the return of Siegfried's memory, shows that this sharpening occurred to Wagner on reflection; the revised chord certainly suggests the idea of waking from a bad dream, when it resolves on to the second inversion of the dominant of E major in the next bar.

Ex. 59 Sketch

There is a more substantial alteration at the end of Siegfried's narration, affecting more than expression or euphony, as always in Wagner. The words 'schlafend ein wonniges Weib' are accompanied in the sketch by sequences based on the Magic Fire ('Waberlohe') motive (which I suggested, apropos of the third act of *Die Walküre*, might better be called the Goodwill motive):

Ex. 60*a* Sketch

200 *315*   In the score they are extended from four bars to eleven and supported by
Freia's Love motive played three times by the first violins in unison. Apart
from its extraordinary beauty, this passage is also a reminiscence of the
violin unison in the third act of *Siegfried*; followed as it is by the repetition
of the chords associated with Brünnhilde's first greeting to the sun, when
Siegfried invokes her name, what we now hear is a magnificent, varied
reprise of that scene.

Ex. 60*b* Score

233 *324*   The changes made in the score to the repeated statement of the Wälsungen motive which launches the Funeral March are apparently slight but
they are very important. Already in the sketch, the first four bars were
transposed down by up to a third, and a slight alteration was made to the
rhythm; in the score they are transposed lower still, by a semitone or a
whole tone. Most significant of all, the second statement is not simply a
transposed, sequential repetition of the first, but a melodic variation of it: ·

Variations on the Funeral March: 1st statement

Ex. 61*a* Sketch I

Ex. 61*b* Sketch II

Ex. 61*c* Score
Hr. Tub.

2nd statement

Ex. 61*d* Sketch

Ex. 61*e* Score
Cl. Fag.

The transition to the C minor of the Funeral March involves the repetition
of the semiquaver triplet figure in the sketch, which is replaced in the score
by the simple unison of the low strings. When Wagner conducted the

Funeral March in Vienna in 1875, Porges relates that, by means of a powerful crescendo on these three quaver notes and a slight variation of the tempo of the intervening rests, making them irregular and somehow alive, he imbued the whole with incomparable significance. 'It was like the human personality rearing up in protest against the superior force of the dreadful, tragic agony threatening to destroy it.'

The Funeral March included in the complete composition sketch cannot, incidentally, be the very first draft of September 1871, to which I have already referred, since it is preceded on the page by Siegfried's last words, which had not been set on the earlier occasion.

Although many of the details are only fleetingly suggested, and although the pencilled notation has been half obliterated, one can still see all the essentials clearly enough, especially where the sketch differs from the score. For instance, where the key changes to G minor the chords of the Death motive still appear as semiquavers in the sketch, whereas in the score they were replaced by quavers (on the horns, violas and cellos). At the same time the triplet figure of the first and second violins, confined to the last beat of the bar in the sketch, is now expanded to the last two beats. Above all, the rather rigid dotted rhythm of the tragic Wälsungen motive which provides the principal melodic line of this passage is relaxed by syncopation in the score:

238 325

Ex. 62*a* Sketch

Ex. 62*b* Score

All these alterations contribute to a resolved, solemn calm. The risk of monotony as the mood persists is averted by the entry of Siegfried's Hero motive, derived from the Horn Call, at the dynamic climax, in a tauter, more 'angular' rhythmic pattern in the score than in the sketch.

248 327

Ex. 63*a* Sketch

Ex. 63*b* Score

Ex. 63*c* Sketch

Ex. 63*d* Score

A note 'bis' in the sketch indicates the repetition of the two C minor bars which end the Funeral March, and there are also four more indistinct bars inserted on the stave above, which would have made up a very final-sounding small Bar, *a–a–b*, with the preceding bars. But Wagner decided to avoid a cadence of that kind at this juncture, jettisoned the extra bars and moved directly into the *pp* horn and woodwind ninth chords, with which Gutrune's motive floats in 'like a breath of wind' (Porges). That is exactly the effect Wagner wanted: cutting Gutrune's solo and continuing straightaway with Hagen's 'Hoiho' is unacceptable.

Scene 3

In contrast to the extreme dynamic and emotional intensity of the Funeral March, Wagner's concern in Gutrune's scene was to induce the sense of uncanny emptiness, of haunted disquiet, by the greatest possible stylization. Her 'Nein!', accompanied by the Ring motive in the sketch, is heard unaccompanied in the score, seemingly lost on the third beat of an otherwise silent bar.

Ex. 64*a* Sketch   Ex. 64*b* Score

'Ich fürchte Brünnhild'' is supported by Brünnhilde's motive in the sketch, while the words are accompanied by nothing more than the dying G♮ of the clarinet in the score:

Ex. 65*a* Sketch

Ex. 65*b* Score

Similarly, her question 'Bist du wach?' is not only completely unaccompanied in the score, but additionally is answered by a whole bar's rest, marked with a fermata.

The overall effect of the scene is, in fact, that of a long 'rest' between the two shattering episodes of the Funeral March and the entrance of the cortège with Siegfried's body. Gutrune's scream at this sight is echoed by a vehement string figure, which plunges downwards *ff* and turns into the motive of her grief. The word 'longer' is written against it in the sketch, and in fact in the score the last two bars are extended, while the rhythmic articulation is revised to transform the figure into an expressive melodic phrase.

274 334

Ex. 66*a* Sketch

Ex. 66*b* Score

This same blending of figuration and motive occurs twice more in somewhat varied forms: at Gutrune's grieving 'Fort, treuloser Bruder, du Mörder meines Mannes', and at her outburst, 'Brünnhilde! Neiderboste! Du brachtest uns diese Not'. In the latter case the statements of the motive dissolve into semiquaver figurations again, in such a way as to suggest an intensifying variation of the motive of her grief.

277–8 336
301 342

From the point of view of compositional technique, this is a perfect example of what Kurth means by a development motive, one that takes on a clearly defined thematic shape and then disperses again into figuration. It is already thus in the sketch, once more confirming an organic, not merely decorative, function. In purely dramatic terms, the composer's concern with Gutrune demonstrates his wish to compensate for what she lacks in immediate dramatic life by adding depth to the musical expression of her grief.

298 342

The setting of Brünnhilde's words, 'Kinder hört' ich greinen nach der Mutter, da süße Milch sie verschüttet', as she enters at the back of the stage and walks 'resolutely and solemnly' forward, was added in the composition sketch after the rest of the passage had been written out. Did Wagner fear that the style of this line of recitative would be disruptive? We have had one instance, in the Wanderer–Erda scene in Act III of *Siegfried*, where he decided against a similar line of recitative for that reason.

Ex. 67 Sketch

A subsequent change to the sketch of the setting of Gutrune's last words, 'Verfluchter Hagen...Brünnhild' war die Traute, die durch den Trank er vergaß!', was occasioned by the need at one point to adjust the accompaniment, which had been written down first, to the vocal part when it was added. The sketch also includes the short orchestral postlude, with its descending sequences on Gutrune's motive, intended, as Wagner explained, to symbolize her death.

Brünnhilde's command to the Vassals, 'Starke Scheite schichtet mir dort', is the start of the tetralogy's great epilogue, whose outstanding difference from the finales of the other parts of the work is that it not only represents the summation of a complex, many-layered action, but also reviews the manifold motivic material and brings it to its conclusion. What Wagner said of Siegfried's Funeral March applies even more strongly to this finale: 'How could words ever call forth the impression evoked by these themes, formed anew?' (DMCW, I, pp. 583f.). The magnitude of the task he had set himself is reflected in his struggle to accomplish it musically, as testified by the alterations to the sketch and by the five versions of the symphonic finale.

Brünnhilde in this scene, in Wagner's words, appears like 'a prophetess of the ancient Germans'. And when Siegfried's *ideal* form is resurrected in her imagination, she feels herself to be transported from her surroundings: 'she says nothing at all to the people present, it is like a glorious vision' (Porges).

324 *348* The first revision comes in the instrumental passage following 'Vollbringt Brünnhildes Wunsch!' ('wish'; changed to 'Wort', 'word', in the score for vocal reasons); it was expanded in the sketch and yet more in the score, so

that it now makes a delicate transition leading into the 'vision'. There is an amazing difference between the sketch and the score in the vocal writing of what follows. The greatly widened intervals, the stressing of 'strahlt' and 'Licht', the substitution of triplets for the simple quaver at the end, all add a victorious exaltation to the line:

Ex. 68*a* Sketch

Other changes include the insertion of a bar's rest in the voice part in the score after 'Wißt ihr, wie das ward?', so that the invocation of the gods in the next line, 'O ihr, der Eide ewige Hüter!', is charged with an even greater ritual force. Similarly, a rest before 'dir', the drawing-out of the syllable itself and another rest following it accumulate the emphasis on Wotan's 'eternal guilt'.

337 *351*

Ex. 69*a* Sketch

345 *353* Finally the sketch shows that the two bars of accompaniment with the motive of Wotan's restless wandering (bass clarinet, cello, double bass in the score) were a later insertion in the sketch, while it was not until the score that he created the dissonance of the voice's A♭ clashing with the sustained G♭ minor chord of the tubas and trombones (*pp*) to give the final cadence its inescapably bitter accent.

Ex. 70*a* Sketch

Ex. 70*b* Sketch (revision of ex. 70*a*)

Ex. 70*c* Score

350 *354* There are two versions of Brünnhilde's apostrophe to the Rhinemaidens, 'Der Wassertiefe weise Schwestern', in addition to the preliminary studies on a separate sheet (cf. p. 180). The need here was to unite beauty of sound with the greatest possible verbal clarity: it is apparent at a glance that the version in the score provides the happier solution. The motivic allusions were selected for their particular power of association, and this, too, is accomplished more effectively and with more exact relevance in the score, where, apart from the 'Weia–Waga' melody, the greatest prominence is given to the sequential repetitions of the phrase 'gebt uns das Gold, gebt uns das Gold' – the very phrase struck up by the six horns when Siegfried emerged from Fafner's cave with the ring on his finger.

Ex. 71*a* Sketch

Ex. 71*b* Score

354 *355*   From '[Ihr in der] Flut löset ihn auf' onwards, the composition sketch
and the score correspond again, apart from minor divergences in the vocal
line; the similarity is quite astonishing when one considers the often abrupt
variations in the motivic combinations throughout this passage, such as the
syncopated thirds of the Ring motive, sliding downwards in combination
with the Curse motive, and then suddenly turning into the striding descent
of the Spear motive, on *ff* trumpets and trombones; or the sudden
emergence of the Gods' Downfall motive from Loge's chromatic motive at
366 *358*   'Denn der Götter Ende dämmert nun [the sketch has the synonym 'jetzt']
auf'. A change in the voice part here seems to be of primary psychological
significance:

Ex. 72*a* Sketch

Ex. 72*b* Score

While the declamatory line is triumphant as it appears in the sketch, the
syncopation and above all the drop in pitch at the end of the line give the

version in the score an impression of breathlessness, as though Brünnhilde has had to summon her last reserves of strength to pronounce the words at all. On the other hand, the apostrophe to Grane is the same in the sketch as in the score, except that the phrase 'vermählt ihm zu sein!' is rewritten to lie higher:

382 *362*

Ex. 73*a* Sketch

Brünnh.

ver - mählt — ihm   zu   sein.

Ex. 73*b* Score

Brünnh.

ver - mählt — ihm — zu   sein! —

The sketch still has a bar's rest after her cry of 'Siegfried! Siegfried!'; the word 'Sieh!' is inserted there in the score, and the last line of all is syncopated and spread out over two bars instead of one: all of this was obviously done to create as much breadth for the voice's last utterance as possible (even the change in the text from the original 'Selig gilt dir mein Gruß!' to 'Selig grüßt dich dein Weib!' is a matter of easing the enunciation rather than of essential meaning).

Ex. 74*a* Sketch

Brünnh.

Sieg-fried!   Sieg-fried!   Se - lig   grüßt   dich dein Weib!

(fort! [sic]

Ex. 74*b* Score

Brünnh.

Sieg-fried!   Sieg-fried!   Sieh! —   Se - lig   grüßt   dich dein Weib!

It was between completing the composition sketch and the orchestral sketch of the *Ring* that Wagner made a significant comment on his compositional technique. The chorus master Carl Riedel had expressed perplexity about the part-writing in bar 758 of the last movement of the Choral Symphony, and Wagner wrote back to him on 4 May 1872:

That passage is an infernal stumbling block! Beethoven wrote it like that, that's quite certain; but it seems no less certain that he must have made a mistake. I know from my own experience that I am meticulous in my working-out, yet as I read something through at the last, or as I play it over, the most peculiar quid-pro-quos suddenly leap out at me, due to the fact that in many cases the conception of the voice part is incompatible with the orchestra.

Clearly he was referring here to his recent experiences in setting *Götterdämmerung.*

The symphonic finale

402ff.
365ff.

Of the three different versions of Brünnhilde's final words,[18] Wagner had decided to use the second, beginning 'Führ' ich nun nicht mehr nach Walhalls Feste' ('If I now no longer go to Valhalla's fortress'), to bring his composition to its conclusion. It was Cosima who advised him to omit the whole passage, on the grounds that it sounded 'rather contrived'. This is the point of a note in the margin of the orchestral sketch: 'Enough! anything to please Cosel!'

The decisive factor was that no words could do justice to the symbolic significance of the myth. Another consideration, in all probability, was that it was as a musician that he had to complete his immense work: to do that a vocal scena would be less appropriate than a symphonic orchestral passage, in which the principal motives of the entire work could be juxtaposed in new, meaningful relationships.

The preliminary sketch (undated, written in pencil on a separate sheet) demonstrates that Wagner already had the fundamental motivic material and how it was to be disposed clear in his mind: rising sequential repetitions of the Valhalla motive, starting in its original key of D♭ major, and enriched by the addition of the Weia–Waga melody and the motive of Redemption through Love, reach a climax at which the first part of Siegfried's theme breaks in and is converted in conclusion into the Redemption motive, restored to D♭ major.

Ex. 75a Preliminary sketch

<hr />

[18] Cf. Otto Strobel, 'Zur Entstehungsgeschichte der *Götterdämmerung*', *Die Musik*, February 1933; Westernhagen, *Vom Holländer zum Parsifal*, pp. 85ff.; Westernhagen, *Wagner*, p. 402. The present text corrects the last of these in certain points.

Ex. 75*b* Preliminary sketch

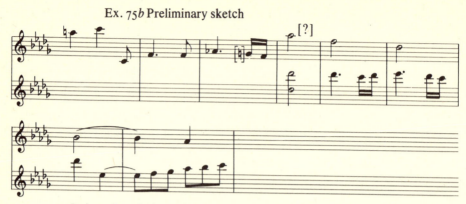

It is quite obvious that this sketch was written out as a spontaneous inspiration; apart from the absence of harmonies, the key signatures are both inexact and incomplete.

In the composition sketch the Weia–Waga melody enters first, in its original key of A♭ major, beginning on the second inversion of the tonic chord; this introduction in the key of the dominant firmly prepares the finale's principal key of D♭ major. There is a hint of the Wave motive as an accompanimental figure in the ensuing bars. The sequences based on the Valhalla motive proceed in the same way in the composition sketch as in the earlier sketch: the opening of the motive is played twice, then the whole motive once, rising each time by a whole tone. This goes on until Wagner is able to bring in the beginning of Siegfried's motive in F major (F minor) and consequently arrive at his goal, D♭ major, after three bars.

Ex. 75*c* Composition sketch

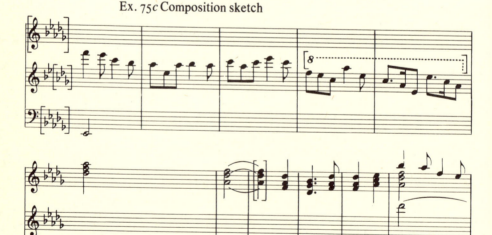

Ex. 75*d* Composition sketch

But the time allowed to reach the climax is too short, and too short-breathed, by comparison with the score. Moreover, as the climax of a sequential progression beginning on D♭ major, F major sounds colourless. Wagner's problem was to find a means of extending the sequences and simultaneously keeping them going until he arrived at a more brilliant key, without thereby losing, as the last note of the Siegfried motive, the D♭ that he needed to start the Redemption motive.

The supplementary sketch on the back of the last sheet of the composition sketch represents his efforts to solve the problem. By changing the sequential progression he contrived to start Siegfried's motive in D♭ major (D♭ minor) this time and arrived in its final cadence on B♭♭ major (A major), that is, on a chord which includes both the last note of Siegfried's motive – B♭♭ (A) – and the first note of the Redemption motive – D♭ (C♯) – but in which they are not identical, do not coincide: as a result this crucial modulation is even weaker in its impact than the earlier version in the composition sketch.

Ex. 75e Composition sketch (revision)

The solution was finally found in the orchestral sketch, though by paradoxical means. Here Wagner's sequential statements of the Valhalla motive go on for even longer until they reach G♭ major, the Siegfried motive starts in G♭ major (G♭ minor) and with its last note suddenly arrives in – D major! Had Wagner mistaken his goal, and overshot it by a semitone? Far from it. He wrote the D major chord as a first inversion, dubbed it the Neapolitan sixth of D♭ major and brought in the descending motive of the Downfall of the Gods, whose Neapolitan harmonization has been familiar to the listener ever since its first appearance in Erda's scene in *Das Rheingold*; with this plagal cadence he moved straight into the D♭ major of the Redemption through Love motive.

This is one of the most inspired uses of the tried and trusted technique of modulation, displaying its genius especially in its combination of musical function with symbolic association: the entry of the Downfall of the Gods motive at this juncture is highly apposite. The orchestral sketch shows that Wagner changed the rhythm of this last three times until, with the fourth and simplest, which he retained in the score, he succeeded in invoking the impression of an inexorable fate. The ensuing D♭ major of the Redemption motive is all the more transfiguring as a result.

Ex. 75*f* Orchestral sketch (reduced)

One practical outcome of the study of the sketches would be that knowledge of the trouble that Wagner took in preparing the entry of the Downfall of the Gods motive and in moulding it in the suitable rhythmic shape might lead conductors to highlight it by making the brass accompaniment play a diminuendo which may not be prescribed but clearly makes sense.

Originally the sequences based on the Valhalla motive were intended to finish as soon as F minor was reached. But as he was writing out the orchestral sketch, Wagner vigorously crossed out everything, including the final cadence, and excepting only the first three chords, and rewrote it all as it now appears in the score, with the sequences continuing until the entry of the entire motive in Db major.

The final pattern of the sequential writing is thus as follows:

A. The whole theme twice – the initial motive three times.
B. The whole theme twice – the initial motive twice.
C. The whole theme once with the final cadence.

This leaves only one difference between the orchestral sketch and the score, which should be mentioned, although on the face of it it is a minor one. Whereas in the orchestral sketch, in section A, the Redemption motive is notated in 12/8 bars which span two of the 6/8 bars of the Weia–Waga melody, in the score it floats on flutes and violins, in complete rhythmic independence of all the other parts, in 2/2, one bar of which is equivalent to two of the 6/8 bars.[19] Not until it is heard in sovereign isolation at the end, after the statement of the Gods' Downfall motive, is it written in 12/8 time in the score.

It is now possible to consider the musical function – as distinct from the poetic and ideal function – of the Redemption and Weia–Waga motives as the accompaniment in section A: the broadening of the Valhalla motive (from 3/4 at its exposition in *Das Rheingold* to 3/2 in the *Götterdämmerung* finale) inevitably emphasizes the symmetrical caesuras, and the unceasing, even flow of the other two motives bridges those caesuras and sustains the music's momentum.[20] In sections B and C this role is assumed by the dotted rhythm of the motive of Wotan's restless wandering in the bass line and maintained with mounting intensity until the dynamic climax (all the strings, reinforced in places by contrabass tuba).

The strength of the associations aroused by the Restlessness motive hardly needs to be pointed out: it recalls not only Brünnhilde's 'Ruhe, ruhe, du Gott!', but above all Waltraute's depiction of the gods and heroes assembled in Valhalla to await their doom, with Wotan silent on his throne.

Lastly, all the melodic phrases which had no more than a connecting function were eliminated in the orchestral sketch, so that the symphonic conclusion, still something of a medley in the earliest sketch, in its final version is a structure of compelling musical logic. As Porges wrote, deeply impressed by the 1876 rehearsals, the performance of it demands 'a grip of iron, the themes and melodies must build up before us like Cyclopian masonry'.

---

[19] In his vocal score Klindworth wrote the Redemption motive in 12/8 to make it easier for the player (p. 366).
[20] Kurth refers to other instances of this technique of bridging before Wagner, e.g. in the work of Mozart, but there it is found almost exclusively in the accompanimental parts of vocal compositions (p. 419).

Conclusion

> There is no profit in just looking at a thing. Each time we look
> at something we start to observe, each time we observe we
> start to reflect, each time we reflect we start to establish
> connections, and so it can be said that every time we look at
> something attentively we are already constructing theories
> about the rest of the world.
> (*Goethe*, Zur Farbenlehre, *preface*)

This analysis of the composition sketches of *Der Ring des Nibelungen* is the
outcome of the attempt to observe and to describe the process of the
creation of the 'most problematical artistic structure of the last millenia', as
Gerhart Hauptmann called it, following the thread provided by the docu-
ments recently made available for research, as one would observe and
describe a natural phenomenon. That this should lead to theorizing of a
more general kind, as Goethe said, is not only inevitable, it is actually
profitable.

The most immediate observation is that each of the sketches individually
was written down in a very short time, and the inevitable conclusion is that
the act of writing was preceded by an age of musical invention and
compilation. A short chronology of the preparatory work done in the
composer's musical imagination will illustrate the extent to which it is
permissible to speak of the 'simultaneity' of the poetic and the musical
creative process.

It is clear from the start that the musician was already making an active
contribution when Wagner abandoned his historical play *Friedrich Bar-
barossa* in 1848 in favour of the mythological subject of *Siegfrieds Tod*. The
difference is already apparent in the language, the foundation on which the
melody was to be constructed, in that the iambics which had dominated the
4/4 metre of *Lohengrin* were now replaced by a freer rhythm, in which each
line has either two or three stressed root syllables, and any number of
unstressed syllables.

In the first manuscript draft of the verse text of *Siegfrieds Tod* (written
12–28 November 1848), there is a musical sketch in the margin against the
stage direction 'the Vassals lift the body on to the shield' which, though of
little intrinsic interest, has symptomatic significance. Houston Stewart
Chamberlain published the page in facsimile in the illustrated edition of his
Richard Wagner (1896) with the comment: 'The master appears to have
turned his sheet of paper sideways under the impact of a sudden inspiration,
and to have quickly drawn two staves and scribbled down these eight bars.
The use of the tenor clef seems to indicate that he was thinking of
trombones' (pp. 267ff.).

Even at that early stage Wagner had formed conceptions about the composition of the whole work that went further than isolated ideas of that kind. The sculptor Gustav Adolph Kietz tells of a conversation that took place after a reading of *Siegfrieds Tod*, just after the text had been completed: when the chorus master Wilhelm Fischer expressed doubts as to the feasibility of setting such a text, Wagner explained the important contribution the orchestra would make to the dramatic expression, and stressed that 'the word' projected from the stage would have to carry more weight than had hitherto been the case.[1]

When Wagner first tried, in 1850, to set the beginning of the text ('to translate it into music', in his own words), as we have seen, he already anticipated the key of the Norns' scene in *Götterdämmerung*, the key of the Valkyries' scene with the Valkyrie motive, and wrote a recognizable prototype of the theme of the Annunciation of Death.

He soon abandoned this essay, ostensibly because he was unable to imagine a singer capable of portraying his Brünnhilde at that time. But a deeper reason was that at this 'most decisive moment' of his life he had to allow everything that was hovering on the edge of his vision to advance into the full light of his consciousness, he had to take complete control of the ideas that welled up in him (letter to Liszt, 25 November 1850). It was at this stage that he wrote his most important theoretical work, *Oper und Drama*, the crystallization of his reflections on the composition of the Nibelungen drama, on declamation, the role of motives, harmony, rhythm, instrumentation, and even mime and choreography.

And while he gradually worked these theories out of his system, as they dispersed 'like a grey mist', he conceived the texts of *Siegfried*, *Die Walküre* and *Das Rheingold*. It was a matter of compositional rather than poetic or textual necessity that he had to round *Siegfrieds Tod* out into the *Ring des Nibelungen*, and in doing so he was able to benefit from all he had learnt from his attempt at setting the earliest of the texts and from writing *Oper und Drama*.

An inner disquiet which drove him to take refuge in illness, to go on hazardous rambles in the Alps, to take an ineffective cure in St Moritz and to visit northern Italy, was merely the symptom of the struggle to discover the starting point from which to launch his composition. At last, on 5 September 1853 in La Spezia, the prelude of *Das Rheingold* came to him in a visionary half-sleep, exactly as it had been gestating in him, waiting its own time to be born.

The five years before that vision were thus a period in which the two activities of writing the text and composing the music had been simultaneous, though in a less overt sense than in the case of *Tristan*. It was a direct result of the five years that Wagner was able to write down the composition sketch of *Das Rheingold*, in all its detail, in nine weeks, as though he was taking dictation.

[1] *Richard Wagner in den Jahren 1842–49 und 1873–75* (Dresden, 1905), p. 70.

He revealed the other secret of this outburst of creative vigour in a 'letter on dramatic art': 'The dramatist who is incapable of imagining the full power of his work in performances he improvises in his own head has been denied the true vocation to drama' (*Brief über das Schauspielerwesen*, RWGS, IX, p. 263). This is particularly apposite to the dramatic composer as exemplified by Wagner himself; the stage directions noted in the composition sketches show how keen his imagination was in that sense, but the most conclusive proof lies in the dramatic strength of his work.

In the essay 'on actors and singers' written immediately before the 'letter', he named the dramatic singer (or singing actress) of whom he was thinking when he wrote the composition sketch of *Götterdämmerung*. As a boy he had been so impressed by Wilhelmine Schröder-Devrient in the role of Leonore that he had written to her that if she should ever hear his name being hailed in the world of art, then she might care to remember that it was she, by her performance that evening, who had made him what he thereupon swore to become. Schröder-Devrient had been dead for years, but she possessed the gift of 'guiding a composer towards the way he must compose, if it is to be worth the trouble to be "sung" by such a woman: she did it by what I call the "example" that she, the mime, set the dramatist, and that I alone, among all those to whom she gave it, have followed' (*Über Schauspieler und Sänger* [1872], RWGS, IX, p. 221). I believe that it is her spirit that breathes in those intangible characteristics of the role of Brünnhilde.

Analysis of the composition sketches has afforded us insights into the composer's stylistic intentions and into the style realized in the work, but with these last considerations we approach mysteries that evade analysis; the best that we can do now is to echo Goethe: 'The greatest happiness of a thoughtful person is to have studied all that yields itself to study, and to reverence what eludes study in tranquillity.'[2]

[2] Sophienausgabe, section II, vol. 11, p. 159.

Bibliography

of the works consulted by the author

Altmann, Wilhelm, *Richard Wagners Briefe nach Zeitfolge und Inhalt* (Leipzig, 1905)

Bailey, Robert, 'Wagner's musical sketches for *Siegfrieds Tod*', in *Studies in music history* [in honour of Otto Strunk] (Princeton N.J., 1968)

Bayreuth, die Stadt Richard Wagners, ed. Otto Strobel (Munich, 1943)

BBL   *Bayreuther Blätter*, ed. Hans von Wolzogen, 61 vols. (Chemnitz, later Bayreuth, 1878–1938)

Bayreuther Festspielbuch 1951, ed. by the directorate of the Bayreuth Festival

Dahlhaus, Carl, ed., *Das Drama Richard Wagners als musikalisches Kunstwerk* (*Studien zur Musikgeschichte des 19. Jahrhunderts*, vol. XXIII) (Regensburg, 1970)

Daube, Otto, '*Ich schreibe keine Symphonien mehr*' (Cologne, 1960)

Droysen, Joh. Gust., *Des Aischylos Werke*, 2 vols. (Berlin, 1832)

DMCW   Du Moulin-Eckart, Count Richard, *Cosima Wagner*, vol. I (Munich, 1929)

Furtwängler, Wilhelm, *Ton und Wort* (Wiesbaden, 1954)

GLRW   Glasenapp, C. F., *Das Leben Richard Wagners*, 6 vols. (Leipzig, 1905–12)

Goethe, J. W. von, *Werke*, Sophienausgabe, section I, vol. 50 (Weimar, 1900)

Guichard, Léon, *La musique et les lettres en France au temps du wagnérisme* (Paris, 1963)

Halm, August, *Von Grenzen und Ländern der Musik* (Munich, 1916)

Hecker, Joachim von, *Untersuchungen an den Skizzen zum Streichquartett cis-moll op. 131* (typescript diss., University Library, Freiburg i. Br., 1956)

Helm, Theodor, *Beethovens Streichquartette*, 3rd edn (Leipzig, 1921)

Hey, Julius, *Richard Wagner als Vortragsmeister 1864–1876*, ed. Hans Hey (Leipzig, 1911)

Ipser, Karl, *Richard Wagner in Italien* (Salzburg, 1951)

Kurth, Ernst, *Romantische Harmonik und ihre Krise in Wagners Tristan*, 1st edn (Bern and Leipzig, 1920)

L'Illustration, February 1933 (Paris)

Lorenz, Alfred, *Das Geheimnis der Form bei Richard Wagner*, vol. I, *Der Ring des Nibelungen*, 2nd edn (Tutzing, 1966)

Die Musik in Geschichte und Gegenwart (MGG), vol. XIV (Kassel, 1968)

Neue Zeitschrift für Musik, no. 5, 1963 (Mainz)

NLRW   Newman, Ernest, *The Life of Richard Wagner*, vols. II and III, 2nd edn
              (New York, 1946, 1948)
           – *The Wagner Operas*, 2nd edn (New York, 1959); English edn: *Wagner
              Nights* (London, 1949)
        Nietzsche, Friedrich, *Richard Wagner in Bayreuth*, various edns
        Nottebohm, Gustav, *Zwei Skizzenbücher von Beethoven aus dem Jahre 1801
              bis 1803*, ed. Paul Mies (Leipzig, 1924)
        Pfitzner, Hans, *Die Ästhetik der musikalischen Impotenz* (Verlag der
              Süddeutschen Monatshefte, Munich, 1920)
        Porges, Heinrich, *Die Bühnenproben zu den Bayreuther Festspielen des
              Jahres 1876* (Leipzig, 1896)
        Riezler, Walter, *Beethoven* (Zürich, 1951)
        Roeder, Erich, *Felix Draeseke*, vol. I (Dresden, n.d. [1931])
        Schuh, Willi, ' *Tristan und Isolde* im Leben und Wirken Richard Strauss'',
              Bayreuther Festspielbuch 1952
        Schweitzer, Albert, *Bach* (Leipzig, various edns)
        Shaw, Bernard, *The major critical essays* (London, 1955)
        Strauss, Richard, *Betrachtungen und Erinnerungen* (Zürich, 1949)
           – *Instrumentationslehre von Hector Berlioz* (Leipzig, 1904)
        Strobel, Otto, *Richard Wagner, Leben und Schaffen: eine Zeittafel*
              (Bayreuth, 1952)
           – *Skizzen und Entwürfe zur Ring-Dichtung* (Munich, 1930)
           – 'Die Originalpartitur von Richard Wagners *Rheingold* ', *Bayreuther
              Festspielführer 1928*
           – 'Die Kompositionskizzen zum *Ring des Nibelungen*', *Bayreuther
              Festspielführer 1930*
           – 'Zur Entstehungsgeschichte der *Götterdämmerung*', *Die Musik*,
              February 1938
           – '"Geschenke des Himmels": Über die ältesten überlieferten *Tristan*-
              Themen', *Bayreuther Festspielführer 1938*
        Uhlig, Theodor, *Musikalische Schriften*, ed. by Ludwig Frankenstein
              (Regensburg, n.d. [1913])
        Voss, Egon, *Studien zur Instrumentation Richard Wagners* (*Studien zur
              Musikgeschichte des 19. Jahrhunderts*, vol. XXIV) (Regensburg, 1970)
        Wagner-Jahrbuch, ed. by Ludwig Frankenstein, vol. V (Berlin, 1913)
        Wagner-Gesamtausgabe, ed. by Carl Dahlhaus, vol. XXX (Mainz, 1970)
        Wagner, Cosima, *Die Briefe Cosimas an Friedrich Nietzsche*, ed. by Erhart
              Thierbach, 2 vols. (Weimar, 1938, 1940)
        Wagner, Richard, *Briefe in Originalausgaben*, 17 vols. (Leipzig, 1912)
           – *Briefe, die Sammlung Burrell*, ed. by John N. Burk (Frankfurt am
              Main, 1953) [Originally published as *Letters of Richard Wagner: the
              Burrell Collection* (New York, 1950)]
           – *Briefe an Hans von Bülow* (Jena, 1916)
           – *Briefe Wagners an Mathilde Maier*, ed. by Hans Scholz (Leipzig,
              1930)
TWLF   – *Lettres françaises...*, publiées par Julien Tiersot (Paris, 1935)
RWGS   – *Gesammelte Schriften und Dichtungen*, vols. I–X, 4th edn (Leipzig,
              1907)

RWGS	– *Sämtliche Schriften und Dichtungen*, vols. XI–XVI, 6th edn (Leipzig, n.d.)
ML	– *Mein Leben*, first authentic edition (Munich, 1963)
	– and Cosima, *Lettres à Judith Gautier*, présentées par Léon Guichard (Paris, 1964)
KLRW	– and King Ludwig II, *Briefwechsel*, ed. by Otto Strobel, 5 vols. (Karlsruhe, 1936–9)

Westernhagen, Curt von, *Vom Holländer zum Parsifal* (Zürich/Freiburg i. Br., 1962)

– *Wagner* (Zürich/Freiburg i. Br., 1968)

Westphal, Kurt, *Vom Einfall zur Symphonie: Einblick in Beethovens Schaffensweise* (Berlin, 1965)

Index

of persons cited in the text

6